RELIGIOUS NATIONALISM

D1636460

RELIGIOUS NATIONALISM

Hindus and Muslims in India

PETER VAN DER VEER

UNIVERSITY OF CALIFORNIA PRESS
BERKELEY   LOS ANGELES   LONDON

University of California Press
Berkeley and Los Angeles, California

University of California Press, Ltd.
London, England

© 1994 by
The Regents of the University of California

Library of Congress Cataloging-in-Publication Data

Veer, Peter van der.
  Religious nationalism / Peter van der Veer.
       p.   cm.
  Includes bibliographical references and index.
  ISBN 0-520-08220-6 (alk. paper) ; 0-520-08256-7 (pbk. : alk.
paper)
    1. Nationalism—Religious aspects.   2. Nationalism—
Religious aspects—Hinduism.   3. Nationalism—Religious
aspects—Islam.   4. Religion and politics—India.
5. Hinduism—Social aspects—India.   6. Islam—Social
aspects—India.   I. Title.
BL2015.N26V44   1994
320.5'5'0954—dc20   93-28079

Printed in the United States of America
9 8 7 6 5 4 3 2

The paper used in this publication meets the minimum
requirements of American National Standard for Information
Sciences—Permanence of Paper for Printed Library Materials,
ANSI Z39.48-1984. ∞

For Jacobien, Jan Anne, and Sjoerd

Contents

Preface

Current events in India reveal the continuing importance of religious nationalism. While much has been written on both Indian religions and Indian nationalism, the religious aspects of Indian nationalisms have yet to receive adequate attention. To study these aspects—movements, discourses, practices—we need a shift in emphasis from the political scientist's study of political parties and voting behavior to the anthropologist's study of religious movements and ritual action as part of historical practice. My aim in this book is modest. I am not able to describe and explain religious nationalism as it occurs in India in its full historical and social complexity. I will thus limit myself to some religious movements, discourses, and practices whose links to nationalism have not, in my opinion, been sufficiently taken into account. My discussion will not provide a straightforward narrative of the development of religious nationalisms but will instead address a set of related issues from a variety of angles. The argument clarifies the transformation of what Eric Hobsbawm calls "protonational feelings of collective belonging" into religious nationalism.[1]

I submit that we should take religious discourse and practice as constitutive of changing social identities, rather than treating them as ideological smoke screens that hide the real clash of material interests and social classes. The study I want to engage here concerns the historical construction of Hindu and Muslim identities in India and, specifically, the transformation of these identities in the colonial and postcolonial periods in the context of the rise of nationalism. My argument is: (1) that religious identity is constructed in ritual discourse and practice; (2) that these identities are not "primordial attachments," inculcated by unchanging traditions, but specific products of changing forms of religious organization and communication; (3) that religious nationalism articulates discourse on the religious community and discourse on the nation; and (4) that Hindu and Muslim nationalisms develop along similar lines and that the one needs the other. An important caveat is that in discussing the contemporary situation I will in general limit myself to India. Scant attention will thus be given to Pakistan and Bangladesh or to post-Independence Muslim nationalism in India.

The claim that something like religious nationalism exists will be rejected by many students of nationalism for the simple reason that both nationalism and its theory depend on a Western discourse of modernity. This discourse constitutes the "traditional" as its antithesis and interprets difference as backwardness. A crucial element of the discourse of modernity is the opposition of the "religious" to the "secular." One point I want to make in this book is that leading theories of nationalism tend to ignore the importance of colonialism and orientalism in the spread of nationalism. To understand religious nationalism in India we need both an analysis of "tradition" that is not prejudiced by the discourse of modernity and a theory of the impact of colonialism and orientalism that does not deny agency to colonial subjects.

My interest in the subject of religious nationalism started with experiences I had in 1984 while I was doing fieldwork in Ayodhya, a Hindu pilgrimage center in Uttar Pradesh, a province in North India.[2] My research focused on the social organization, religious orientations, and ritual performances of the two most important groups of specialists in Ayodhya, the Ramanandi monks and the Brahman priests. In focusing on these two groups, I was concerned to assess the values and identities of the religious specialists in this center who receive pilgrims, and how these have changed over time. While my work explicitly tried to take a historical perspective by looking at large-scale political and economic processes, it did not seem necessary at the time to take the rise of religious nationalism during this century into account. I saw Ayodhya as an important religious center, but, at least in the twentieth century, as a political backwater, far removed from the main arenas of political activity, such as Delhi, Lucknow, and Kanpur.

Whatever the value of these considerations—and the argument

of this book places them very much in doubt—at the end of my research period in 1984 I was jolted out of my complacency. Of course, I was aware that Ayodhya had a site that had been long under dispute between Hindus and Muslims. It was an old mosque, built on the very spot that, Hindus claimed, was the birthplace of Lord Rama, the premier god of Ayodhya. One could not fail to see the mosque in Ramkot, the center of Ayodhya, where the most important temples are located. Entering the compound of the mosque one encountered a police picket, intended to ensure that no one tried to enter the mosque, which was itself closed off by a gate with an impressive lock. On a platform in front of the mosque a group of Hindu monks would sit and chant. Pamphlets saying that this was the birthplace of Lord Rama and should be returned to the Hindus were handed out, and donations solicited. Despite this form of "agitation" and the presence of the police, though, the site had always struck me as rather serene during the period that I regularly visited Ayodhya, from 1977 to 1984. The disputes seemed to have more to do with who among the monks would receive which part of the donations than with any attempt to launch an attack on the mosque.

In 1984, however, the relative peace of the place was suddenly disrupted when a campaign "to liberate the birthplace of Lord Rama" was launched.[3] The initiative was taken not by local monks but by a Hindu nationalist movement with branches all over the country. Since then, the site has developed into one of the hottest issues in Indian politics today. Hundreds of people have died in riots between Hindus and Muslims. The issue precipitated the fall of the Indian government in 1990, and a major opposition party subsequently embraced the issue very successfully in its electoral campaign. The issue continued to be contested after the elections, and on 6 December 1992 a Hindu mob marched on the mosque and succeeded in demolishing it. This event was again followed by rioting, with heavy loss of life and property, especially among Muslims, in many parts of the country. Hindu temples in Pakistan, Bangladesh, and Great Britain were attacked in retaliation. Indeed, the Ayodhya case reflects all the elements of religious nationalism in which I have come to be interested. While this book is not principally about Ayodhya, the Ayodhya case is taken here as the main illustration of my argument.[4]

Ayodhya is a site (*tirtha*) for pilgrimage (*yatra*) and the campaign related to it consists of religious processions (also called *yatra*). As I will try to show, movement and the definition of space and territory are central elements in religious nationalism. This also pertains to the transnational migration resulting from the demands of the labor market, which plays a significant role in the construction of nationalism "at home." Theories of nationalism often assume a sharp opposition between the traditional, parochial community and the modern, larger framework of the nation. What I want to show is the extent to which larger frameworks than that of the locality were already available in India before the colonial era, and the extent to which religious nationalism builds on these earlier frameworks and transforms them. My argument is that conceptions of a larger world emerge both in religious travel, primarily pilgrimage, and in migration. Although these two types of movement may seem very different, they reinforce each other in important ways. Given that pilgrimage is, by definition, a ritual of the larger community, it is easily incorporated into religious nationalism.

The relation between nationalism and transnational migration is also relevant here since, in the campaign for "rebuilding" the temple in Ayodhya, the involvement of Hindus who live outside of India has proved crucial. Migrants who leave India but continue to have ties with their homeland are confronted with challenges to their identity that are often met by nationalist activism. Instead of encouraging a sense of world citizenship, the transnational experience seems to reinforce nationalist as well as religious identity. It is the ambiguities of the dialectic between nationalism and transnationalism that constantly draw one's attention in contemporary politics.

The mosque-temple issue did not arise "naturally." Rather, it has depended on conscious, planned action by religious and political movements and is, as such, related to a changing political context that I will try to sketch. The arguments of the participants in the dispute focus on two problems: the relation between Hindus and Muslims, and the nature of the Indian nation-state. Most important, they concern conflicting interpretations of history. Religious discourse tends either to deny historical change or else to prove its ultimate irrelevance. It is my argument that religious nationalism combines this antihistorical feature of religious discourse with an empiricist search for "facts" that has been highly influenced by orientalism. Nationalism has a very urgent and contradictory need to show, in a historical account, that the nation has always existed, a need that emerges clearly in the attempt to "rebuild" the temple in Ayodhya.

My earlier work was largely devoted to the study of the development of one Hindu monastic order, the Ramanandis, whereas in this book I look, from a comparative perspective, at the development of Hindu, Sikh, and Muslim religious communities. My goal is to demonstrate that religious nationalism builds on a previous construction of religious community. This is not a version of the two-nation theory, which says that the Hindu and Muslim (or Sikh) nations are primordial entities, long predating the nationalist era. Rather, I will argue that religious nationalism in the nineteenth and twentieth centuries builds on forms of religious identity and modes of religious communication that are themselves in a constant process of transformation during both the colonial and postcolonial periods. The spread of religious orientations in India has always been largely dependent on holy men and their networks of sacred centers, while the expansion of religious groups through conversion is clearly a process of long duration, continuing down to the present day.

Much of the literature on the emergence of nationalism in nineteenth-century India focuses on the dual role of the colonial state and the "colonized" middle class. We should not reserve agency only for the "bourgeois project," however, but also pay attention to movements and discourses that do not seem to have a narrow bourgeois support. The main issue here is the connection between the reformist religion of the bourgeoisie and the religion of the "other half." There is a kind of Protestant reformation in Indian religion that entails a "laicization" of organization and leadership, as Richard Gombrich and Gananath Obeyesekere have observed in their study of Sri Lankan Buddhism, where they demonstrate the importance of the emergence of "Protestant Buddhism" for Sinhalese nationalism.[5] A similar development can be found in Indian Hinduism and Islam. One instance of this is the saintly behavior of the politician, as in the case of Mahatma Gandhi. Other instances include the marginalization of Sufi saints in Islam and the "ethicization" of conduct among the Muslim laity.

Very important also is the historical formation of Hindi as a Hindu language and Urdu as a Muslim language, as well as the relation of these languages of everyday life to the sacred languages of Hinduism and Islam, Sanskrit and Arabic. As I will seek to show, the sacredness of the languages of the scriptures is, in the context of religious nationalism, attributed to national languages—a form of "laicization" of sacred communication. A similar process is at work in the use of religious imagery in films shown in movie theaters and on television.

Not only are the sacred scriptures adapted for cinema and literature in the age of nationalism but ritual communication itself is transformed. In religious communities ritual communication plays a crucial role in forging an identity among people with very different class backgrounds. This sociological observation entails an understanding of ritual as a political process in which identity is discursively constructed and contested. With this in mind, I will examine the ways in which the ritual construction of gender is taken up in the nationalist construction of the nation as "brotherhood." The question I want to ask is whether the Hindu veneration of mother cow and the Muslim elaboration of gender separation become operative in similar ways in the new discursive space of nationalism.

One of the great problems in writing about culture and nationalism is the strong tendency to reify one's object of discussion. There is clearly much truth in Richard Handler's argument that "boundedness, continuity, and homogeneity encompassing diversity" dominate both nationalist and social-scientific discourse equally.[6] No doubt, studies of "aspects of culture," and especially of "traditional culture," do much to freeze and objectify culture as heritage, as a tangible sign of a common identity. This problem is even more overwhelming in the case of a work, such as the present one, that generalizes about a huge society over a large time period. It is hard to escape from speaking about "the Hindus" or "the Muslims" if one does not intend to provide a detailed, contextualized case study. Therefore I am certain that parts of this book will have fallen prey to the very essentializations my argument attempts to problematize.

Another important problem is that, writing about another culture, one tends to claim an objective outsider's viewpoint on matters for which other people die. I am, by definition, an outsider to Indian affairs because of my Dutch citizenship, and having recently gone through the intricate machinery of obtaining permanent residency in the United States, I would be the last to claim that borders and nation-states do not exist. However, India and Holland belong to a world system of nation-states, and within that context I have been privileged to study India for the last two decades. "India" has thereby become part of my personal identity, an area of emotional involvement. In that sense I do not think that I am totally "outside" the phenomenon I discuss in this book, although I would not claim to be writing "within."[7] In fact, I would argue that the decision about what is "within" and what is "outside" is the very subject of nationalist debate. Those who have read my earlier book, *Gods on Earth*, will hardly have come to the conclusion that I romanticized Ayodhya. Still, I had a romantic attachment to its peaceful way of life and now feel pained when I see that the troops of monkeys on the roofs of Ayodhya's temples have been replaced by policemen with semiautomatic guns. Confronted with the anguish and fear of my Muslim friends during recent visits to Surat I feel even more the tragedy of what is happening in India. Nevertheless, it is hard for me to take sides and exchange the position of outsider for that of partisan. Obviously, this has to do with my relative distance from events and my personal safety in respect to them. But I also find it genuinely difficult to adopt the "liberal" position of condemning religious nationalists. In fact, I want to escape from that position in order to be able to understand religious nationalism. Of course, I am in favor of "nonviolence," but my analysis in this book has led me to understand the ambiguities of Hindu "tolerance" and Gandhian "nonviolence."

On the intellectual side, I do recognize the power of the discursive formation in which we think and argue about ourselves and the world. I have been influenced by a more general critique of the narrative of modernity that became influential in the 1980s—but much of this critique is completely Eurocentric. This book thus attempts to redirect attention to discursive traditions that are affected by the European ones but not derived from them. It is my hope that what I have to say will problematize some of the main issues in contemporary politics not only in India but on a world scale.

This is a book of synthesis. My intellectual debts are therefore innumerable and recorded in the footnotes. The subject is huge, and the present book is only one among many. Particularly pertinent to its subject matter, however, are three recent books: Partha Chatterjee's *Nationalist Thought and the Colonial World: A Derivative*

Discourse? (1986); Sandria Freitag's *Collective Action and Community* (1989); and Gyanendra Pandey's *The Construction of Communalism in Colonial North India* (1990). More generally, I feel very much indebted to the perspective on religion and politics developed in the numerous writings of Talal Asad.

An early impetus to this work was given by a series of discussions carried out under the auspices of Wilder House at the University if Chicago. I am grateful to David Laitin, its director, for his encouragement. Barney Cohn was present on one of these occasions, and his sharp questions prodded me to do some further thinking. At the University of Pennsylvania Arjun Appadurai commented on the early drafts of the first two chapters. To work with him, Carol Breckenridge, and David Ludden was a true pleasure. Finally, at the University of California Press I owe special thanks to Lynne Withey for her early encouragement and to Pamela MacFarland Holway for her careful attention to the manuscript. I am also indebted to the anonymous readers of the manuscript for their many incisive comments. In general, however, I have taken little advice and am myself to blame for inaccuracies and inconsistencies.

Chapter One

Religious Nationalism

Babar's Mosque or Rama's Temple?

The cover of the 15 May 1991 issue of *India Today*, India's leading newsmagazine, shows Lal Kishan Advani, the leader of the Bharatiya Janata party (BJP), with bow and arrow in hand, vermilion on his forehead. His posture, immediately recognizable to all Hindus, imitates that of the icon of *kodanda* Rama, the god Rama with bow and arrows. In the national elections of May and June 1991, in which 511 seats were contested, Advani's party won 119 seats and 20 percent of the vote. This meant that the BJP had nearly doubled its share of the national vote and had emerged as India's largest opposition party by far.[1] Perhaps even more significant, it won the state elections and formed a government in Uttar Pradesh, India's most populous state of some 100 million people.

The political success of the BJP depends squarely on its alliance with two Hindu nationalist movements, the Vishva Hindu Parishad (VHP), an organization of religious leaders, and the Rashtriya Swayamsevak Sangh (RSS), a militant youth organization. This alliance allows it to use religious discourse and mass-scale ritual action in the political arena. The party's program stresses *Hindutva*, Hinduness, a term explored by the Hindu nationalist leader V. D. Savarkar in the 1920s: "A Hindu means a person who regards this land of Bharat Varsha, from the Indus to the Seas, as his Father-Land as well as his Holy-Land that is the cradle of his religion."[2] The term *Hindutva* equates religious and national identity: an Indian is a Hindu—an equation that puts important Indian religious communities, such as Christians and Muslims, outside the nation.

1

The argument for the term stresses that Hindus form the majority community in the country and that, accordingly, India should be ruled by them as a Hindu state (*rashtra*).

All this is not new. From its very beginning in the nineteenth century nationalism in India has fed upon religious identifications. This is true not only for the two most important religious communities in India, Hindus and Muslims, but also for groups like the Sikhs and, in Sri Lanka, the Buddhists. In all these cases nation building is directly dependent on religious antagonism, between Hindus and Muslims, between Sikhs and Hindus, between Buddhists and Hindus. At Independence this antagonism led to the most important political event of twentieth-century South Asian history, the formation of Pakistan as a homeland for Indian Muslims. This history also provides the background to the issue that was responsible for the recent success of the BJP: a dispute between Hindus and Muslims over a building in the city of Ayodhya, in Uttar Pradesh.

In the North Indian pilgrimage center of Ayodhya is an old mosque, known as the Babari Masjid, which was built in 1528 by a general of Babar, founder of the Mughal dynasty. The dispute centers on a local (hi)story, according to which the mosque was built to replace an even more ancient Hindu temple to the god Rama, which had occupied the spot from the eleventh century A.D. The temple commemorated the place where Rama, the god-hero of the great epic poem the *Ramayana*, had been born. After destroying the temple, the general built his mosque, using carved pillars that had been taken, the story goes, from the temple ruins. I heard this story when I visited Ayodhya for the first time in 1977. The British also recorded it when they took control over the city. After the annexation of the regional realm—to which Ayodhya gave its name (Awadh)—in 1856, the British decided to put a railing around the mosque and to raise a platform outside on which Hindus could worship, while Muslims were allowed to continue their prayers inside.

This situation seems to have continued until Independence. Following the partition of India and Pakistan in 1947, the Indian government placed a guard outside the mosque, which was now declared out of bounds for both communities. However, during the night of 22 to 23 December 1949 an image of Rama was placed in the mosque by a group of young Hindus, who have never been caught and tried. The next day a rumor spread quickly that Lord Rama had appeared in the form of an image to claim the mosque as his temple. Riots ensued, which were quelled by the army, but the image was never removed. Leaders of both Hindu and Muslim groups subsequently filed suits to claim the place as theirs.

In 1984 the Vishva Hindu Parishad, a Hindu nationalist movement, began to demand that the lock on Rama's birthplace be opened. *Tala kholo!* ("Open the lock!") was their battle cry. A procession started out from Sitamarhi (the birthplace of Sita, Rama's wife), reaching Ayodhya on Saturday, 6 October 1984. The procession consisted of little more than a few monks in private cars and a truck bearing large statues of Rama and Sita under a banner inscribed with the slogan *Bharat mata ki jay* ("Hail to Mother India"). The next day, VHP leaders and local abbots made speeches in Ayodhya. But none of this was very impressive. When the procession arrived at the state capital, Lucknow, however, it attracted considerably more attention. From Lucknow the procession moved on to Delhi, where the VHP intended to stage a huge rally, but it was caught in the aftermath of the murder of Indira Gandhi by her Sikh bodyguards, which turned national attention away from the Ayodhya issue. Nevertheless, in the following years the VHP continued to put pressure on politicians, which resulted in a decision by the district and session judge of Faizabad on 14 February 1986 that the disputed site should be opened immediately to the public. This decision triggered off communal violence all over North India, and on 30 March 1987 Muslims staged in New Delhi their biggest protest since Independence.

After the decision by the Faizabad judge the temple-mosque issue came to occupy an increasingly central position in the platforms of various political parties, ultimately playing an important role in the elections of 1989. Even the leader of the Congress party, the late Rajiv Gandhi, who was then leader of the opposition, insisted in a rally in Faizabad-Ayodhya that he supported the VHP case. But the issue was made absolutely central by the Bharatiya Janata party. At least from this point onward—and probably already in 1986—the political agenda of the BJP cannot be separated from that of the VHP. There is a direct coordination of rituals, agitation, and political maneuvering by the high command of the BJP, the

RSS, and the VHP—who in fact overlap to a significant degree. Vijaye Raje Scindia is a vice president of the BJP and a leader of the VHP; Lal Kishan Advani and Atal Behari Vajpayee are leaders of the BJP but have a background in the RSS; an important leader of the RSS, Manohar Pingle, has the VHP in his portfolio. Significantly, the VHP leadership also draws extensively on the experience of retired members in the higher echelons of the Indian bureaucracy, such as former director-generals of police, former chief judges, and former ministers: it is not simply an "extremist" organization, far removed from the mainstream of Indian society. Obviously, the support of persons with strong links to the bureaucracy is critical in the planning and execution of mass-scale demonstrations.

Beginning in September 1989 the VHP engaged in the worship of the "bricks of Lord Rama" (*ramshila*) in villages across North India, organizing processions to bring these sacred bricks to Ayodhya, where they would be used to build a temple on the site of Rama's birthplace, in place of the mosque of Babar. It is estimated that some three hundred lives have been lost in connection with these "building processions." The heaviest casualties occurred in Bihar, where the Muslim population of the town of Bhagalpur was almost wiped out. Ultimately, the VHP was allowed to lay its foundation stones in a pit outside the mosque on so-called undisputed lands. Remarkably, some of the stones most prominently exhibited come from the United States, Canada, the Caribbean, and South Africa, as if to emphasize the transnational character of this nationalist enterprise.

In 1990 there were two major political developments that affected the course of action regarding Ayodhya. In the first place, the Kashmir issue flared up again, bringing with it such unprecedented violence against the Hindu population that large groups of people were forced to leave that part of the country. The BJP took a strong anti-Pakistan stance on the situation in Kashmir—and, in India, this is always related to an anti-Muslim stance. Second, in September, V. P. Singh's government decided to implement an earlier report of the Mandal Commission that suggested a considerable increase in the number of places reserved for the so-called backward castes in educational institutions and government service. These reservation policies are among the most important political instruments in the modern Indian state. In South India these policies have led to the result that the great majority of the population is now listed as "backward." In northern and western India the policies have resulted in large-scale violence, which in a number of cases (Ahmedabad in 1985, for example) escalated into Hindu-Muslim riots.

Following the Mandal decision, widespread antireservation riots took place, during which a large number of students immolated themselves in what was for India a new form of protest. Since the agitation around the reservation issue imperiled the Hindu agenda of the VHP/BJP/RSS, Lal Kishan Advani, the leader of the BJP, decided to start a ritual procession that would pass through ten states—from Somanatha, in Gujarat, to Ayodhya, in Uttar Pradesh—with the goal of constructing the new temple to Rama on 30 October. Advani's posturing as Rama, with which this chapter opened, took place in the context of this campaign. His initiative met with great enthusiasm all over the country. Members of a recently established youth branch of the VHP, the Bajrang Dal, offered a cup of their blood to their leader to show their determination. All this ignited a kind of time bomb, which ticked louder with every mile taken in the direction of Ayodhya. Mulayam Singh Yadav, the chief minister of Uttar Pradesh, took a vow that he would not allow Advani to enter Ayodhya, and indeed, before 30 October, Advani was arrested in the neighboring state of Bihar by Chief Minister Laloo Yadav's government. This did not prevent Advani's followers from marching to the mosque, but they were stopped when the police opened fire. To appreciate the firm stance of the two chief ministers, Mulayam Singh Yadav and Laloo Yadav, who were backed by V. P. Singh's central government, one has to take into account that they are low-caste leaders of an upwardly mobile backward caste—*yadav* is a synonym of *ahir*, "shepherd"—that would benefit considerably from the implementation of the Mandal report. Moreover, V. P. Singh and his colleagues allied themselves with the prevailing tradition of institutional secularism. The government of India could not allow the radical alienation of its Muslim population by an attack on the Ayodhya mosque. Notwithstanding all the political strategy involved, then, the secularism of the state was at stake. It is highly doubtful that a Congress government would have acted in a different manner. Nevertheless, the actions taken by V. P. Singh's government resulted in its loss of the BJP's support in parliament and its subsequent fall on 16 November.

The VHP continued its agitation with a highly effective video and audio cassette campaign on the events in Ayodhya on 30 October. According to its claims, thousands have been killed by the police and the evidence suppressed. The bones and ashes of Ayodhya's martyrs were carried in special ritual pots (*asthi kalashas*) throughout the country before finally being immersed in sacred water. In Ayodhya itself a major ritual sacrifice (*mahayajna*) was sponsored by the VHP, with Vijaye Raje Scindia as the principal sacrificer.

As we have seen, this ritual campaign led to the BJP's electoral success in 1991 and to a BJP government in Uttar Pradesh. The problem then shifted to a standoff between the union government, formed by the Congress party, and the state government of Uttar Pradesh, formed by the BJP, the main national opposition party. This delicate situation was exacerbated by the fact that the VHP, which is relatively autonomous from the BJP, continued to press for a swift demolition of the mosque and building of the temple. There were signs that the BJP wanted to distance itself somewhat from the VHP, since it feared that the government might remove the BJP from power in Uttar Pradesh if it failed to restrain the VHP. At the same time, the VHP single-mindedly pursued its goal.

In 1992 the government of India, formed by Congress (I), attempted to resolve the issue by organizing direct negotiations between the VHP and the Muslim Babari Masjid Action Committee, but these negotiations proved fruitless. Then, on 6 December 1992, a rally in Ayodhya, organized by the VHP and the BJP, resulted in an attack on the mosque and its subsequent demolition. Although BJP leader Lal Kishan Advani, who was present at the site, immediately tried to distance himself from the act of demolition, there can be little doubt that the entire event had been well planned in advance.

The government of India took some strong action in response, imposing president's rule in Uttar Pradesh immediately after the demolition. This was followed by the dismissal of BJP governments in Madhya Pradesh, Himachal Pradesh, and Rajasthan. India's prime minister, P. V. Narasimha Rao, expressed the government's intention to rebuild the mosque. Finally, the government decided to ban several Hindu organizations, such as the RSS, the VHP, and the Bajrang Dal, which had played leading roles in the demolition campaign. These decisions were challenged by the BJP's attempt to organize a huge rally at the Boat Club in Delhi on 25 February 1993, which the government banned and successfully prevented from taking place.

Despite these vigorous actions by the government, the destruction of the mosque provoked immense communal violence, especially in Bombay, Ahmedabad, Surat, and Calcutta. More than a thousand people—most of them Muslims—were killed in Bombay alone. The pogroms in Bombay were led by the Shiv Sena, a fanatic Hindu political party active in the Bombay region, which, although banned, was, according to a number of reports in English-language news media, actively supported by the Bombay police force.[3] The participation of the police in the attacks on Muslims has also been documented in other areas, such as the east Delhi neighborhood of Seelampur.[4] The events in India had, moreover, international repercussions. They were followed by riots in Pakistan and Bangladesh, Muslims in these countries as well as in Great Britain setting fire to Hindu temples in retaliation.

Religious issues, such as the temple-mosque controversy, generate passionate feelings and violent action. A common fallacy is that these passions are "natural" and that the violent struggle is an explosion of pent-up feelings. I want to argue that, although passions are certainly involved, their very "naturalness" is produced by a political process. The temple-mosque controversy did not evoke strong feelings between 1949, when the image of Rama was installed, and 1984, when the VHP started its agitations. By transforming the mosque in Ayodhya from a local shrine into a symbol of the "threatened" Hindu majority, however, the VHP has been instrumental in the homogenization of a "national" Hinduism. This is not to say—as it often is—that this kind of religious controversy is only a smoke screen, behind which we can find the "real" clash of material interests and social classes. Nor is it simply a political trick conjured up by leaders for their own benefit. Such arguments simply overlook the importance of religious meaning and practice in the construction of identity. What we have to understand is how certain issues are promoted as "naturally" crucial to the "self-respect" of a collectivity that is portrayed as a homogeneous whole, as if it were an individual. If we want to penetrate the very real passions and violence evoked by the temple-mosque controversy, we must understand how this controversy is related to fundamental orienting conceptions of the world and of personhood, which are made sacrosanct. This implies that we have to analyze not only the ideologies that produce these conceptions but also the historical context in which they are produced.

Before the VHP started its campaign, Ayodhya had already been adopted in a scheme to promote indigenous tourism that included the building of hotels and the publication of tourist information, which would be made available in India's many tourist offices. It would be an exaggeration to claim that the spirit of pilgrimage has been replaced by that of state-sponsored tourism, but it is an important development that politicians have decided the state should provide for the middle-class needs of those on pilgrimage. Beginning in 1985 the state government of Uttar Pradesh embarked on an ambitious and extremely expensive scheme to beautify the waterfront of Ayodhya's sacred river, the Sarayu. In the middle of the stream a platform was raised, which can be reached from the bank of the river. Called "Rama's Footstep," it is an imitation of a similar platform in the Ganges at Hardwar. Likewise, the involvement of the state government of Uttar Pradesh in the decision of the Faizabad judge to unlock the mosque can clearly be interpreted as a move in a struggle for the control over Hindu places of pilgrimage, which are more and more included in middle-class tourist itineraries.

A parallel development is the success of religious stories in Indian cinema and, more recently, on Indian television. In South India movie actors have for some time been leading politicians, setting the stage for a cinematic populism through the use of religious imagery. This has now become a trend throughout the country. Playing a saint or god in a movie qualifies a person for saintliness or godliness on the political stage. Besides that, there is clearly a penchant among the public for the struggle between good and evil on the screen, which, in the past, was satisfied with nonreligious themes. But the new discovery is the dramatization of religious tales. A major event in the history of Indian television was undoubtedly the broadcasting of the *Ramayana* in the form of a serial rivaling the length of "Dallas" or "Dynasty," starting in January 1987. This has done more than anything else to make a standard version of the epic known and popular among the Indian middle class. Moreover, it greatly enhanced the general public's knowledge of Ayodhya as Rama's birthplace and therefore as one of the most important places of pilgrimage in Uttar Pradesh. In this way the controversy concerning the mosque built "on Rama's birthplace" has become an issue that is highly loaded with affect in the popular imagination.

For Muslims the issue has also become loaded. First of all, a mosque is sacred space. It cannot simply be demolished or removed. The very idea that a mosque should make room for a temple, in which images are worshiped, sounds like an utter defeat of Islam and is therefore highly repugnant to Muslims. Second, there is the (hi)story according to which Babar was involved in the building of the mosque. This provides even more reason for at least some Muslims to demand its preservation, since their pride and self-esteem is bound up with the glorious past of the Mughal empire. The decline of that empire is often construed as the decline of the Muslim community itself. In the Muslim view, the "facts" of this glorious past stand squarely opposite to the "fictions" of Hindu mythology. Babar and his general were historical figures and the mosque obviously a real building, while Rama and his birthplace are myths. The great importance of the Shiʿa nawabs for the expansion of Ayodhya as a Hindu center is as much underplayed by Sunni Muslims as by Hindus. The idea that the period of the Mughal empire's decline was at the same time the golden era of the nawabs of Awadh is too much connected with Shiʿa-Sunni strife to be considered in the construction of a Muslim history.

As far as the demolition of the temple is concerned, two different opinions are heard among Muslim leaders. The more radical version denies that there ever was a temple. In fact, it tries to deny the whole history of Hindu oppression by Muslims, calling it a Hindu fiction. The other version accepts the demolition of the temple as a historical fact but argues that Muslims had the duty to destroy places where icons were worshiped in a country that was under their sovereignty. Once it was built, the mosque became a consecrated place for them, which everyone had to respect. In their argument, a secular state must protect the right of religious minorities and cannot reverse events that happened almost five hundred years ago on the basis of majority sentiments. For Muslims the mosque is a symbol of their glorious past but also of their threatened present.

While much of the Muslim response is indeed a reaction to initiatives taken by the Vishva Hindu Parished, their position is not simply that of a beleaguered minority. Undoubtedly, the situation of the Muslim minority, who make up around 12 percent of the Indian population, cannot be properly understood without taking its relations with Pakistan and Bangladesh and with the wider Muslim world into consideration. In the construction of the Muslim "other" by Hindu nationalist movements, Muslims are always referred to as a dangerous "foreign element," as not truly Indian. The partition of 1947, as well as the events both leading up to and following it, have given this construction a strongly "realistic" aspect. First of all, the traumatic experiences of partition stirred up long-standing feelings of distrust. Second, such feelings have not been allayed by the subsequent history of unfriendly relations between India and Pakistan, which has led to a series of wars and other, more minor hostilities. In these events Indian Muslims could easily be portrayed as a foreign hand weakening India from inside. Third, the growth of labor migration (largely Muslim) to the Middle East, these laborers sending their remittances back to India, as well as the support given by countries in the Middle East to Islamic institutions and even to missionary activities in India, have again reinforced the foreignness of Indian Muslims in the eyes of some of their fellow citizens. Moreover, the assertion of Islamic identity in the politics of nearby states also awakens old fears among Hindu politicians. Finally, there is a perception of the Muslims as a homogeneous community, since they are seen to vote in elections as a bloc. As a result of all this, Muslims are readily stereotyped as a foreign element in Indian culture and society. When in power, they oppressed Hindus; now, out of power, they continue to withhold fundamental rights from the Hindus via the democratic system, as well as to act as the agents of pan-Islamism on Indian soil.

The temple-mosque controversy in Ayodhya has thus become a symbolic focus of Hindu and Muslim identities within the Indian nation-state. Hindu nationalism demands that the state be the instrument of the political will of its Hindu majority, and its choice of actions gives Muslims a justified feeling of being an endangered minority. It does not seem exceptional that it is the control over religious centers as material embodiments of beliefs and practices that is so crucial in religious nationalism. Similar controversies take place between Hindus and Jains in western India, and between Tamil Hindus and Buddhist Sinhalese in Sri Lanka.[5] I would also include in this category the many examples of attempts by the state to control religious centers, such as the *gurdwaras*—and especially the Golden Temple—of the Sikhs, the Hindu temple complexes in South India, and the Sufi shrines in Pakistan.[6] Moreover, it seems that this kind of contest is not only typical for the Indian case but for religious nationalism in general. One could cite many examples here, but let me refer only to one well-known bone of contention, Jerusalem's Temple Mount/*har habayit*/*al-haram al-sharif*.[7]

Sacred centers are the foci of religious identity. They are the places on the surface of the earth that express most clearly a relation between cosmology and private experience. A journey to one of these centers is a discovery of one's identity in relation to the other world and to the community of believers—a ritual construction of self that not only integrates the believers but also places a symbolic boundary between them and "outsiders." This is not an unambiguous boundary, however, but a contested and negotiated one. It allows for negotiation, revision, and reinterpretation, signaled, in the study of religion, by such terms as *conversion, syncretism,* or *reform*. The ambiguities of these terms are those of the social process of boundary maintenance.

Although it is in the nature of religious discourse and practice that sacred centers are alleged to transcend history, it is clear that, over the course of religious history, they are "invented"—"found" as well as "founded"—and also "lost" or "declining." Control over sacred centers and ritual action is not only crucial for the power of religious elites but is a source of continuous struggle between religious movements. The important role played by sacred centers in the construction of religious communities in India is continued in the construction of Hindu and Muslim nationalism. However, many students of nationalism will object that there is no such thing as religious nationalism—that, in fact, it is a contradiction in terms, since the nation-state is a secular entity. The notion that religious nationalism is somehow flawed or hybrid is at the heart of the discourse of modernity, which divides societies into "modern" and "traditional." But the connection between secularism and nationalism is a product of the Enlightenment. Before we can even try to understand Hindu and Muslim nationalisms in India, then, we must examine this connection in some depth—a discussion that will lead us into the problem of the colonial-orientalist impact on India.

The Great Divide

The temple-mosque controversy highlights the issue of the viability of secularism in contemporary Indian society. More than forty years after the founding of a secular state, Indian intellectuals, facing controversies such as that in Ayodhya, increasingly question the desirability of secularism as a basis for state policy. One argument by the anthropologist T. N. Madan runs as follows: Secularism is a value that developed in connection with Protestantism and individualism. In Protestantism salvation is an individual concern, rather than being mediated by the church, as in Catholicism. Combined with the rationalism of modern science, Protestantism has thus given rise to a secularizing process. Modernization theory then made this particular Western development into a universal feature of the transition from a "traditional" to a "modern" society. However, despite rapid industrialization and urbanization, as well as the spread of educational institutions—all aspects of "modernization"—secularization has not been very successful in India. Instead, there is a rapidly growing religious activism in politics. This being the case, T. N. Madan suggests that India's religious traditions should be protected from "secularist" attacks and used for the construction of an Indian nation-state that would not be alienated from Indian culture.[8]

I am in general agreement with this line of argument, and I want to pursue it somewhat further. However, Madan's suggestion ignores the extent to which Hindu religious traditions have, from the start, been creatively used for the construction of the idea of an Indian nation. Therefore, he cannot avoid the question of which traditions should be protected and used for the construction of a truly Indian nation-state. One has to acknowledge that some of these traditions are mutually antagonistic and thus have to be managed, rather than simply protected. Moreover, I do not see much evidence of a ruthless state policy to secularize Indian society. The problem is rather the state's diminishing capability to arbitrate

conflicts, such as the temple-mosque controversy, in a society characterized by a plurality of cultures. Nevertheless, Madan is right
in suggesting that to understand the specific ways in which the idea
of the nation is adopted in discourse about Indian society we have
to get away from the tyranny of modernization theory. The secular
nation-state as sign of modernity must be recognized as an ideological notion, which can be contested by other notions. Modernization
theory attempts to show that a particular blueprint of "the" modern
nation-state is the inevitable outcome of the history of capitalism;
its attraction lies precisely in its mixture of historical facts and social
ideals. Before we can understand the internal Indian debate on the
nation, then, we have to deconstruct discourse about the relation
among modernity, secularism, and nationalism.

Anthropological discourse about nationalism relies heavily on a
particular conceptualization of historical developments in Europe.
The emergence of the European nation-state is commonly seen to
depend on three connected processes of centralization: "the emergence of supra-local identities and cultures (the 'nation'); the rise of
powerful and authoritative institutions within the public domain
(the 'state'), and the development of particular ways of organizing
production and consumption (the 'economy')."[9] In a recent study,
Ernest Gellner connects these three processes in a characteristically
sweeping manner.[10] He argues that modern industrial society depends on economic and cognitive growth, which, in its turn, requires a homogeneous culture. A crucial factor is the centralization
of resources by the state in order to run an educational system that
can instill a standardized, literacy-based "high" culture. The industrial division of labor is an objective imperative for a shared culture,
that is, nationalism, and nationalism holds together an anonymous,
impersonal society made up of mutually substitutable, atomized
individuals.[11] That culture is by definition secular, since economic
and cognitive growth is only possible when the absolutist cognitive
claims of the earlier agrarian (namely, preindustrial) age are replaced by open scientific inquiry.[12] The industrial transformation of
an agrarian world thus brings a nationalism that comes packaged
with individualism and secularism.

Gellner's argument is not limited to European history but pur-
ports to offer a sociological analysis of what modernization entails
everywhere in the world. Though the industrial transformation and

the emergence of nationalism occurred first in Europe, it was spread
to the rest of the world via colonialism, namely, the expansion of
the European industrial society. As Sally Falk Moore rightly observes in her thorough critique of Gellner's position, his argument
contains a teleological assumption: the coming of nationalism may
not be smooth everywhere, but, in the end, nationalism definitely
will come and yield the fruits of modernity.[13]

Of course, it is plausible that there are significant relations between the emergence of an industrial economy and the gradual
homogenization of culture through a state-controlled education system. But Gellner exaggerates the universal success of homogenization and simplifies its nature. Gellner's argument subsumes a
variety of local histories under the mechanical laws of a universal
history. The history told by Gellner unfolds all by itself, independent of human agency. It is the story of the victory of a fetishized
historical force, capitalism, which celebrates objective imperatives
and ignores meaningful and innovative action by the individuals
and groups who make history in everyday life. Gellner pays little
attention to the contradictions of homogenization or to the forms of
resistance it meets. The basic flaw of the modernization theory
espoused by Gellner, as well as that of many Marxist analyses of the
expansion of capitalism, is the assumption that a shared culture (or
ideology) is necessary to integrate the social system. While it can
be seen that both the social constraints of the division of labor and
the physical constraints of political force to some extent produce
what we can call a "social order," there is no need to assume that
the social order depends on common culture and moral consensus.[14]

It should be clear that centralization and homogenization create
their own counterforces. There is an internal dynamic in these
processes such that what is at one point an antinational rebellion
may become, at another, a successful nationalist movement that
results in the formation of a nation-state. There is not much reason
to believe that this process will eventually reach a saturation point.
Nor is it sufficient to speak, as Gellner does, of entropy-resistant
traits, such as, for instance, race, that are barriers to mobility and
equality and can thus become politically important.[15] In other words,
the centralizing force of nation building itself sprouts centrifugal
forces that crystallize around other dreams of nationhood: nationalism creates other nationalisms—religious, ethnic, linguistic, sec-

ular—but not a common culture. The modernization paradigm makes too much of homogenization, while it overlooks "antagonization" and "heterogenization." The forging of identity always simultaneously creates diversity.

Gellner's text is important, though, in that it presents a picture of nationalism that is typical for an entire commonsense way of thinking. Crucial is the way in which the secular nation-state is presented as a sign of modernity. To a considerable extent the discussion of nationalism is thus narrowed down to the dichotomy between "traditional" and "modern." Tradition is what societies have before they are touched by the great transformation of capitalism—and what seems to characterize "traditional" societies most is that they are under the sway of "religion." Such a misleading conception is also fundamental to Benedict Anderson's ground-breaking discussion of nationalism. According to Anderson, nationalism appeared when the two large cultural systems that had preceded it—the religious community and the dynastic realm—disappeared.[16] In his view, the great sacral cultures with their sacred languages—Latin, Sanskrit, Pali, Arabic, Chinese—made religious communities such as Christendom and the Islamic *umma* imaginable, inasmuch as the religious specialists who mediated between Latin and the vernacular, for example, according to a medieval conception of the world shared by virtually everyone, also mediated between heaven and earth.[17] Nationalism as a "modern" phenomenon could only arise from the ruins of a "traditional" world, characterized by a religious worldview, by religiously imagined communities (using sacred languages), and by hierarchically structured dynastic realms under the rule of a sacred king.

Anderson and Gellner both present a view of the traditional predecessor of modern culture that is typical for an entire sociological tradition dealing with the great transformation brought by capitalism. The first difficulty with Anderson's argument is similar to one we have already encountered in our discussion of Gellner. Anderson often slips, almost unwittingly, from an interpretation of European history into the elusive category of world history: "In a word, the fall of Latin exemplified a larger process in which the sacred communities integrated by sacred languages were gradually fragmented, pluralized, and territorialized."[18] Anderson goes on to argue that models of nationalism—of European and American origin—were pirated by colonial nationalists in the second half of the nineteenth century.[19] The relation between this idea and the argument that "traditional" cultural conceptions had to disappear "first in Western Europe, later elsewhere" before nationalism could arise remains unclear.[20] On the one hand, we have the specific impact of colonialism, which is barely discussed; on the other, there is the modernization of Europe, which is universalized.

As I have shown above, the major problem with this kind of argument is that it is based upon an ahistorical and essentializing treatment of culture as either "traditional" or "modern." I want to illustrate my objections with a short discussion of the jajmani system, a classic topos of the tradition-modernity dichotomy in the study of India. This system is often seen as a "moral economy" fundamentally different from the modern "rational economy," or capitalism. What is described in the literature as "the jajmani system" is a system of exchange in Indian villages, confined to highly local arenas, whereby high-caste landowning families called *jajmans* are provided ritual and nonritual services by lower castes in exchange for products of the land (shares of the "grain heap"). According to the anthropologist Louis Dumont, who stresses complementary rights and the hierarchical interdependence of castes, this system is hierarchically oriented to the collectivity as a whole. Moreover, "This view of an ordered whole, in which each is assigned his place, is fundamentally religious."[21] In Dumont's view, then, "traditional" society in India is characterized by a religious ideology that encompasses a politicoeconomic domain.

Despite the considerable controversies surrounding Dumont's theory of the Indian caste system, anthropologists and historians have in general accepted the idea that India's jajmani economy is determined by traditional cultural conceptions. Nevertheless, there is quite a good deal of awkward evidence to show that the jajmani system as the economy of "traditional" India is largely a myth. This evidence—of the use of money, of the existence of property and of a market in landed property, of considerable labor migration, of great regional differences in precolonial and early colonial India— is either not considered at all or is presented as "peripheral" or "external," and thus not interfering with the fundamentally "autarkic" nature of village economy.[22] According to Frank Perlin, in later colonial times this evidence is treated as "invasions by the cash nexus, by commercial imperatives, the market, capitalistic relationships, of weanings away from jajmani, and of the decay of traditional circuits and obligations, and so forth."[23] As Perlin points out, however, this process is shown by various authors to be taking place at any time between the sixteenth and twentieth centuries. It is therefore entirely unclear when and where "traditional India" with its jajmani system can be found. The jajmani system is best seen as a convenient metaphor to describe a society that is not "modern" and that, in the name of progress and enlightenment, was "invaded" and destroyed by the arrival of capitalism in the colonial era.

In an attempt to bridge the gap between materialist and culturalist explanations of societal organization and change, Perlin argues that "the pre-industrial world remains a catch-all category in which the culturalist equation, in its several varieties, continues to manifest itself."[24] Only after capitalism has "invaded" a "traditional" society do materialists begin seeking material explanations for social phenomena. Culture matters in custom-bound "traditional" society, it seems, but rationality—economic and otherwise—dominates "modern" society. Only in the case of Western society, however, does the "traditional" culture safely become a thing of the past in a more or less definite historical period, that of the Enlightenment. In the rest of the world the transition is so vague that an anthropologist like Dumont can describe twentieth-century India as a "traditional" caste society. But this perspective is basically ahistorical: it makes the study of Indian history—and all other histories of the "traditional"—seem irrelevant. Within this framework all the comparative questions about societies and their development are already answered before they are explored.

Nationalism is generally assumed to belong squarely on the "modern" side of the "great divide." It is the result of the demise of "traditional" society and is therefore a sign of modernity. But there is a tension between this view and the observation that, in many societies, nationalism is the product of diffusion. In the latter case the "modern" is not the result of a historical transition; rather, the "modern" invades the "traditional." According to Dumont, this leads to a period of uneasy combinations, as exemplified by Indian communalism, which combines religion and nationalism.[25] Ultimately,

communalism will disappear only when the society is made truly
"modern." As we will see later, this view is shared by "secularists"
such as Nehru among the Indian nationalists.

To solve the conceptual muddle arising from Western cultural
discourse about "modernity," it is helpful, in the case of India, to
distinguish two separate, though connected, processes. First, there
is the development of supralocal identities. This is related to the
formation of states and other powerful centralizing institutions, as
well as to the expansion of networks of economic interdependence—
processes that are very much present in precolonial societies such
as India. Precolonial India had its own pattern of change, which
has, to an important extent, continued in the colonial and postcolonial periods. No doubt, colonialism and the expansion of the world
system impinge on these processes, but they do not determine
them. There is no reason to reduce multiple histories to the success
story of capitalism by denying the historical agency of the people
involved. Second, there is the introduction of a Western discourse
in which individualism, equality, and secularism are combined in
what we might call the religion of the nation. This type of nationalism offers an ideological blueprint of an imagined social order
deriving from the West. As a blueprint it has great force, but it is
constantly contested and certainly not dominant. What we have to
understand is the way in which this Western discourse is engaged
by Indian discursive traditions. Partha Chatterjee is right in asserting that Indian nationalist discourse is derived from the European
type but is, at the same time, different because of the colonial
context in which it has arisen.[26]

Colonialism and Orientalism

To describe in detail the impact of colonialism and orientalism on
Indian nationalism would require an account of the history of some
hundred years, from the mid-nineteenth century to the mid-twen-
tieth century. I will only be able to make a few general points here.
Let me start by making an admittedly false, but nonetheless helpful,
distinction between the impact of the colonial state on Indian society
and the impact of the orientalist study of India on Indian self-
perception.

The impact of the colonial state and its various institutions on

Indian society came into its own in the early nineteenth century. After suppressing a widespread civil revolt in northern India during 1857 and 1858, the British established their dominance officially by making Queen Victoria monarch of India. The nineteenth century saw a massive state project undertaken by a small group of British officials to enumerate, classify, and thereby control a quarter of a billion Indians. In this project categories like caste, religious community, and race were variously applied, but two elements are of particular importance: the collection of data on caste and the division of the population into religious communities. The census operations, begun in 1872 to collect facts about the population of India, made use of a classification of endogamous groups—castes—ranked in a hierarchical order. This classification was derived from classical Hindu texts, but the census operations succeeded in making it a contemporary reality.[27] They established an official discourse of caste that enabled officials to rule Indian society but that also had a deep impact on the way Indians came to perceive their relations with one another on an all-India basis. Some have argued that the British invented caste, but this seems an exaggeration.[28] Caste society did exist before the colonial period, but the census operations did much to make caste divisions more rigid and to encourage the application of all-India categories. This resulted in the enhanced importance of caste in dealings with the state and led to the emergence of caste associations (*sabhas*).

The division of the Indian population into religious communities was an aspect of colonial thought from the beginning. When the British sought to apply indigenous law, they made a clear-cut division between "Hindu" and "Muhammedan" law. This conceptual division was further institutionalized in the census operations, which established a Hindu "majority" and a Muslim "minority" that in turn became the basis of electoral, representative politics. The "establishment" of both the Hindu majority and the Muslim minority as social and political categories, however, was largely the result of the manner of classification, not of preexisting facts. To some extent one may say that the project of the colonial state created these facts. Again, this is not to say that there was no division of Hindu and Muslim communities in the precolonial period. There was: the division was not a colonial invention. But to count these communities and to have leaders represent them was a colonial novelty, and it was fundamental to the emergence of religious nationalism.

At the same time I would argue that too much is currently made of the colonial construction of caste and religious communities and too little of the precolonial basis for these categories, on which the colonial state had its impact. Much of the argument in this book is intended to demonstrate that contemporary Indian nationalist politics is to a significant degree "indigenous." To see the "foreign hand" as the only explanation of the origin of religious nationalism concedes too much ground to both colonialist and secular nationalist views of Indian society. The colonialist view denies Indians political agency in creating their society. Religious nationalist action is "passion," "the frenzy of the mob," not consciously chosen political behavior guided by a specific worldview. The secular nationalist view argues much the same but with the twist that this mob behavior is alleged to result from a political strategy on the part of the colonial rulers to "divide and rule" the Indian people.

The orientalist impact on the way Indians perceive themselves is also far-reaching. The orientalists saw India as an ancient Hindu civilization, in which Brahmanical authority was paramount. On the one hand, they stressed that Western and Hindu civilization had the same Indo-European roots and that the study of the Vedas was crucial for the understanding of Western civilization. On the other hand, they emphasized the decline of Hindu civilization under Muslim rule and saw themselves as protectors of their Hindu "brethren" against the oriental despotism of Muslims. Their study of Muslim civilization did not focus on India but on the Arab heartland. To the extent that Indian Muslims were studied, it was not a religious or cultural account but a political history focusing on the decline of the Mughals and intended to legitimate British rule. It is fair to say that Indian Islam was simply regarded as part of the great Islamic civilization centering on the Middle East, while Hindus were the true natives of India, whose ancient, pre-Islamic civilization was worth attention but whose present condition was deplorable.

Orientalist discourse found its way easily into religious reform movements and into religious nationalism. Hindu reformers like Dayananda and Vivekananda harped on the theme of decline and called for a revitalization of ancient religion. Since they saw the

West and their British representatives as part of the problem, they also called for a nationalist struggle. Muslim reformers like the founders of Aligarh University, but also reformist ʿulamaʾ in Deoband, called for a revitalization of a defeated Islam. Many of the arguments used here were directly derived from orientalism. However, we should be wary of giving orientalism hegemonic force, as Edward Said has done in his important book.[29] I do not agree with Said's notion that colonialism and orientalism created the reality in which Indians had to live. This notion is in itself an orientalist fallacy that denies Indians agency in constructing their society and simplifies the intricate interplay of Western and Indian discourses. As I will argue in chapter 2, both Hindu and Muslim reform continue discourses that have a precolonial tradition. What can be demonstrated is that orientalism has transformed them and has placed them in a new political context.

Colonialism, orientalism, and nationalism are discourses that derive from the Enlightenment. One of the most powerful arguments used to legitimate colonial rule was that the British were an enlightened race who had a duty to lead and develop the Indian people, steeped in ancient prejudices as they were. An important utilitarian element of this argument was that the British were a secular Christian nation who had a rational interest in a useful morality. Hindu society, on the contrary, was completely under the authority of priests and given to endless, absurd rituals.[30] The Muslims of India were at the same time "backward" and "bigoted," prone to zealous revolutionary activism.[31] It is curious that this colonialist argument continues to play such an important role in modernization theory as well as in Indian secular nationalism, although it is understandable, if we recognize it as a legacy of the Enlightenment. The colonial regime was to play the role of a modern, secular state in a society torn by religious and civil strife, just as it had in seventeenth-century Europe. Accordingly, the colonial state would only play a temporary role, until Indian elites were "enlightened" enough to assume their historic role as leaders of their own people.

There can be no doubt that Western discourse on the nation, derived from the Enlightenment and refracted through the lenses of colonialism and orientalism, had a great influence on Indian secular nationalism in both the colonial and postcolonial contexts.

The continuing force of this nationalist discourse is, to an important extent, related to the fact that the institutional framework of the colonial state, which has been inherited by the postcolonial state, is based upon this ideology. Moreover, in the postcolonial period it was adopted by a significant section of the Indian elite who took over power from the British. Nevertheless, secular nationalism remains a discourse that is necessarily linked to social movements the strength of which depends, at least partly, on historical context. Secularism did not prevent the founding of Pakistan, while in the Indian case we are witnessing the gradual weakening of secular nationalism at the present juncture.

In India the most important imaginings of the nation continue to be religious, not secular—although secular nationalism does exist as an ideological force. It is espoused by parts of the Congress party and by the communist and socialist parties. Among these secular nationalists, there is a strong tendency to call religious nationalism "communalism," a term used as a political insult. As Gyanendra Pandey has rightly pointed out, "communalism" is an orientalist term, coined to describe the "otherness" of politics in the "East" but now employed by secular nationalists to indicate the "illegitimacy" of religious nationalism.[32] In the heat of political struggle communalism is often taken by its opponents to be antinationalist, but it should be clear that communalism is only a form of nationalism. In communalism it is a common religion that is imagined as the basis of group identity; in nationalism it is a common ethnic culture that is imagined as such. Political will, expressed through a democratic process, a "common" history, and a "common" territory are characteristics of both the communal and nationalist concepts. One can go even further by acknowledging that, like all concepts of the nation, both are ultimately derivative of Western post-Enlightenment discourse. If there is a crucial difference between nationalism and communalism, it lies in their respective imagining of the content and practical implications of "common ethnic culture" and "common religion." Rather than as utterly opposed ideological forces they should be be seen as "moderate" and "radical" tendencies within nationalism. The moderates accept cultural pluralism and equality among different religious communities within the nation, while the radicals see the nation as the community of coreligionists.

Except for those of the Marxist left, Indian dreams of the nation always take religion as one of the main aspects of national identity. Even Nehru's version of Indian nationalism had to accept the significance of religious community in Indian culture. Likewise, an important part of the political discourse of the Congress party depends on the Gandhian legacy, which stands, as we shall see, in the Hindu discursive tradition. This political discourse is not secular, but it imagines a common ethnic culture of India in terms of religious pluralism. In this moderate view the different communities that populate the nation have to be represented in the state. This implies that the legal system has to acknowledge pluralism in personal law and that the educational system has to pay attention to a plurality of languages and religions. When conflict arises between groups with different ethnic and/or religious identities—that is, between subnationalities—the state is seen to represent a superior common interest and to stand above the conflicting parties, so that it is able to arbitrate. At the same time, the state must promote the idea of religious tolerance in a pluralist society, which it can only do by emphasizing the commonality of spiritual pursuits. Thus the state is not secular. Rather, it promotes a specific view of "religion" as a universal characteristic of Indian ethnicity. The different religions are only refractions of one great Indian spirituality, which the state provides equally for in its education system.

However, there is a considerable gap between these pluralist intentions and the actual functioning of the Indian state. While it is evident that conflicting communities do resort to negotiation, arbitrated by the state, it is also clear that the state does not transcend society. Indeed, if there is a shared view of the state in India it is that "others" have captured it and use it against "us." This view is highly damaging for the arbitrational role of the state in conflicts such as the temple-mosque controversy in Ayodhya. Important in all types of Indian nationalism is a perception of a transcendent state that is modeled on "traditionalizing" constructions, either of the "Hindu kingdom" or of the "Muslim sultanate." When a pluralist state can no longer project its transcendent, arbitrational image, conflicts can only be solved through violence.

The radical version of Indian nationalism takes one religion as the basis of national identity, thereby relegating adherents of other religions to a secondary, inferior status. The idea here is that one religion is superior to all others and that this fact should be expressed in control over public life. The movements that carry this radical message differ considerably. Some are political parties, like the Muslim League and the Hindu Mahasabha in the colonial period, both of which tried to maximize political power using the democratic process. But there are also religious movements that remain, at least partly, outside the democratic process and seek to expand their control over public life in other ways. They resemble one another in their aggressive drawing of symbolic boundaries between the religious community and "the others."

The temple-mosque controversy is only the latest in a series of struggles over the appropriation of religious symbols in which "party politics" is merely involved in a secondary way. However, these controversies touch the heart of the construction of religious identities, which form the premise of politics in South Asia. The expansion of religious movements and the transformation of the way they communicate "national" religious identities is crucial for both the radical and moderate versions of nationalism in South Asia. It is these movements that I will discuss in the next chapter.

Chapter Two

Religious Formations

In this chapter I want to discuss the formation of religious communities through the expansion of networks of families of saints and ascetic orders. Though we will see certain general patterns in the formation of Muslim, Hindu, and Sikh communities, there are also some important differences, so that, when we come to speak of Muslim, Hindu, and Sikh nationalisms, the "nations" projected by these nationalisms will each have unique features. These processes of conversion and expansion began long before the onset of the colonial era but have continued in the colonial and postcolonial periods, during which they have been transformed through the influence of reform movements. As I will argue, it is not so much the religious message of reform movements on which the discourse of religious nationalism builds. Rather, religious reform makes certain religious discursive traditions available for nationalist discourse. Moreover, religious reform movements do not have to replace earlier forms of religious organization and discourse to do so. While the first part of the chapter is mainly devoted to the *longue durée* of the evolution of religious organization, the second part focuses on the role of reform movements in the production of religious nationalism.

Expansion and Conversion

Muslim conversion has been a highly politicized subject ever since the first British census operation in 1872.[1] The census made it clear not only that South Asia had a very considerable Muslim population but also that this population could not entirely derive from descendants of Muslim immigrants. It had been a long-standing colonial myth that Indian Muslims were originally a group of immigrants who had ruled over the great Indian masses. The implication of this myth is obvious: the British replaced Muslims as just another ruling group coming from outside, because India needed control from outside. In an evolutionary perspective, the British, as representatives of an enlightened civilization, had to replace the Muslims, whose rule showed the signs of decline. This colonial myth was supported by a sharp distinction, drawn by the Muslim landed elite itself, between a ruling class of immigrant Muslims with high status and converts with low status. The great masses of Muslims converts who did not claim an origin outside of India became important only with the shift from elite politics to mass politics in Indian nationalism. The Muslim elite did not "represent" the Muslim masses; it ruled over a certain territory, along with its population. To be able to rule it had to forge alliances with Hindu elites as well, although the general idiom of legitimacy remained Islamic.[2]

It is hard to overestimate the impact of the concepts of "majority" and "minority" on modern Indian society. Obviously, these concepts are directly related to the enterprise of counting and classifying India's population undertaken by the British in the census gatherings. While this can be interpreted as a project that enabled the British to collect basic information in order to rule over India, at the same time it set the modern notion of "representation" on a numerical footing. The odd effect of the census was that it simultaneously cut the society up into infinitesimal units and yet created a huge "Hindu majority," together with several "minorities," of which the most significant was the Muslim. Political elites, who had to respond to the new facts of life, tried both to enlarge the communities they "represented" and to define their boundaries more clearly. For example, Gandhi coined the term *harijans*, children of the god Hari (Vishnu), for untouchable castes that had been relegated to the outside of "pure" Hindu society for most of history. According to Robert Frykenberg, Gandhi did this to make untouchables part of the "Hindu majority."[3] Likewise, Sikhs were counted as part of the "Hindu majority." All this was, of course, also contested in political arenas. A major leader from an untouchable caste, Dr. B. R. Ambedkar (1892–1956), argued against the Gandhian construction of a Hindu majority and ultimately organized a movement that encouraged untouchables to convert to Buddhism.[4] Currently, the separatist Khalistan movement among the Sikhs attempts to draw a sharp boundary between Sikhs and Hindus.

In this new configuration Muslims found themselves in a "minority," whose number and voting behavior became the new "facts" of representational politics. The Pakistan movement concluded from these facts that Muslims could only live safely and with dignity in a "homeland," where Muslims would form the majority. Ultimately, on the basis of the number game, North India was cut up during partition into regions with Hindu majorities and regions with Muslim majorities. However, this was not the end of it. The growth of the Muslim population continued to be one of the most vexing political issues in the new India.

The issue of the growth of the Muslim population has two aspects. The first is the politics of reproduction. The fertility rate among Muslims, according to the 1981 census, was 4.1 and among Hindus 3.6. One of the most tenacious Hindu myths in this connection is that the fertility rate among Muslims is much higher than among other groups of the population because Islam allows men to have more than one wife. This myth, which links religion to sexuality and politics in a very suggestive way, is crucial in contemporary Indian political discourse.

The second aspect of the issue is that of conversion. There is considerable controversy in both scholarly and public opinion—characteristically intertwined with what is called common sense—about Muslim conversion. One school of thought argues that Muslims sought the "submission" of those vanquished in holy wars (*jihads*). In this view conversion is an act of political violence. A related view is that conversion took place for pragmatic reasons and did not involve an act of faith. Another school of thought has it that conversion was a result of missionary activities by Sufi saints. Here, conversion did involve a change of heart or mind of individuals won over to the spiritual attractions of Islam. A third school of thought, which I have often encountered among Indian Muslims, offers a combination of the first two. It argues that a primary conversion through the sword was followed by a secondary one through Sufi influence.

Whatever the different views of conversion, the issue is not

merely a historical one but also involves a constant passionate debate about Muslim missionary activities—whether imaginary or
real—in contemporary India. After the oil crisis there was an explosion of allegations and violence centering on the idea that Muslim
conversions had been induced by oil money. The most important
of such conflicts related to Meenakshipuram, a South Indian village
in which an untouchable community converted to Islam in February
1981. Whatever the motives of the untouchables of Meenakshipuram to convert en masse to Islam, evidence indicates that they
were not forced by their poverty to go for paid conversion. On the
contrary, these converts were relatively educated and upwardly
mobile and claimed that the humiliations of the Hindu social system
were an important reason for their conversion.[5] Nevertheless, the
conversions were immediately perceived in the Hindu press as
induced by "oil money" and as a threat to "Indian unity." The union
government and its leader, Indira Gandhi, issued stern statements
against the Muslim conspiracy. The most significant result, however, was the growth of Hindu nationalist organizations, such as the
VHP and the RSS. Clearly, a feeling of being besieged was created
among Hindus, who can only be a "majority" as long as huge disenfranchised groups such as untouchables and tribals do not openly
declare themselves to be outside that majority. In this connection
it is important to see that "Gandhians," as well as members of the
RSS and the VHP, do not take the Hindu identity of untouchables
and tribals for granted but are actively engaged in the so-called
uplift of those sections of the Indian population. This social reformist
effort can, in my opinion, be seen as part of a long-term process of
"Hinduization" in India.

Indeed, most striking in the attention given to Muslim conversion is the tacit assumption by almost everyone that Hinduism is a
"natural given" on Indian soil.[6] It is simply taken to be the native
religion of India, while Islam is seen as coming from "outside" to
convert Hindus. Moreover, the project of conversion to Islam is
essentially seen as a failed one, if one portrays Hinduism as a
"sponge" that simply absorbs invaders and missionaries and turns
them into Hindus.[7] This set of assumptions is naturally highly det-
rimental to the position of Muslims as both genuine Muslims and
genuine Indian citizens when the Indian nation is defined as the
"sons of the soil." This is not to say that "foreignness" is an identity

mainly imposed from outside to mark off a Muslim minority. On the contrary, as we have seen, it is also an identity that confers status within the Muslim community, while the universal community of Muslims is a reference point, which in varying degrees has had its importance for Indian Muslims throughout history. Nevertheless, from an observers's point of view there is no good reason to insist that those who have a Muslim identity are either foreigners or converts, whereas the Hindu identity is natural or given. Hindu and Muslim are blanket terms that have been used to "identify" large and internally divided groups of people at various periods in Indian history. In the case of both Islam and Hinduism this implies a process of expansion and conversion. While "foreignness" always plays a role in a process of expansion, it is interesting to note that not only do Muslim elites refer proudly to their "foreign" origin but Hindu elites do so as well. South Indian Brahmans point to their North Indian origin, and all fair-skinned high castes claim an origin outside of India as an "Aryan" people that conquered South Asia and brought Hinduism with them. Such notions, which relate external origin to high status, have been stimulated by orientalist racism.

Another important misunderstanding is that the fundamental political cleavage between "Hindu" and "Muslim" communities is only the result of political developments in the late nineteenth century. The general view is that in the precolonial and early colonial periods Muslim and Hindu elites had shared interests and that this was what mattered politically. Moreover, the argument runs, there was a Hindu-Muslim syncretistic culture of the "masses." There are three important arguments we have to engage here, and they differ in their interpretation of what made religious difference emerge as the major line of political cleavage. Paul Brass argues that Muslim elites started to ask for preferential treatment in re- action to electoral politics, which in turn induced Hindu elites to mobilize the Hindu population for political action. This is an elite-focused rational choice approach. A second argument, put forward by Francis Robinson, has it that there existed long-standing essen- tial differences between Hindus and Muslims. Then, when new arenas of local power came into existence, in which local social conflicts could be played out, political entrepreneurs started to emphasize religious differences in their approach to the British

administration. A third argument more or less puts the blame on
the hegemony of the colonial state. In Indian secular nationalist
historiography it is the "divide and rule" policies of the British that
created the cleavage between Hindus and Muslims. A more so-
phisticated account is given by Gyanendra Pandey, who points out
that the British constructed a "communalist" narrative to interpret
the disconnected and highly divergent events with which they were
confronted.[8]

But if we focus on recent political history, narrowly understood—
whether as elite politics, essentialized religious antagonism, or colonial hegemony—the *longue durée* of the construction of religious
identities escapes our attention. There are a number of difficult
problems here. If we say that religious differences "become politicized" at the end of the nineteenth century, we seem to assume that
they were not political before. If we say that "communal" identities
are forged in this period, we seem to assume that people had very
different identities before and acquired new ones as a consequence
of political manipulation by elites or by the state. I would argue
that to understand the growth of religious nationalism we cannot
reduce the content and the formation of religious identities to the
maximizing behavior of elites, essentialized value systems, or the
hegemonic project of the colonial state.

Instead, I would propose, first, that if we want to take religious
discourse and practice as relevant to the project of religious nationalism, we have to attempt to understand religious identities as
historically produced in religious institutions that are in a constant
process of transformation. Second, I would argue that there is little
reason to speak of the "politicization" of religion in the era of nationalism, since religion is always produced, as Talal Asad argues,
by particular social forces, in other words, by power.[9] No doubt,
the colonial state introduced new political arenas based on electoral
representation, which called for broader political mobilization.
However, I would like to draw attention to the relative autonomy
of the historical transformation of religious institutions. Religious
identities are produced in religious configurations, which are related to other more comprehensive configurations, such as the state.
I would argue that the formation of religious communities is certainly affected by state formation but cannot be reduced to it.

Obviously, it is impossible to ignore the role of the state in the formation of nationalism. It is clear that nation and state are directly connected. Nationalism seeks control over the political unit, the state. Thus far, Muslim nationalism is the only religious nationalism that has been able to capture the state. Sikh nationalism has not (yet) been successful in creating that political reality, and Hindu nationalism is even further removed from that goal, if perhaps only because so much of the culture of the Indian state is already Hindu, in its "pluralist" version. The Muslim community can be accommodated by this type of nation-state, as it has been since Independence. The question is, however, whether the Hindu majority will be willing to adopt a more "singularist" version of Hindu nationalism. This can, in my opinion, be achieved only by a further demonization of the Muslim "other," resulting in an escalation of violence that in turn will cause a new Muslim nationalism to grow. There is nothing teleological in these processes, and there is no way to predict them.

While nationalism may try to capture the state, the state is often seen as the producer of nationalism. In Ernest Gellner's theory it is the state that centralizes economic resources in industrializing societies, thereby to making education in a national language and culture possible.[10] He is speaking here, as elsewhere, about the modernizing state in Europe. In nineteenth-century India, of course, a "colonial society" is produced by a colonizing state that was also engaged in creating a national identity "at home." Indian nationalisms are formed in resistance to this colonization but are also deeply affected by it. Incidentally, the element of resistance is certainly not limited to nationalism in colonial societies. Revolutionary nationalism in France placed "the people" in opposition to the absolutist monarchy, and settler nationalism in North America placed the settlers in opposition to the British state. In many cases it is in the dialectic of state projects and resistance to them that nationalism is produced.

In a series of fascinating papers, Bernard Cohn has focused on the documentation project of the Indian colonial state, which he sees as "both totalizing and individualizing."[11] This project created the totality of the people to be governed ("the Indians") but also marked off religions, languages, ethnic groups, and castes. In Cohn's work the study of the social history of colonial India is primarily the study of the construction of knowledge about India by the colonial state. Colonial data collection for the production of dictionaries and grammars, to be used in educational institutions, played an important role in the construction of language communities. Codifications of Hindu and Muslim law organized the relations between the state and religious communities. The census operations were crucial in the definition of castes and religious communities.

A crucial question is, of course, to what extent Indian national identities have in fact been constructed by the production of colonial knowledge. The emphasis on the colonial construction of communalism ignores the extent to which precolonial state formation had been involved in the construction of religious community. The destruction of the Vishwanath temple in Banaras by the Mughal emperor Aurangzeb (1618–1707), along with his imposition of taxes on Hindus, remains an important example of state-induced community formation. Together with Mysore's Tipu Sultan, Aurangzeb has become a symbol of Muslim political bigotry in the narrative of Hindu nationalism. The fact that this is rhetoric with a present-day political purpose cannot, however, obscure the existence of such community-based state policies in the precolonial period. On the Hindu side we might mention Jai Singh II of Jaipur (1688–1743), whose attempts to create a society based on Hindu ideology (*varnashramadharma*) remain a prime example of precolonial Hindu state policies. Another fascinating example is the *Muluki Ain*, a state treatise of 1854, in which the rulers of Nepal— which had not been colonized by the British—tried to ensure the purity of their Hindu society by documenting and certifying a hierarchy of social species and their interactions.[12] Muslims were categorized as a low caste in this state-imposed order. The independent Nepalese state has until recently portrayed itself as the flag bearer of Hinduism in relation to its colonial neighbor, British India, and its postcolonial neighbor, secular India. It is, of course, nonsense to say that the later religious nationalisms of the subcontinent are a linear development from these state attempts to create Hindu or Muslim societies. However, the point is that before the colonial period and independent of colonial intervention there were constructions of religious community in which state institutions were involved.

The societies that precolonial states attempted to build were not nations. Let me emphasize here that it is only in the nineteenth century that the discourse of nationalism gains influence and affects "protonational" discourses on community. Richard Burghart shows, in the case of Nepal, how notions about the relations between ruler, land, and people were only gradually transformed into the concept of the nation-state.[13] It should also be clear that in the precolonial period state projects were often contradictory and had only limited effect, since resources were not sufficiently centralized for states to have the power to control society. There can be no doubt that the colonial and postcolonial states have much more power to exert such control, but still it is important to realize that such power remains limited.

Students of the postcolonial Indian state often comment on the fragmented nature of political institutions in a way that reminds one of historians' assessments of the precolonial Mughal empire. Where students of contemporary India see a "breakdown" of institutions as leading to widespread violence, historians of the eighteenth century see the "twilight of the Mughals" as the cause of endemic violence. Where other writers who deal with the present period see violence as resulting from a monolithic modernizing state, some historians of the eighteenth century point to Aurangzeb's Mughal state and its constant military campaigns. The descriptions of the role of the state remain the same, whether one is describing the precolonial or the postcolonial state.

Without denying the importance of state projects in the construction of communities, the argument in this chapter tries to escape from the hegemony of the discourse on state hegemony. Community formation can be traced to a variety of sources, but in the case of religious nationalism we have to focus more than we normally do on religious movements and institutions, as well as on the disciplinary practices connected to them. There are, I would suggest, striking parallels at particular moments in history between the expansion of religious organizations and state formation, and between the formation of religious communities and nation building.[14] I will try to illustrate these parallels by discussing the evolution of Sufi, Hindu, and Sikh modes of organization in North India.

Sufi Cults

Saints, traders, and soldiers were the agents of Islamic expansion in South Asia. These three categories are sometimes difficult to distinguish. Sufi centers were at the same time centers of religion, trade, and political power. In the coastal areas Arab traders from the Persian Gulf were the first to introduce Islam, while Turkish armies brought Islam to the north. Whether the expansion was via trade or via conquest, however, Sufi saints were always among the first to explore the frontier. When I speak of Sufis I do not refer to something as vague as "Islamic mystics," but to brotherhoods (*tari-qat*) of people initiated by a vow of spiritual allegiance (*bai'at*) to a saint (*pir*) who claims to belong to a spiritual lineage going back to the founder of the brotherhood and ultimately to the Prophet himself. Most brotherhoods were founded outside of South Asia in places like Baghdad, but some, such as the Chishti brotherhood, are almost exclusively South Asian.

The expansion of Sufi brotherhoods was a crucial aspect of the Islamization of South Asia, since Sufism was largely coextensive with Islam until the nineteenth century. This expansion always had a military aspect. The South Asian landscape is studded with shrines for warrior Sufis, who are revered as religious soldiers (*ghazi*) and martyrs (*shahid*). Sufi saints were the leaders of military bands, made up of their spiritual disciples. They were constantly engaged in military combat with non-Muslims, but they also fought amongst themselves in the frontier areas of Islamic military and political expansion. Richard Eaton observes that the warrior Sufi disap-peared from the stage when a Muslim state was firmly established.[15] This observation is based on fourteenth-century material from the capital of the Muslim state of Bijapur in the Deccan, but it ignores the inner frontiers within such states. We have evidence from eighteenth-century North India that military bands of Muslim fakirs continued to exist, collecting tribute by force, until they were wiped out by the British at the beginning of the nineteenth century.[16] There is little reason, then, to support Eaton's argument that "the Warrior Sufi appeared only briefly in the subcontinent's Islamic frontier, being the product of unique historical circumstances. The disappearance of the Warrior Sufi may be credited partly to the assimilative character of Hindu civilization, which has usually suc-ceeded in at least modifying if not fully absorbing the many foreign elements that have been introduced into the subcontinent, and partly also to the establishment from the mid-fourteenth century of stable Indo-Muslim states on the Bijapur plateau." Eaton believes that the combined force of the warrior and virtue of the saint is an essential characteristic of Arab Islam but is not found in India after the fusion of Islam with a "reflective, syncretic, and sentimental" Hinduism. This argument derives from a misunderstanding of "Hinduism" and of religious expansion. As we will see later, "the combined force of the warrior and virtue of the saint" is as much part of Hindu and Sikh expansion as it is of Islamic expansion.[17]

Muslim state formation and Sufi expansion can be seen as dialectically connected. Often it was Sufis who penetrated "tribal" areas and established centers of healing and sacred power, long before Muslim states were established. Sufi fakirs were "wild men" who controlled the powers of the wilderness, of the forest. The legends of buried *pirs* in South India resemble those of non-Islamic warrior divinities.[18] These Sufis "converted" large groups of the population to a form of Islam. Especially in the Punjab and in East Bengal Sufi centers were eminently successful. When armies were able to incorporate these areas into a realm under a Muslim king, the new rulers inevitably sought association with preestablished Sufi centers to obtain legitimacy as well as crucial support.

By creating centers around tombs (*dargahs*) Sufis formed a constituency of lay followers. Essential in the Sufi brotherhoods is the relation between the spiritual master, *murshid* or *pir*, and the disciple, *murid*. Sufis use a telling image to express this relation: the disciple in the presence of his master should be like a corpse in the hands of a washerman. The code is one of total surrender to the authority of the *pir*. Although the *pir* is really only an intermediary between God and believer, he is often worshiped in his own right as a god on earth. This worship continues after his death, which is seen as merely a death of the body, while the spirit lives on to meet the Beloved God. The day on which the saint died is annually celebrated as a wedding ceremony (*'urs*).

The main feature of the *'urs* is a procession led by the living saint toward the sacred tomb.[19] It expresses the liveliness of a marriage procession, as if to deny death by celebrating the wedding of the saint with his beloved Allah. It is an occasion of great spiritual power, since the cosmological message is that the *pir* is still alive and has an unhindered access to God, in whose court he will now intercede on behalf of his supplicants. By implication, the distinction between the saint who is buried and his saintly descendant (*pirzada*) who comes to celebrate is unmade by this denial of death and by the assertion of the timelessness of saintly genealogy. The living saint, the spiritual head of the brotherhood, is, in his restrained behavior amidst an unruly procession (in which people sometimes get possessed), almost a replica of the tomb.

The saint's day provides a theater in which the saint appears as a sacred center, an icon of devotion. While in general his knowledge and behavior set an example to the followers, special emphasis is given to the power inherent in his body. Muslims and Hindus come to see and touch the saint in the same way they come to see and touch the tomb. The participation of Hindus is often taken to be a sign of syncretism, but there is reason for caution in using that term.[20] What is crucial in my observations is that Hindus and Muslims appear to have rather similar ideas about power and saintliness but that the participation of Hindus in the celebration is restricted. The saint's day is an occasion of power, and Hindus are permitted to benefit from it, but only within clearly defined limits. Women, both Muslim and Hindu, are also allowed to participate in the celebration but, again, often under strict conditions. Of course, these conditions are subject to varying Sufi traditions and to change.

The main virtues of the saint reside in the purity of his blood and the refinement of his behavior. These virtues depend ultimately on his exemplary family life. While ascetic celibacy, along with the power derived from it, is found in Sufi tradition, it remains marginal. In general saints are family men, and their honor (*izzat*) depends on the modesty of their women. No doubt this is true for every South Asian Muslim, but the seclusion (*purdah*) of women in saintly families is in general much stricter than in the rest of Muslim society. As Patricia Jeffery has shown in her study of the Nizamuddin Chishti shrine in Delhi, this can be partly explained by the marriage politics of the saintly families. It is extremely important to keep the blood "pure" when one derives one's power from descent. The traditional Muslim elite of South Asia claims descent from the Prophet via his daughter Fatima. Seclusion of women is part of the high-status behavior of that elite, of which the saintly families form a section.[21] In the religious idiom of my own Sufi informants, however, their policy of strict seclusion and consequent stringent limitations on the movement of women was portrayed as exemplary behavior (*adab*) for all Muslims to follow.

Public prayer, veneration of the saint, and listening to the example of the Prophet inculcate a sense of identity in Muslims. They form a community (*umma*) that may primarily be felt as local, as in the case of a localized saint's cult, but has some features that transcend the local boundaries. This is true both for the Sufi brotherhood and for the community of Muslims who go to a particular local mosque. I do not think in fact that the brotherhood is a more localized phenomenon than the mosque community, for both refer to a tradition that extends beyond local boundaries. The examples of the saints and the Prophet organize one's emotions and show one the proper way of life—even the proper way of dressing and the proper hairstyle. It is in his body rhythm, including his emotions of shame, honor, and desire, that a Muslim man feels part of a community.

In religious practice, however, there is a shift when one proceeds from shrine to mosque. The shrine is an open public space, which, though under Muslim control, leaves interpretation and practice to a great extent undetermined. The shrine and the veneration of the saints create a community that is hierarchized in terms of the degree of its involvement in the brotherhood. Hindus do participate, as people who benefit from the flow of saintly power, but they remain at the outer fringe of public ceremonies such as the saint's days. However, in terms of tone and atmosphere, a saint's day is entirely different from that other form of public worship in Muslim life, prayer in the mosque. The latter is an exclusive Muslim affair, which takes place within an enclosure that hides the prayer from the eyes of the infidels. The boundary between the community of believers who submit unanimously to Allah and the rest of the world is clearly drawn. This is not to say that the communal prayer in itself creates a universal community of Muslims, since there are various debates about how the prayer should be performed.[22] Nevertheless, those who pray together ideally form an egalitarian community of believers, clearly demarcated, spatially and religiously, from unbelievers such as Hindus or Christians.

Sufis do not see an opposition between the shrine and the mosque. There is often a mosque attached to a Sufi shrine. Granted, while the procession to the tomb is a show of openness, the prayer is an exclusive affair. While the procession centers on the powerful body of the saint, the prayer stresses the community and equality of those who jointly perform it. Both rituals, however, teach the participants an essential Islamic attitude of "submission." On the saint's day the disciples go together with their saint, as good Muslims, to pray in the mosque. Usually the saint is their leader in the prayer (*imam*), but that is not necessary. Celebration of the saint's day and prayer in the mosque belong together.

The distinction between tomb and mosque resembles that between the exoteric sciences (*zahiri*), such as the knowledge of the law (*shari^cat*), and the esoteric sciences (*batini*), such as the practice of meditation. The *^culama[,]* are the experts in the first type of sciences, while Sufi saints command the second type. In fact, however, until the nineteenth century this was a purely analytical distinction. The sciences belong together, just as *^culama[,]* and Sufi saints form one class of religious leaders.[23] Gellner's argument about Islam, which essentializes an opposition of "doctors" and "saints," cannot be accepted for the period before the nineteenth century, and even after that period it has to be highly qualified as an opposition between "reformists" and "traditionalists."[24] The same can be said about the opposition of shrine to mosque. As we will see, reformists oppose the shrine and see the mosque as the focus of Muslim practice. Their definition of the community is entirely an exclusive one, while the Sufi definition is inclusive, with a clear sense of hierarchical distance.

The tombs of famous saints and their descendants form a hierarchical network of shrines over a landscape they have sanctified. Saintly charisma is inherited through blood relation, and there mainly through primogeniture. There is also scope for personal charisma, but even in such cases some (imputed) connection with established lineages is important. The saint's cult is primarily a cult of power (*barakat*). The Sufi saint is a miracle man who has great powers, some of which—such as healing powers—are very much in demand. It is a commonplace that people turn to Sufi shrines for solutions to practical problems, such as the desire for children or the healing of diseases. The powers of a shrine and a *pir* family are broadcast through oral and written narratives that are spread by followers. These hagiographic tales provide answers to the problems of later generations as well as models of behavior. An especially successful medium of communicating the powers of a saint is music, especially devotional songs. Shrines draw great gatherings of people who come to hear the music and the poetry in praise of the saint and his family. Some of India's most important musical and poetical traditions find their origin in these gatherings.

Some observers emphasize tomb cults rather than the veneration of living saints as central to Sufism.[25] But in the eyes of followers the distinction between the tomb and the living saint who is currently on the throne (*gaddi*) is artificial.[26] The story of Sufi expansion is the story of tomb cults and the spiritual lineages connected to them. The most important tomb cult in India is that of Mu'in al-din Chishti, who was buried in 1233 in Ajmer, an important city in medieval Rajasthan, strategically located along the trade routes that connected coastal Gujarat and the city of Delhi, in the interior.[27] Almost nothing is known about the buried saint around which the shrine complex has grown.[28] It was only in the sixteenth century that the shrine became really important, thanks to the active patronage of the Mughal emperor Akbar, who visited the shrine fourteen times. From then on, the Mughals continued to support the cult of Mu'in al-din. But even in the colonial and postcolonial periods Ajmer remained the main Sufi center of pilgrimage for both Hindus and Muslims. Its fame transcends the national borders between India and Pakistan. My visit to the shrine, in 1986, coincided with that of Zia ul Haq, then president of Pakistan, whose pilgrimage seemed a conscious attempt to place his regime in the tradition of the Mughal emperors.

While this tomb cult is an overwhelming success, there have of course been a great number of failures. It is not easy to determine the causes of success or failure, although a few points can be made. The first concerns the relation between state formation and cult expansion. There is often a definite link between ruling dynasties, the formation of a regional realm, and a tomb cult. Political and religious history are clearly intertwined. Second, continuous propaganda, heralding the specific accomplishments of a shrine, such as the healing of particular diseases, and spread by a network of fakirs and subsidiary shrines, is essential to sustain a shrine's clientele.

The great success of Mu'in al-din Chishti's tomb in Ajmer depended on a combination of factors, including its strategic geographical position, the patronage of the most important Muslim dynasty of India, and its fame as spread through a large order of fakirs and through a network of Chishti shrines. Mu'in al-din's saint's day is not only celebrated in Ajmer but in shrines all over the country.

These shrines are hierarchically connected with one another. In particular, the ceremony of investiture of a new incumbent (*dastar bandi*) at a shrine is one major performance in which this hierarchy is visible, in that the incumbent of a "senior" shrine has to be invited to tie a turban for the new incumbent of the "junior" shrine. Finally, the cults of some of Mu'in al-din's direct descendants, such as Farid al-din, the third in succession, and Nizam al-din, fourth in succession, have won an enormous following in their own right, which has made Chishti Sufism one of the most important forms of Indian Islam.

The tomb cult of Farid al-din Chishti (d. 1265) has been thoroughly studied, which enables us to trace Sufi expansion and conversion in some detail.[29] The tomb is in Pakpattan, a place on the banks of the river Sutlej in Punjab. Pakpattan means "holy ferry," and it is remarkable that both its location and its name continue the Hindu image of the sacred center on the riverbank as a *tirtha*, a ford whereby one can cross over to the other bank of ultramundane existence. Baba Farid's shrine is a religious center that dominates a sacred region (*vilayat*). A constant flow of goods and services (*nazrana*) comes to the shrine in exchange for religious favors such as female fertility, good crops, and relief from illness. Very important as a system of redistribution is the free communal kitchen (*langar*), which testifies to both the wealth and the spiritual power of the cult.

The followers of the shrine and its saintly lineage have a history of how they became followers, and by implication, how they were converted to Islam. Several clans in the region are collectively adherents of the shrine, so that descent and religious identities merge. I see this as a point of major importance. When the ideologies of descent and conversion cannot be separated in a group's identity, the veneration of the saint is one of the foci of social solidarity. Moreover, as Gellner has shown in his study of Morocco, the saints can act as intermediaries among several tribes and thus create a religious unity that encompasses tribal diversity.[30] In fact, what we see here is the creation of a regional identity around the symbolic cluster of a tomb cult. The point is that not only do states play a decisive role in determining the identities of their subjects but religious regimes do the same. When the British tried to make their construction of "tribal identity" and "tribal customary law" the basis of colonial politics in the Punjab, they were opposed by Muslims who emphasized Islamic law (*shari'at*) and Muslim identity.[31] Both the construction of a tribal system by a colonial state and the opposition against it can be interpreted as the transformation of an identity, in which the principles of descent and spiritual allegiance were merged by a religious Sufi regime. In this transformation not only British policies but also Islamic reform played a decisive role.

Historically, the establishment of Baba Farid's shrine was instrumental in the transformation of this region from a non-Islamic into an Islamic one. This transformation was not simply the result of conversion. Before the colonial time one can say that the descendants of Baba Farid, the Chishti clan (*biradari*), ruled their realm sanctioned by the paramount powers in Delhi. Their followers formed armies with which they defended and expanded their territory. In the nineteenth century their political power was only contained by that of the Sikhs, who were succeeded by the British. To some extent this pattern continued under the British, who used the saints' authority in a system of "indirect rule." Part of that authority was no doubt spiritual, deriving from being in the line of descent from Baba Farid, but part of it was also material, since the descendants were landlords and the followers their tenants. The spiritual hierarchy of a saintly lineage (*pirzade*) with its lineages of disciples (*murid*) is at the same time a social hierarchy of high-status patrons and low-status clients. This hierarchy was not only sustained by patterns of spiritual patronage but also by patterns of marriage and kinship. The families of tribal chiefs gave their daughters to the Sayyid families of Baba Farid's clan, while these families kept their daughters within the clan—a hypergamous pattern commonly found in northern India and related to a hierarchical worldview, in which the status of bride-givers is seen as lower than that of bride-takers.

Despite a high degree of congruence between being a spiritual follower and being a tenant, a would-be follower had to take an oath of allegiance (*bai'at*). To accept a *pir* as one's spiritual master is culturally conceived as a matter of personal choice, however constrained by circumstance. The question is whether, by taking this oath, a non-Muslim becomes a Muslim. I would argue that the oath's implication is that one becomes a follower of Baba Farid and by that token a Muslim.[32] While an initiation ritual is thus symbolic of conversion, it is only the initial stage in a long process of Islamic socialization that extends over several generations and is subject to historical context. There is clearly a temptation to see this as a teleological process of which the outcome is a kind of Wahhabism, a "purist" or "reformist" Islam. But this would certainly be incorrect. What one might suggest is that those who have been initiated as Sufis gradually come to be socialized in a Muslim world, in which knowledge of the Qur'an and an awareness of the need for communal prayer in the mosque is important. That this socialization was indeed happening long before the advent of nationalism in the nineteenth century is apparent from the attempts to transmit the message of Islam in the local language, as is attested as early as the sixteenth century by the *puthi* literature in Bengali.[33] Sometimes this literature went far in trying to accommodate both Hindu and Islamic concepts, but the aim remained to convey Islam rather than to create a new, syncretistic religion. Nor were the Bengali attempts to reach the masses accepted by everyone. In this and other cases an internal debate among Muslims about the issue of orthodoxy remained important. Although the participation of the laity in these debates was limited, the fact of their socialization as Muslims made participation possible in principle and allowed for the later notion of representation, which would provide the basis for nineteenth-century reform and nationalism.

The demonstration of an identity shift remains a thorny historical problem, since so much depends on cultural debates about the self, inner and outer, as well as the boundaries between the two. Richard Eaton has pursued an interesting, quantitative approach to the overall rate of change from any given religion toward Islam among the followers of Baba Farid.[34] He counts masculine given names in genealogical charts and enumerates the frequency with which Muslim names occur. The Siyal clan of Jhang district, which he takes as his example, has a tradition that their founder was converted by Baba Farid. In the twenty generations stretching from the thirteenth century, in which the founder lived, to the nineteenth century, in which the charts were gathered into a book, there is a remarkable shift in the occurrence of Muslim names. Until the fifteenth century only Punjabi secular names occur, and it is not until the middle of the seventeenth century that Muslim names achieve parity with Punjabi secular names. The data also indicate that by the early nineteenth century Punjabi secular names had totally disappeared. If we take the bestowing of a name as an external sign of conversion, then the process of conversion in this example spanned a period from the fourteenth to the nineteenth century. If we ask ourselves "What's in a name?" the answer might be that names are very significant parts of one's social identity. Here, the documented change in names reveals a very slow homogenization of the identities of tribal followers of Baba Farid. Such Islamization is, as we will see below, not different from a process of Hinduization or Sikhization.

The evidence of a gradual process of Islamization should not make us forget that identity formation works by a dialectics of inclusion and exclusion. It is often observed that Sufism has open boundaries, that its beliefs and practices are syncretistic, allowing room for local customs. While this is true, it should not be exaggerated. There have always been mechanisms for boundary maintenance within Sufism that stress Islamic exclusivity. Throughout history, many Sufis have never been interested in attracting anything other than Muslim followers. Moreover, what the identity of a true Muslim should be has always been contested by Sufis of different persuasions. Central to that debate has been the notion that a true Muslim must be able to demonstrate some sort of continuity with the past.[35] Not only did the very spiritual lineages of Sufi saints go back to the roots of Islam, but the masters were always concerned with "true practice" and "true belief" according to Islamic law (*shari'at*) and the exemplary practices (*sunna*) of the Prophet. There has thus been constant debate about "orthodoxy" throughout Islamic history, but, as we will see, the shape of this debate was transformed in the nineteenth century.

Hindu Devotionalism

Saints, traders, and soldiers are as much the agents of Hindu expansion as of Islamic. Contrary to the popular Western belief, Hinduism cannot be characterized by an ethics of pacifism. The Hindu notion of nonviolence (*ahimsa*) derives from a theologically grounded opposition to animal sacrifice. In that sense it is the ideological basis of vegetarian practices but not of a general pacifism. Hindu saints (*sadhus*) have always been soldiers as well as traders, and fighting ascetics (*nagas*) form important military sections of most Hindu monastic orders. Their organization into regiments and armies is probably a development of the eighteenth century, but these *nagas* represent a long tradition within asceticism.

Ascetics have until recently also been important traders. In the eighteenth century they were even the principal traders in several parts of North India. As Bernard Cohn points out, Shaivite ascetics were the commercial leaders of the important North Indian commercial town of Mirzapur.[36] He argues that these ascetics had at least two great advantages as traders. They could both pool and build up their resources, especially since they were not forced to squander them in conspicuous consumption during the great status ritual of marriage or to divide them up among their inheritors. Moreover, they could use their pilgrimage circuit, which ran from Hardwar in the north through the Gangetic plain to Bengal and Puri in Orissa, as a trading network. Christopher Bayly has put the point succinctly: "Using a combination of military and commercial power, they could link up areas of supply and demand in the stable and productive zones and provide their own protection on the difficult routes between them. Their corporate savings and investment habits enabled them to form and direct the uses of capital with great efficiency. By the 1780s, the ascetic sects seem to have comprised the dominant money-lending and property-owning group in Allahabad, Benares and Mirzapur."[37]

It is important to state here that although we have very clear evidence of the combination of trade, soldiery, and asceticism in the eighteenth century, there is no reason to surmise that this combination was a result of the "twilight of the Mughals"—since we also have scattered evidence that this combination existed in earlier periods.[38] What seems to have happened in the seventeenth century is that Mughal rule, which was at its height before 1720, stimulated the expansion of communications in large parts of India. Moreover, the emergence of powerful regional realms, such as that of Awadh, in the early eighteenth century did not put a brake on this development—as theories about the decline of the Mughal empire have often supposed—but in fact did much to encourage it. There can be little doubt that this expansion of communications allowed the related phenomena of pilgrimage and trade to thrive in the eighteenth century. This explains the oral accounts of growing competition among several Hindu orders in that century and also the incipient military organization of various groups of fighting ascetics. Violent clashes among several orders occurred regularly at the great monastic gatherings during the bathing festivals (*kumbh melas*) that took place on auspicious occasions. Even today the order of precedence in taking a bath is a matter of conflict between the orders, but the battles of the eighteenth century were directed at the control of the sacred centers at which these bathing festivals were held. These centers were nodal points in a system of both pilgrimage and trade.

The Hindu "saints," the *sadhus*, are organized into monastic orders. The origin of the orders is unclear, but Hindu asceticism probably originated in the same era as the great ascetic religions of Jainism and Buddhism, namely, in the middle of the first millennium B.C. The most striking development in early Hinduism is the gradual growth in importance of the devotional cults of two male deities, Vishnu and Shiva, cults that incorporated the cults of various female deities ("mothers"). The spread of Vaishnavite and Shaivite cults depended largely on ascetics.

Some authors argue that there is a structural tension in Hinduism between Brahmanism, the religion of the Brahmans, and renunciation, the spiritualism of the ascetics.[39] I am not convinced by that argument. On the contrary, most ascetic orders have been founded by Brahmans, and some orders consist entirely of Brahman ascetics. After all, one's caste status does not become irrelevant after one has chosen to become an ascetic. To some extent, the relation between Brahman priests and ascetic gurus resembles that of 'ulama' and *pirs* in pre–nineteenth-century Islam. They form a combined religious elite with high social status but divergent ritual and spiritual practices. In both cases this elite maintains rather tenuous relations with groups of "wild" ascetics and fakirs, who reject all worldly status distinctions. To be really successful, though, the orders have to be supported by dominant, high-status groups—who tend to have more respect for high-status Brahman ascetics than for non-Brahmans, who may have a lower social status than they themselves have. An even more important explanation of Brahman domination is the fact that the worship of images of "high" gods like Vishnu and Shiva is preferably left to men of higher ritual status.

The first half of the second millennium A.D. witnessed the expansion of ascetic orders, along with the cults of their gods, throughout the Indian subcontinent, as well as the development of temple worship, mostly with Brahman officiants. Hinduism, as we see it today in India, focuses on the devotional worship of images of a personal savior-god (Vishnu or Shiva), who is the husband-lover of the mother deity, or on the imageless worship of a transcendent world soul. It is not a religion centered around a powerful church, but it has an internal coherence that justifies its identification as "Hinduism." Hinduism can be seen, very much like Islam, as a not fully integrated family of ideas and practices spread by ascetics and priestly families over an enormous region inhabited by very different populations. Although there is no churchlike organization, there are long-term processes of centralization and homogenization. These parallel processes remained, however, largely confined to particular regions and particular peoples until the present century.

By and large the expansion of Hinduism is not different from that of Sufism. A crucial difference, however, is the ultimate reference of Sufi orders and *'ulama'*, with their different beliefs and practices, to one revelation and one Prophet, which allows for a greater degree of centralization. The story of Hindu expansion is therefore more complicated than that of Indian Islam, but, when we restrict ourselves to the observation of Hindu and Islamic expansion in the same region (North India) and period (1400–1900), it is remarkably similar. In both cases the regime building of orders and brotherhoods led by spiritual masters is crucial.

What are Hindu ascetic orders? Hindu saints or monks (*sadhus*) are initiated into an ascetic and/or devotional tradition (*sampradaya*) by a spiritual master (*guru*). Those who are initiated by the same guru form a family (*parivar*) and belong to a spiritual lineage going back to the god of the order. In the process of initiation one loses one's name and one's worldly connections. Moreover, a monk takes a vow of celibacy (*brahmacarya*). The organization of Hindu orders, like that of the Sufi brotherhoods, is loosely structured around the personal relationship between guru and spiritual disciple. The relation between the order and a supporting laity is also organized around the dyadic relation between guru and disciple. The layman is initiated in the same way as the monk, except that he does not take the vow of celibacy. While the choice of a guru is optional, there are in many cases traditions that connect families with lineages of gurus. In the literature dealing with Hinduism these collectivities of lay followers clustered around a nucleus of ascetic lineages are often called sects, although this term has a number of problematic connotations deriving from its use in the history of Christianity.

Celibacy is, however, a contested phenomenon in Hindu devotional groups. Many of these groups exhibit a tendency toward the marginalization of ascetic celibacy once they settle in holy places and abandon their migratory style of life. Most Krishnaite religious communities (Krishna is an incarnation of Vishnu), although founded by celibate ascetics, are led by families of gurus who trace their ancestry to the married successors of the founders. These families closely resemble those of the descendants of a Sufi saint (*pirzade*). Besides these families there are groups of celibate ascetics who go around the countryside to spread their message. Both the lineages and the ascetics are supported by the gifts of a supporting laity. What little documentation exists shows that the social identity of that laity is largely formed by their allegiance to the gurus of the community.[40] However, a caveat is in order here. Some guru lineages have been better able than others to bind a self-reproducing lay community to them. There are also cases in which the allegiance to a guru is restricted to only one generation, while, in other cases, different members of one family may choose gurus from different orders.

The importance of peripatetic ascetics lies in their instrumentality in the spread of devotional cults and the incorporation of non-Hindu cults. This expansion generally took the form of the "discovery" of places that had been lost in an earlier, mythic era (*yuga*). This method ensured an aura of great antiquity to the newly established center. In many cases the discovery implied violent struggles with other claimants, ascetics of rival orders.[41] Also important is that the orders established their cults in places where other cults (of mountains, snakes, or trees, for example) already existed. In all these cases the cults have at least two layers: a lower stratum, made up of the superseded religious beliefs and practices, and an upper stratum, formed by the general patterns of theology and ritual of the monastic orders. This is attested by evidence from all over South Asia but has been particularly well researched in the Braj area near Mathura in North India. Charlotte Vaudeville shows that, in the sixteenth century, the ascetics who developed the worship of Krishna in this area incorporated in various ways older forms of worship within their cult.[42] It is striking that so many of the older forms have remained so clearly visible down to the present day, to the point where the upper stratum of Krishnaite beliefs is often not much more than a thin veneer. In the course of almost four centuries of Krishnaite dominance the orders have no doubt woven a web of Krishnaite signification through which the older icons and their worship are interpreted, but the process of conversion is still unfinished. Incorporation of older forms within a new cult is often effected by arguing that the icon worshiped is really a manifestation (*avatara, vyuha*) of the new deity. In Braj, however, this interpretation did not reach large groups of the population, who still did no more than superficially acknowledge Krishnaite interpretations.

One feature of Hindu ascetic organization is its resistance to centralization. Every guru has his own followers and is not, in principle, subject to a higher authority. Nevertheless, important historical attempts at centralization have occurred. A majority of Shaivite ascetics accept the authority of four leaders who have their monasteries in four different parts of India. In addition, Shaivite centralization was encouraged by the existence of an army made up of regiments of fighting ascetics (*nagas*), which has a long history. From the eighteenth century we have evidence that some Shaivite ascetic groups could also be hired as mercenaries, even by Muslim rulers. The army of the nawabs of Awadh, the greatest Muslim power in the eighteenth century, depended on Shaivite ascetics. Two of Nawab Shuja-ud-Daulah's three most powerful generals were Shaivite ascetics. By 1760 they held in readiness a combined force of twelve thousand men.[43] Anupgiri (1780–1804), alias Himmat Bahadur, a Shaivite ascetic general, followed a career as a condottiere, which made him one of the most influential power brokers in North India.[44]

A significant degree of military organization was also found among other ascetic groups, such as the Dadupanthis, who even served as regular soldiers in the army of Jaipur until 1938. Very important was an attempt to integrate ascetic groups who worship various manifestations of Vishnu into a Vaishnavite brotherhood with an attached army. This was largely the effort of the king of Jaipur, Jai Singh II (1688–1743), one of the most powerful rulers in North India.[45] Jai Singh tried to create a homogeneous Hindu community of Vaishnavite persuasion by forcing the religious leaders of the

Vaishnavite communities to collaborate in spiritual affairs and to combine their armies. There can be no doubt that Jai Singh tried to implement Brahmanical political theory (*varnashramadharma*) by demanding that the communities follow caste regulations and that ascetic celibacy be postponed until the last stage of life. His own role was clearly that of the *dharmaraja*, the "righteous king" and "protector of the socioreligious order." But this attempt at religious state formation proved abortive. There is more than one reason for its failure. Jai Singh tried to force leaders of different, though related, religious communities to combine under a new, all-embracing banner. The theological, ritual, and organizational differences were just too large, however, for such an outside initiative to succeed. Moreover, there was too great a disparity among the different Vaishnavite groups, who catered to the religious needs of groups of people with different socioeconomic positions, and in places as far apart as Bengal in the east and Gujarat in the west.

The military and economic power of the ascetic trader-soldiers declined among all the diverse religious regimes—Hindu, Sikh, and Sufi—in the nineteenth and twentieth centuries during the Pax Britannica. While the eighteenth century had seen the greatest expansion of this power, this era came to a characteristic end in the so-called Sannyasi Rebellion in Bengal and Bihar, in which Hindu *sadhus* and Muslim fakirs fought the British in a protracted battle for control over tax collection that lasted from 1770 to 1800.[46] Some of the peasant rebellions against the British that flared up in the same region later in the nineteenth century were again led by ascetics.[47]

Although in general the British wanted to get rid of their ascetic competitors, there were exceptions. In Gujarat the British sought the support of a religious regime that had a pronounced a military character. Swami Narayan, the leader of an important Vaishnavite community, was seen by the British as one of the most critical centralizing and pacifying forces in large parts of Gujarat. Since the British were not able to suppress banditry and marauding in areas like Kutch and Kathiawar on their own, they accepted the Swaminarayanis as partners in their enterprise.[48] When the swami met an Anglican religious leader, Bishop Reginald Heber, he was accompanied by two hundred horsemen and a large number of armed disciples. Much of the military power of Swami Narayan had been built up in the face of violent opposition from other Vaishnavite groups who were already established in the area, as well as dynasties like that of Ahmedabad. Nonetheless, the Swaminarayanis' partnership with the British in controlling large parts of Gujarat did pay off considerably. Their gurus started to attract groups of upwardly mobile peasants, who benefited greatly from agrarian reform, especially the growing of cash crops. The Swaminarayani gurus also played a crucial role in "civilizing" and organizing what was to become a leading elite in Gujarat, the Patidar community.

There is no doubt that the expanding influence of groups of saints led to the conversion of enormous groups of people to some form of Hindu identity. Nevertheless, Hindu devotional communities remained bound to certain regions and social groups, so that Hindu identity continued to be fragmented. To the extent that there is a common denominator, it can be found in the discourse and practice of devotionalism. There is a constant dialectic between celibate renunciation and domesticity that is played out in the myth-models of the most important Hindu gods, Shiva and Vishnu, the latter in his two principal manifestations, Rama and Krishna.

Shiva can be seen as the grandiose self-sufficient ascetic, whose erect phallus (*linga*) is the ambiguous symbol of ascetic chastity and erotic life-giving power. His mythology abounds with the tension between his asceticism and the claims of domestic life with wife and child. Krishna's mythology centers on two myth-models. The first shows Krishna as a spoiled, male child, doted on by his mother. It thus deals with the mother-son symbiosis that is so important in Hindu culture. In the second, Krishna is the great lover who has endless relations with the cowherd girls (*gopis*). This myth-model deals with free love, but love is theologically interpreted not as sexual gratification (*kama*) but as selfless devotion (*prema*). The emotion of love is thus sublimated into devotional worship. In contrast to the erotic abandon that characterizes much of Krishna mythology, Rama's story deals largely with the sacred marriage of Rama and his wife, Sita. Rama is the ideal of the detached husband, of chastity within marriage; Sita is the ideal loyal wife.

The myth-models of all three gods are played out, celebrated, and developed in devotional discourse. There is no clear-cut restriction of the myth-models to certain communities that worship a particular god, although every community approaches these myths from its own angle. Rather, it is a fairly open discourse in which the main theme of chastity and detachment within marriage is presented from different sides and repeatedly reworked by the creative use of different myth-models. The guru, whether a celibate monk or a family man, reveals in his behavior the ideal of a detached life.

How does ritual practice communicate the devotional myth-models through which a person's sense of identity is constructed and his private experience objectified? The devotee should cultivate humility, equanimity, and detachment, study and listen to the scriptures, and most of all immerse himself in a devotional mood. One does so by joining a community of faithful and by following the instructions of the guru. All this seems very internalized and private, but in fact devotional practice is a public theater of the emotions. Central is worship of the image of the deity in a temple, which includes the celebration of festivals, whereby the image is offered all the good things. This form of worship is called "service" (*seva*) and requires constant attendance upon the deity. The image is perceived as a living presence of the god, endowed with human feelings and tastes. It is interesting that the guru, the living leader of the community, is often equated with the image as a living presence of the god. The word *murti*, "image," is also applied to the guru. Likewise, the attendance to all the needs of the guru replicates the service for the image. The immediate worship of the image of the deity itself is in the hands of male Brahmans, who are ritually pure. While nobody but the Brahman priests may touch the image, the "looking at the images" (*darshan*), the music, and the offering of food are public performances that create a sense of community. Listening to devotional songs and to stories told or performed in theater plays (*lilas*) is also essential in the construction of a Hindu devotional identity. Though these performances are to a great extent open to the larger public, there are also certain boundaries.

One of the most important boundaries is that which excludes untouchables. This is, of course, of crucial importance for the construction of a Hindu community, since untouchables form some 15 to 25 percent of the Indian population. Their exclusion thus presents a major obstacle for the expansion of Hinduism. It is a very complicated matter to decide what untouchability meant in the precolonial period. Perhaps at the village level untouchable groups did participate in the worship of the gods, while they were excluded

from at least some devotional cults that were firmly in the hands of
Brahman priests. The crux of the matter seems to lie in the ritual
supremacy of the Brahmans as priests who, in their obsession with
purity, were generally against the integration of castes who had to
perform polluting services for the community, such as scavenging.
Thus, legislation introduced by both the colonial and postcolonial
state that would permit untouchables free entry into Hindu temples
has been primarily (and often exclusively) attacked by Brahmans
afraid of losing their ritual supremacy.[49] But worship of the deities
has not in any way declined owing to the "defilement" caused by
the entry of untouchables. Moreover, the idea that untouchables
should be made part of a Hindu community is one of the most
important issues in the ideology of present-day Hindu nationalist
movements such as the Vishva Hindu Parishad. Untouchables are
rhetorically incorporated into the Hindu nation, though, as a group
of people who, like the tribals, have to be "uplifted" by a program
of social reform.

The other group excluded from participation in the direct worship of images is the Muslims. They are "barbarians" (*mlecchas*),
outside the pale of Hindu society. "Idolatry" is the most significant
symbolic marker of the boundary between Hindus and Muslims.
Muslims can and do participate in Hindu festivals. They can and
do seek the blessings of powerful gurus. They can as patrons support
the building of Hindu temples, but they cannot go into a temple
and worship an image without losing their identity as Muslim. It is
therefore the imageless devotion (*nirguna bhakti*) that is most com-
patible with Muslim beliefs and practices. In the communities that
follow this kind of devotional practice, such as the Kabirpanthis,
the Dadupanthis, and the Sikhs, it is again the saint-guru who is
central. Worship of the guru in Hindu devotionalism and of the
saint in Sufism are similar modes of religious communication. Their
messages are also very similar. Both deal with the interplay of
authority and transformation through humility, as well as with the
construction of masculinity and feminity. It is, however, not difficult
to find the symbolic markers that clearly demarcate Hindus from
Muslims. They are located in the ritual enclosures of temple and
mosque and in the direct worship of god through prayer.

Although devotionalist discourse and practice unite Hindus of
different movements, under certain conditions a Hindu religious

community can evolve in a direction that allows it ultimately to assert itself as "non-Hindu." This is the case in the Sikh community, which not only practices imageless devotion but also has replaced the authority of the guru with that of the community—a step that has been crucial in strengthening the notion of the "community," which has in turn been crucial in the formulation of a religious nationalism.

The Sikh Nation

The Sikhs are a religious community. The word *Sikh* means "spiritual disciple," and the disciples form together a community, or *panth* (spiritual path). This community was founded by guru Nanak (1469–1539). Nanak belonged to a group of *sants* (saints) who propagated the worship of a shapeless (*nirguna*) world soul and of the guru as a manifestation of transcendent reality. The *sants* are often seen as mediators between Islamic imageless worship of the one god and Hindu polytheism, but Islamic influence does not have to be invoked in order to understand the emergence of the *sant* traditions. The dialectics of transcendence (imageless) and immanence (with images) can be accounted for simply by looking at the development of Shaivite and Vaishnavite religious methods.[50] Nevertheless, the rejection of images and the concomitant ritual authority of the Brahmans on the part of the *sant* tradition amounted to a major break with the dominant Hindu tradition of temple worship.

Nanak's successors belonged to a small circle of the Khatri clan, while most of the lay members derived from a larger social category, the Jats. Jats are peasants with a tradition of militancy who, according to a hypothesis of the historian Irfan Habib, were originally pastoralists.[51] Their changeover to a sedentary way of life may have been accompanied by parallel processes of Hinduization and Sikhization. In the case of the Sikh Jats, we may have a process of gradual conversion to Sikhism that resembles the formation of a Muslim community through allegiance to the *pirs* of Baba Farid in Pakpattan, described earlier. It is important to bear in mind that social identities like Jat or Rajput are widespread in North India, and rather disparate groups are covered by these names. Some Jat groups, however, went through a more radical process of identity formation by becoming disciples of Nanak and his successors.

The community of Sikhs closed its ranks in the eighteenth century. In some ways the Sikhs went through the same process of militarization and centralization as did Hindu ascetic orders, described above. The main difference, however, seems to have been that there was much <u>less of a sharp distinction among the Sikhs</u> <u>between lay community and religious specialists</u> than in the Hindu orders—or that the Sikhs made a radical move in obliterating that distinction. The Sikhs were organized into <u>mobile military bands</u> (*jathas* and *misls*) that came together during religious festivals. These bands ultimately formed the Sikh military brotherhood (*khalsa*). In 1699, the tenth guru, Gobind Singh, who inaugurated the brotherhood, declared that he was the last in the succession of Sikh gurus and that from then on the authority and unity of the Sikhs would lie in the sacred teachings of the gurus (preserved in the sacred scripture of the Sikhs) and in the judgment of the entire brotherhood when gathered in a meeting. The formation of the Khalsa was a major development that later enabled the Sikhs to formulate their own nationalism, distinct from that of the Hindus. From then onward, Khalsa Sikhs can be clearly distinguished from those followers of Guru Nanak who did not opt to become part of the Khalsa. Their code of conduct (*rahit*) prescribes that they have a beard and uncut hair, worn with a wooden comb, and wear a turban, a steel bangle, a sword, and a pair of breeches.

Up until the advent of the British, no ruler in Delhi had been able to subjugate the Jat population of the Punjab—partly because the Jat armies could always withdraw into the Shivalik hills, in which the last five gurus of the Sikhs had also taken residence. Indeed, the history of the Sikhs is one of almost constant struggle with the Mughals. One of the gurus, Tegh Bahadur (1644–1675), was arrested and executed, thereby becoming one of the most potent symbols of Sikh martyrdom in the face of religious oppression. The conflict with Muslim rulers in the seventeenth and eighteenth centuries set a pattern of considerable hostility between Sikhs and Muslims. Although this hostility became less prominent in the eighteenth century, it was revived during the horrible events of partition, in which the Sikhs and Muslims of the Punjab found themselves in the middle of the turmoil.

The Sikh heartland in the Punjab had long had a sort of regional autonomy under the control of feuding Jat lineages who gave their spiritual allegiance to Sikh gurus. This internecine warfare came to an end when one war band, under Ranjit Singh, gained ascendancy. The ultimate authority of the brotherhood was temporarily suspended when Ranjit Singh appointed himself maharaja of the Punjab in 1801 and founded a powerful Sikh state, which was annexed by the British in 1839.

The Sikh case is an excellent example of the influence of British colonial policies on the development of a communal identity. The attraction of becoming a member of the Khalsa declined significantly in the years following the annexation of Ranjit's kingdom (*khalsa sarkar*). The forces leading to the founding of a Sikh state and the building of a Sikh brotherhood had been defeated. The governor-general of British India, Lord Dalhousie, observed in 1849 that the Sikhs "are gradually relapsing into Hinduism, and even when they continue Sikhs, they are Hindouified more and more."[52] However, in the period between 1881 and 1921 the Sikh population in the Punjab increased significantly. During this period the British reversed their anti-Sikh policy and began to recruit Sikhs for the army. A recruiting officer reported during the First World War that "it was almost a daily occurrence for say Ram Chand to enter our office and leave it as Ram Singh—Sikh recruit."[53] Those who were not initiated into the Sikh brotherhood were defined as "Hindus" in the British census and were not considered to be as "sturdy" and fit for military service as those who were Sikhs. If someone wanted to enlist in the army, he had to become a Sikh—a process of conversion and the changing of names that can be followed closely.

In a recent book Richard Fox emphasizes the British construction of Sikh identity in a way that is fairly typical of many historians' and anthropologists' discussions of the colonial construction of religious identity (whether Hindu, Muslim, or Sikh).[54] According to his argument, the British attempted to integrate the Punjab into the world economy. In the process they created a class of petty commodity producers at the village level and traders in the urban areas. The British also promoted the Khalsa identity, as we have seen, which was increasingly adopted by this particular class. In that way a loosely integrated culture, in which "Sikhs" had a variety of multiple, overlapping identities, was replaced by a more strongly in-

tegrated Khalsa culture based on "Khalsa" identity, which formed
the basis for religious nationalism. Fox argues, in fact, that the Sikh
Khalsa identity is based on a tradition invented by the British.

It should be clear from my exposition thus far that Fox's view
runs counter to the body of evidence we have about the formation
of the Khalsa identity in the eighteenth century. What emerges in
the Sikh case is that, first, it is an example of successful religious
state formation, and that, second, after its initial defeat the brotherhood was revived by British colonial policies. The Sikh brotherhood in fact amounts to a form of religious state formation. There
is the emergence of a supralocal religious identity, the rise of powerful and authoritative institutions that control the public domain,
and the development of particular ways of organizing production
and consumption. But this is a gradual and unfinished process. The
most important step was taken in the eighteenth century, when
Gobind Singh abolished the line of succession of spiritual leaders,
while laying authority in the hands of the entire brotherhood. This
made the boundary between Sikhs and non-Sikhs much easier to
maintain. The members of the Khalsa were called "hair-wearing"
(*kesdhari*), that is, unshorn "real" Sikhs, in distinction from those
who followed the Sikh teachings but were not initiated.

Religious Reform

In many studies on the emergence of nationalism in the colonial
world special attention is given to the role of religious reform
movements in the production of a nationalist ideology. This is done
for good reason. Let me summarize some of the arguments. In
ruling South Asia, the British made use of indigenous elites who
were urbanized, often English-educated, and partly Westernized.
These elites came to form a national middle class, owing to the
growth of the population and the spread of education. But this was
a class that resented British domination and resisted the attacks on
indigenous culture and religion by Christian missionaries. In Weberian terms this class became the "carrier" of reform movements.

Middle class religious ideology, whether Muslim, Sikh, or Hindu,
shows some common features. First, it incorporates aspects of orientalist essentialism. In the eyes of orientalists, the civilizations of
the East were great in the past but are decadent at present and thus

in need of Western domination. Decadence has led to the acceptance of all kinds of irrational beliefs and practices that pollute the
pure, transcendent essence of religious truth. The reform movements then take up this theme of decadence and defeat by blaming
the superstitions and backwardness of the population for the superiority of Western civilization. But they also attempt to purify the
primeval truth in their religions from "later, irrational accretions"
that derive from the influence of the religions of outsiders. The last
notion is particularly important. By condemning practices and beliefs, especially in the field of healing, that were shared by large
groups with very different social origins, exclusive community
boundaries are sharply drawn. Religious nationalism draws upon
that exclusivity.

Different aspects of reform are highlighted by two arguments
that can, to some extent, be combined. The "modernization" argument has it that "reformed" religion, carried by the middle class,
is simply better suited to a modern society in which mass education,
urbanizing, and industrialization are on the increase. The world
becomes "disenchanted," and the various forms of "traditional" religion experience a decline of social relevance as a consequence of
modernization. The "hegemony" argument pays more attention to
the way in which the rising middle class, empowered by its place
in modern capitalism, tries to use reform to gain a cultural hegemony. It does so by taking control over centers for the production
of religious meaning, such as temples and pilgrimage places. "Reformed" religion becomes a reference system toward which larger
sections of the population gradually orient themselves. It produces
a national identity with clear ethnic boundaries, without threatening internal class differences.

These arguments, although important, are not entirely adequate.
The main difficulty is that even though the "middle class" is seen
to be the carrier of reform, it is evident that only a relatively small
section of the middle class really is converted to one or another
version of reform. At the same time, condemned practices, such as
healing, spirit-possession, and the worship of saints, are not only
continued by the lower, uneducated classes but also by members
of the middle class. Rather than accept in one way or another the
ideological distinction between "popular" and "elite" forms of religion, between "fundamentalism" and "syncretism," between the

bourgeoisie and the rest of the population, we should see these as directly connected.[55]

Similarly, although nationalism may at certain points be promoted by bourgeois elements, its success depends on the extent to which it can motivate large sections of the population. Therefore, more important than reformism's direct success in terms of, for example, recruitment of members or attendance at meetings seems to be their indirect success in creating a political discourse in defense of "our threatened religion."

Another difficulty is that, despite the similarities between the ideologies of the various reform movements, they often have a very different logic and social effect. While there may be a rejection of certain "irrational" or "magical" practices in some cases, in other cases similar practices are accepted but brought under the control of the powers that be. These points can be best illustrated by an examination of what reform accomplished in the cases we discussed earlier.

Islamic Reform

Who is a Muslim? In one sense, whoever declares himself a Muslim is a Muslim, and yet this declaration also has to be accepted by others. This has been the subject of continuous debate—a debate that, to some extent, itself constructs the Muslim community. In the nineteenth century this debate was given a new impetus by the spread of reformist movements. These movements questioned the genuineness of the conversion of large sections of the Muslim population, as well as the Islamic knowledge of the religious elite, both *'ulama'* and *pirs*. They wanted to put a renewed emphasis on the unity of God (*tawhid*), the example of the Prophet (*sunna*), and the canonical law (*shari'at*). This brought them into direct conflict with the Sufi worship of saints and tombs, which they condemned as innovations (*bid'a*).

Basically, there are two ways of looking at nineteenth-century Islamic reform movements. The first sees them as a continuation of an earlier South Asian reform movement, the Naqshbandi Mujaddadi, founded by Ahmad Sirhindi (1564–1624), which was already fervently opposed to saint- and tomb-worship.[56] This movement was very active in the eighteenth century not only in the northern heartland of South Asian Islam but also in the South.[57] In Delhi it influenced the reformist thinker Shah Waliullah (1703–1762), to whose ideas nineteenth-century reform movements constantly refer. No doubt it is true that much of the thrust of the reformist argument was already found in these thinkers and movements, but one has to keep in mind that critics like Sirhindi were themselves Sufi *pirs*. Their criticism was "internal," not an anti-Sufi one—although this changes gradually in the nineteenth century.

This leads to the second view on nineteenth-century reform, which stresses a radical break with the past. In this view nineteenth-century reform in South Asia was heavily influenced by Arab Wahhabis.[58] A movement like the Tariqa Muhammadiya, founded by Sayyid Ahmad Barelwi (1786–1831) and active all over North India, seems, compared to earlier movements, much more radical and also much more interested in securing the support of the masses for political action. Rafiuddin Ahmed has documented the vehemence of the debate in Bengal between these radical reformists and their "traditional" opponents, which created great interest among the illiterate masses in issues that had previously been confined to theological circles. Cheap religious tracts were published and widely distributed. As Ahmed points out, "Islamization of the masses was the key-note of this literature."[59] This was indeed a most significant development, and it has all the ingredients of "protonationalism." The problem with the argument that the shift toward reform was only brought about by contact with the Arab Wahhabites is that it resembles rather closely the colonial theory of the international "Wahhabi conspiracy." One has to appreciate the complexity of the situation. Only some reformist movements in nineteenth-century India seem to take their ideas more or less directly from the Wahhabis. Others continue to be less radical and to stress Sufi ideas while attacking saint worship. Down to the present day important Sufi saints in history are accepted by all parties as the leading scholars of their time. Even the leaders of the important Indian reformist University of Deoband in the nineteenth century, which has in retrospect come to be regarded by many Muslims as a stronghold of anti-Sufism, considered themselves as practicing Sufis who followed the Chishti mode of spiritual training.[60] They wanted to reform Islam by making Sufism an individual mysticism purified of public displays of religious power, an argument that can often be heard in contemporary India.

I think that the gradualist view and the one that sees a rupture can be reconciled when we accept the notion that Muslim reform movements emerged in every part of the Islamic world close on each other's heels during the nineteenth century. They resembled one another in a number of ways, including the fact that they transformed older debates by bringing them to the masses. The hajj to Mecca obviously played an important role in giving reformists from many places an opportunity to meet, but we should remind ourselves that this was not new. Earlier reformers, such as Shah Waliullah, had also been influenced by their visits to Mecca. Moreover, Sufis also visited Mecca.

What explains the shift in the old debate about orthodoxy is not a "Wahhabite conspiracy" but the colonial transformation of India and other regions of the world. It is this transformation that brings the debate to a larger audience and creates a "Muslim community," based on the older allegiances of shrine and mosque. An important question for us therefore becomes what happened to Sufi religious regimes firmly entrenched in a regional system, such as described earlier, when touched by that broad transformation.

There is a considerable amount of empirical data concerning the gradual marginalization of Sufi brotherhoods and the veneration of saints and tombs throughout the Islamic world in the nineteenth and twentieth centuries. Some anthropologists argue that Sufi brotherhoods suffered a decline in social relevance as a result of urbanization, education, and the emergence of a national middle class.[61] This argument does not imply that Sufism disappeared but that the veneration of the tombs of dead saints was separated from its moorings in the brotherhoods, becoming a popular religion of the peasantry or the urban illiterates, condemned by the dominant groups in society.[62] These more or less Weberian interpretations of the nature of the local debate about Sufi practices depend on a master narrative of "modernization," "rationalization," and "marginalization."

In my view this master narrative should not be used to obscure significant differences that are pertinent to specific local narratives. I do accept the notion that, from the nineteenth century onward,

Sufism no longer defines "the" Islamic way of life in the Muslim world, but this observation does not warrant the assumption that Sufi brotherhoods and the saint cults they organize have everywhere lost their social relevance. First of all, not all brotherhoods are the same. Some are connected to shrines of regional, national, or even international importance. There is, for example, little evidence to suggest that a major shrine, such as that of Mu'in al-din Chishti at Ajmer, has suffered much decline. In other shrines and brotherhoods the leadership of Sufi saints is directly related to their position as landlords and power brokers. To expect that land reform and changes in the political structure may affect the position of saints and diminish the social relevance of these brotherhoods is not unreasonable. Nevertheless, as Katherine Ewing shows in her study of Sufism in Pakistan, even in such cases marginalization and decline is by no means certain.[63] There is, in fact, good evidence for the continued importance of these larger shrines with their landowning saintly lineages.

Second, it is important to heed Gananath Obeyesekere's observation that modernization creates an increase in the level of aspiration not only for educated peasants but also for the sons of white-collar workers, although it does not always offer pathways to the achievement of those goals.[64] To expect that we will discover a clear correlation between socioeconomic position and either the acceptance or rejection of Sufi beliefs and practices is definitely mistaken. We simply cannot locate allegiance to Sufi saints among the "marginalized," powerless groups and opposition to them among the "successful," dominant groups. Laborer, entrepreneur, jobless person, and doctor—all may be followers of these saints. One might argue that at a very general level what these people share in a rapidly changing world may be a sense of inadequate control over their own lives in the rurban market. However, this can hardly be related to the choices they make about religious practice.

Despite the objections I have against the "Weberian" master narrative, I do accept the notion that colonialism brought about a major transformation of Indian society. It is true that in the nineteenth century the earlier debate about orthodoxy was taken up with renewed force and that increasingly modern forms of communications were used to spread reformist thought. Another, somewhat related development is that debate about religious belief and practice began to take place within the context of the assertion of religious community. In the colonial world Muslim discourse about religion comes almost inevitably to be linked to discourse about the nature of the nation-state.[65] In the postcolonial period this debate has continued and has been directly influenced by political elites in the newly emergent nation-states that use Islamic discourse in their search for legitimacy. Compared to the rest of the Muslim world, colonial India was exceptional in having the largest Muslim population in the world that was at the same time a minority. Much of the discourse on the nature of the Muslim community or nation and its relation to the state in the colonial era thus has to do with the political assertion of a Muslim minority community against a Hindu majority.

In historical writing on Indian Islam during the colonial period the reformist attempt to define Islam by condemning certain established Sufi practices is interpreted as being linked to the political assertion of boundaries between the Muslim community and the Hindu community. Emphasis on the social and cultural exclusiveness of the Muslim community was used in the political struggle for a separate Muslim state.[66] The dominant historical theory about Hindu-Muslim relations used by Muslim separatists before Independence was that Hindus and Muslims did not share values and thus formed two separate nations. With Independence this theory led to the formation of a "homeland" for Muslims, Pakistan, creating an enormous migration to and from Pakistan, even though a considerable Muslim community chose to stay in India. Whereas in Pakistan the postcolonial state became an important actor in the arena in which reform and Sufism are debated, in the Indian context the role of the self-proclaimed secular state is much less clear.

In post-Independence India the debate among Muslims about reform and Sufism can no longer be linked to a political movement striving for a separate Muslim nation-state. Indian Muslims are in general very outspoken in proclaiming their Indian nationalist feelings. While my informants in Surat agreed on the fact that Hindus and Muslims form fundamentally different communities, they argued for the possibility of peaceful coexistence under the umbrella of a secular state that does not interfere with the religious practices of the different communities. This kind of argument is related to a discourse on Indian society as essentially "pluralist" and "tolerant."

In that connection I found an eclipse of the old theme of "Hindu influence" and "Hindu participation" in the debate about saint worship. This can be seen as a deliberate decision to disconnect—rhetorically, at least—the debate about "orthodoxy" from the definition of the boundaries between Hindus and Muslims.[67]

In Pakistan the situation seems to be different in some respects. Although Sufi shrines continue to be important, their relation with the state is much more significant than in India and is subject to constant, public debate. The relation with Hindus has, however, ceased to be an issue. State officials try to use the appeal of the shrines for their purposes but also attempt to integrate them into a reformist, fundamentalist view of Islam. Pakistani Muslims always have to deal with the presence of a strong anti-Sufi political element in the country.

The most important exponent of this element is the Jama'at-i-Islami.[68] The success of this movement has largely depended on the charismatic qualities of its founder, Maulana Sayyid Abul A'la Maududi (1903–1979), one of the most influential thinkers on Islamic politics in this century. Maududi, born in Hyderabad, received a religious education but was not trained as a religious scholar ('alim)—a simple fact that explains much of his uneasy relation with the religious establishment in Pakistan. He became a journalist and editor of a number of important Muslim newspapers and magazines. In the pre-Independence period he rejected nationalism as a Western conspiracy and argued that Muslims should adhere to Islamic universalism. Society and state should be subordinated to the authority of the Qur'an and the example of the Prophet. In 1941 he founded the Jama'at-i-Islami as a tightly and hierarchically organized revolutionary force, run on almost Leninist principles. It has always remained an organization small in numbers but highly effective. Its members belong to the educated middle class, and it is significant that the Jama'at has attracted more support from students in Pakistan's universities than any other organization. Despite his opposition to the Pakistan movement, partition forced Maududi to move to Lahore. Here the Jama'at became a political party, which, however, like Hindu nationalist parties in India, was typically unsuccessful in the elections it contested. Nevertheless, it built up a considerable influence on Pakistani politics—especially in campaigns for an Islamic constitution and laws against un-Islamic practices.

Maududi's views build on the reformist tradition in Islam in its emphasis on the law (*shariᶜat*) and the example of the Prophet (*sunna*). But Maududi transforms this tradition in his emphasis on the "laicization" of Muslim leadership, which has to pass from the hands of the ᶜ*ulama*ᵓ to university-trained laymen, on the use of the electoral process to express the true will of the Muslim community (*umma*), and on the active role of the state in achieving the objectives of Islam. Although the advocacy of revolutionary methods may perhaps not directly derive from Maududi's writing, both his idea that the state should be taken over by Islamic workers and used for the Islamization of the society and his skill in organizing a highly disciplined force have had considerable influence on revolutionary movements elsewhere in the Muslim world, such as the Ikhwan, and the Muslim brotherhoods of Egypt and the Sudan.

It is interesting to follow Mumtaz Ahmad's comparison of the Pakistani branch of the Jamaᶜat-i-Islami with the Indian branch. In contemporary India there is, of course, simply no possibility of an Islamic state. The Indian Jamaᶜat accommodates this by referring to the early antinationalist stance of Maududi. There is, however, a crucial difference in the attitude of the two branches toward "secularism." In the Indian context secularism is seen as a religiously neutral policy of the state that protects minorities, while in the Pakistani context secularism is seen as an evil force. The extent to which the attitude of the Pakistani Jamaᶜat is similar to that of "radical" Hindu nationalists in India is striking.

Hindu Reform

Just as radical Muslim reformist movements mushroomed all over the Islamic world in the nineteenth century, Hindu and Sikh movements also emerged with sometimes similar programs for "purifying" their religions. The connection with the colonial transformation is even clearer in the Hindu and Sikh cases than in that of Islam. A recurring theme in nineteenth-century Hindu reform is that of Hindu weakness. Hindu society has to be defended against "external" weakness, caused by conversions to "foreign" religion, and against its "internal" weakness, caused by differences and conflicts among Hindus.

The theme of Hindu weakness derives from nineteenth-century discourse on "foreign rule." The Vishva Hindu Parishad (VHP) per-petuates an argument about the decline from a golden age in which a just society based on Hindu dharma (moral law) gave way to a long period of barbaric oppression, first by Muslim rulers (from 1200) and then by the British (from 1800). While this argument is related to a more common Hindu belief that we live in the most degenerate age, the *kaliyuga*, there is a strong activist element here that says that this decline has to be stopped and Hindu society redeemed. One way of doing this is through religious reform.

This theme is most eloquently elaborated by the Arya Samaj, the most significant reformist movement in Hinduism. The Arya Samaj was founded in 1875 by Swami Dayananda Saraswati, a Shaivite ascetic from Gujarat. He preached a return to the religion of the Vedas and, accordingly, elaborated perhaps the most central and certainly the most elusive theme of Hindu discursive tradition: the authority of the Vedas. While Hindus establish the timeless truth of every innovation by linking it in one way or another to the Vedas, Dayananda took this reference to the Vedas literally by condemning the post-Vedic accretions to contemporary Hinduism. What Daya-nanda wanted to create was a "religion of the book," like Christianity or Islam. The Arya Samaj blamed post-Vedic (so-called *pauranik*) Hinduism, which in fact included much of Hinduism's existing discourses and practices, for the decline of the Hindu nation. It urged Hindus to abolish image worship, a crucial feature of devo-tional religion, to abolish caste divisions, and to change their rites of passage.

It is important to see that Dayananda's message combines the traditional reverence for Vedic authority with nineteenth-century orientalism. The emphasis on Vedic *texts*, reconstructed by histor-ical research, the message of socioreligious reform, and the rejection of contemporary Hindu discourse and practice are all supported by orientalist knowledge. The very "foreignness" of this discourse, with its emphasis on textual purity rather than on the purity of the text's interpreters and its repudiation of practices such as image worship, greatly limited the appeal of the Arya Samaj. Owing to its funda-mentalism and its emphasis on scripture, the Arya Samaj remained a marginal movement rather than becoming the Hindu answer to modern times. It is striking that its major appeal is limited to the Punjab, where the attack on image worship fell on fertile soil, prepared by centuries of Sikh traditions of imageless devotion.

I would therefore argue that the major importance of the Arya Samaj is not to be found in its direct message or appeal but in its impact on Hindu discourse in general. The "orthodox" opponents of the Arya Samaj had to defend their discourses against the reformist attacks, which led both groups to the organization of "orthodox" religion (*sanatana dharma*) in the direction of a unified system. In this process the Arya Samaj and their opponents discovered that they had a common ground in their "defense of the Hindu nation."

For example, the Arya Samaj shared with its "orthodox" detractors the notion of the sacredness of mother cow. By organizing "cow protection societies" it shaped the defense of Hinduism against British and Muslim "butchers." Even more important, it set a model for the communication of Hindu nationalism. The Cow Protection Movement, though initiated by Arya Samaj reformists, had nothing to do with reform but much to do with religious nationalism. The Arya Samaj demonstrated the power of activism to stop Hindu weakness and decline, a message that was also received by those who strongly opposed reformism. What we must appreciate here, however, is that while reformism historically plays an important role in emerging Hindu nationalism, it is not synonymous with it. A revivalist, but not reformist, strategy is pursued in creating a discourse on "Hindu spirituality" and "Hindu tolerance" as the main characteristics of the Hindu civilization, which embraces many spiritual styles. This discourse is primarily an apologetics of the strength and vitality of Hinduism but does not necessarily call for scripturalism in the Arya Samaj style. This discourse has, moreover, gradually come to be the mainstream representation of Hinduism to both Hindus and outsiders and is fundamental to Hindu nationalism of all varieties.

However, I would suggest that the discourse has a specific orientalist history. Religious tolerance as an ideal in the West derives from an abstraction and universalization of religion that is part of the Western discourse of "modernity." The move in seventeenth-century Europe to produce a universal definition of "natural religion" as existing in all societies indicates a fragmentation of the unity and authority of the Roman Church but also the rise of new discourses and practices connected to modern nation-states.[69] A growing emphasis on religious tolerance as a positive value is thus related to the marginalization of religious institutions in Europe. At the same time it replaces the violence between religious groups by the violence between nation-states. This discourse is then brought to bear on the Muslim and Hindu populations incorporated in the modern world-system. Muslims, the old rivals of the Christian West, are labeled "fanatic" and "bigoted," while Hindus are seen in a more positive light as "tolerant." At the same time, this labeling explains why Muslims have ruled Hindu India and why Hindus have to be "protected" by the British. In short, what I want to argue here is that the attribution of "tolerance" to Hinduism is a product of a specific orientalist history of ideas.[70] As such, it has also come to dominate Hindu discourse on Hinduism, to the point where tolerance is now viewed as one of the most important characteristics of Hinduism, even though as a doctrinal notion it had no specific place in Hindu discursive traditions.[71] Wilhelm Halbfass argues convincingly that the step to reconcile all religious and philosophical traditions was not taken prior to the colonial period. The earliest available document of such an attempt is in a "Preliminary Discourse" of the pandits who compiled the collection of law texts that became the basis of N. B. Halhed's *Code of Gentoo Laws* (1776): "The truly intelligent well know, that the differences and varieties of created things are a ray of his glorious essence, and that the contrarieties of constitution are a type of his wonderful attributes. . . . He appointed to each tribe its own faith, and to every sect its own religion. . . . He views in each particular place the mode of worship respectively appointed to it; sometimes he is employed with the attendants upon the Mosque, in counting the sacred beads; sometimes he is in the temple, at the adoration of idols; the intimate of the Mussulman, and the friend of the Hindoo; the companion of the Christian, and the confidant of the Jew."[72] It would hardly be possible to give a better example of the collusion of Brahmanical theology and orientalism in the production of "Hindu tolerance." It could be argued that there had been earlier attempts to create Hindu-Muslim consensus. The so-called *sant* tradition of medieval Hindu devotional poetry is often thought to contain a number of such attempts, but in fact they are rather different from the later "tolerance." For example, the famous Maratha poet Eknath (1553–

1599) put a Hindu-Turk debate into verse, which he ended on a note of harmony. He does this, however, only after minutely recording all the differences and hostilities between the two communities.[73]

As the Indologist Paul Hacker has observed, "tolerance" is a poor term for what he thinks is in fact Hindu "inclusivism," a form of hierarchical relativism.[74] There is the Hindu idea—often repeated by the VHP—that there are many paths leading to god and that there are many gods. An important underlying conception here is that of hierarchy.[75] The many gods and paths are manifestations of the One who is formless—but some of these manifestations are higher than others. Moreover, they perform different functions, and in a hierarchical order. The general idea seems to be that other paths do not have to be denied as heretical but that they are inferior and thus cater to inferior beings. This relation between the devotee and his chosen god is thus one of what I would like to call "co-substantiality."[76]

This might be one of the reasons that Hindus visit Muslim shrines for rituals of healing, since Muslim saints are said to control the powers of darkness.[77] At least in some contexts this is an attribution that brackets Muslims with those very powers. Some Muslim practices are thus included in a Hindu cosmological framework but given an inferior position. At the same time this inferiority has always excluded Muslims (and "untouchable" peoples) from practices in higher Brahmanical temples. The point here is that modern Hindu thinkers have come to interpret hierarchical relativism in Hindu discourse in orientalist terms, as "tolerance." This leads, in a universalist version, to an inclusion of all religions in the Vedanta, the spiritual "essence" of Hinduism in its philosophical form, as in the philosopher-president Sarvepalli Radhakrishnan's famous formula: "The Vedanta is not a religion, but religion itself in its most universal and deepest significance."[78] In the more narrow version of the VHP, this interpretation stresses "tolerance" within but excludes the religions that "came from outside" and are intolerantly bent on converting Hindus.

Perhaps the most important expounder of the doctrine of Hindu spirituality was the founder of the Ramakrishna Mission, Vivekananda (1863–1902). The intellectual background of Vivekananda lies in the so-called Bengali renaissance of the nineteenth century. Bengali

intellectuals were among the first in India to receive Western education, which allowed them to enter administrative positions. They
were initially very much stimulated by the colonial encounter and
regarded Western civilization as superior. However, their attempts
to imitate Englishness and Western customs were derided by Indians and British alike as "*babu* culture," the culture of clerks. In a
second phase Bengali intellectuals became more and more critical
both of British attitudes and of what they saw as the problems of
contemporary Indian society. Instead of simply accepting the criticism of their society from missionaries and British officials or openly
defending their culture, they came to formulate specific programs
of religious reform. Especially the Brahmo Samaj of Keshabchandra
Sen played a significant role in creating a reformist discourse. Its
appeal, however, remained confined to the Western-educated in-
telligentsia of Bengal and was spread over India only through Bengali networks. An encounter with Keshabchandra Sen in Calcutta
led Swami Dayananda to found his own reform movement, the Arya
Samaj, discussed above. Keshabchandra Sen also played a significant role among the Calcutta elite by endorsing the charismatic
appeal of an illiterate saint, Ramakrishna Paramahamsa, the priest
of a Calcutta temple in which the goddess Kali was worshiped.

The encounter with this saint had a transformative impact on the
young Narendranath Datta, who adopted the name Vivekananda
when he took his ascetic vows. Vivekananda was an extremely
talented student who had been thoroughly educated in contemporary Western thought. As Tapan Raychaudhuri emphasizes, however, Vivekananda was "more than anything else a mystic in quest
of the Ultimate Reality within a specific Indian tradition."[79] This
tradition was vividly presented to Vivekananda not by the learned
discourse of which he himself was a master but by the charismatic
presence of his guru, Ramakrishna, whose trances had first been
treated as insanity but were later regarded as a sign of possession
by the goddess. Vivekananda came to personalize the transformation of Hindu tradition (in a specific Bengali version) in its encounter
with Western thought.

Vivekananada's typical strategy was to systematize a disparate set
of traditions, make the result intellectually available for a Westernized audience and defensible against Western critique, and incorporate it into the notion of "Hindu spirituality," borne by the Hindu

nation, which was superior to "Western materialism," brought to
India by an aggressive and arrogant "British nation." His major
achievement has been to ground Hindu spirituality in a systematic
interpretation of the Vedanta (the Upanishads and the tradition of
their interpretation). As we have seen, this project has been carried
forward by Sarvepalli Radhakrishnan.

Vivekananda's main accomplishment, then, was to create a discourse that became fundamental to Hindu nationalism in all versions. It was specifically developed by Mahatma Gandhi, but it was
also a major source of inspiration for the RSS/BJP/VHP brand of
Hindu nationalism. A good example of Vivekananda's impact on
Hindu nationalism is his effort to systematize disparate notions of
ascetic practice in an "ancient system of yoga," which is now India's
main export article on the "spirituality market." This systematization
of ascetic practice was one of the most significant steps in promoting
"Hindu spirituality" as healthy for the body and spirit of the individual as well as for the nation as a whole. It is also noteworthy that
Vivekananda's project received a major impetus when he was en-
thusiastically received in Europe and the United States. His visit
to the World Parliament of Religions in Chicago in 1893 not only
made him a celebrity in the United States but strengthened his
opinion of India's contribution to world civilization. We will see in
chapter 4 how the activities of gifted individuals like Vivekananda
outside of India have played a crucial role in the formulation of
Hindu nationalism. A major element in Vivekananda's revivalist
message was indeed nationalism. He saw his project very much in
terms of a revitalization of the Hindu nation, and his movement,
the Ramakrishna Mission, was founded so that ascetics could ded-
icate all their energies to this task. Most important, Vivekananda
focused on the "uplift" of the poor, low-caste masses, a focus inherited by Mahatma Gandhi. However, this could only happen when
India was freed from "foreign oppression." National self-determi-
nation, social reform, and spiritual awakening were all linked in his
perception.

My analysis of the concepts of "Hindu tolerance" and "Hindu
spirituality" could also be applied to Gandhi's famous concept of
"nonviolence." It is sometimes difficult for Westerners to grasp the
violence perpetuated by Hindu monks who speak and act militantly,
since the notion of "nonviolent" otherworldliness is persistently

attributed to Hindu "spirituality." As I have said before, "nonviolence" had a place in Hindu discursive traditions as a rejection of
the violence of animal sacrifice, which resulted in the adoption of
vegetarianism among some groups. However, the idea that Hindus
would be religiously prevented by a doctrine of "nonviolence" from
pursuing their interests by violent means is Gandhi's construction
of Hindu spirituality. Hindu monks, in particular, have a long and
interesting history of warfare related to trading, which continues to
the present day. There is also considerable historical evidence of
violent struggle between different Hindu religious groups as well
as between Hindus and Buddhists, Hindus and Jains, and Hindus
and Muslims. The considerable martial tradition of Hindu India is
in fact perpetuated in one of the most important organizations of
Hindu nationalism, the Rashtriya Swayamsevak Sangh (RSS).

The RSS was founded in 1925 by K. B. Hedgewar, a physician
from Maharashtra. Although the organization has long been dominated by Maharashtrian Brahmans, it has spread over the entire
Hindi-speaking region. The Maharashtrian connection is nonetheless of great importance, since Hedgewar did not take his inspiration
from religious traditions but from that of the Maratha war bands
led by Shivaji and his successors, who were the main rivals of the
Mughals and later of the ascending power of the British. The Maharashtrian tradition has it that Shivaji was the ruler of a Hindu
kingdom that fought successfully against Muslim and British rulers.
It is this militant tradition of the Hindu state—very similar to that
of the Sikhs—that was developed by the RSS. The movement
accepts most of the discourse on Indian spiritual superiority but
emphasizes that spirituality does not imply physical weakness. In
so doing, the RSS continues an important Hindu tradition that
relates physical prowess to spiritual accomplishment. Discipline
and physical training to attain a healthy body and a healthy mind
are stressed. The healthy body of the individual is identified with
the healthy nation.

The RSS is very much a youth organization. Young men go to
their camps for training. When they grow older and get married,
they stop doing so but continue their ties with their age set. A
number of devoted, older men, who are often unmarried and lead
an ascetic life, form the top echelon of the movement. In this way
cadres are formed, distinguished by their discipline, that are active

in RSS-dominated organizations, the so-called RSS family (*pari-var*).[80] The history of the BJP has been marked by a debate about the extent to which the party has been—and still is—dominated by the RSS. Important BJP politicians of today, such as L. K. Advani and A. B. Vajpayee, have an RSS background. The RSS has also been instrumental in founding and solidifying the VHP, and it is fair to say that without RSS support the mass-scale rituals of the VHP could not have been successful.

Training in martial arts and wrestling is very much a part of the youth culture of northern India. Nita Kumar sees these activities as aspects of working-class culture, but I am not convinced that the class division is a more salient characteristic than the religious one.[81] Both Hindus and Muslims have wrestling gymnasiums, but, as far as I know, they are entirely separate. Wrestling gymnasiums are called *akharas*, a word that betrays their roots in the tradition of militant ascetics, whose "camps" and "fortified temples" have that name. Hanuman, who is the patron deity of the Hindu wrestlers, is the principal deity for the militant *sadhus* of Vaishnavite persuasion. Celibacy and physical strength (*bal*) are combined in the Hindu notion of power (*shakti*), which refers both to a sociological concept and to a religious, spiritual concept.[82] Celibacy is the condition of young Hindu males before marriage, and it is they who participate most in the wrestling culture. After interviewing Hindu wrestlers in North India, Joseph Alter found that they connect the healthy body with the health of a nation, from which the corruptions of modern life, such as fashion and the cinema, have been removed.[83] However, wrestling culture is, like the ascetic one, individualistic and body-focused. The RSS draws upon this culture of austerity but transforms its ideas of physical strength and spiritual purity by relating these ideas to a more political vision of the social hygiene of the nation. The transformation is obvious when one compares the wrestling pit with the RSS training grounds. The wrestler trains on his own and fights other wrestlers to win, while the RSS cadres, dressed in uniforms, engage in mass gymnastics.

There is very little explicit Hindu ritual in the RSS. Its main celebration is the Hindu festival of Dassehra, which has a warrior tradition. It is the celebration of the final victory of the god Rama over the demon-king Ravana and features the burning of the demon and his palace. It is also a festival in which the weapons of warriors are blessed. Very important also is the Hindu festival of guru worship. On that day every Hindu who has chosen a guru worships him, whereas RSS members worship the RSS banner.

From its founding the RSS has played an active role in anti-Muslim militancy. The danger of its "radical" view of Hindu nationalism was only fully understood in the aftermath of the partition riots, when Mahatma Gandhi was killed by a Maharashtrian Brahman who had previously been a member of the RSS. Gandhi was clearly too much a "pluralist" for the liking of these militants, and to the present day there is a considerable antipathy against Gandhi in these circles. The RSS was banned for one and a half years, and its leader at the time, M. S. Golwalkar, put in prison. After this sobering setback, the RSS has been able to gather strength again and is routinely connected to Hindu-Muslim riots in many parts of India.

What is striking about the RSS is that it has firm roots in Hindu militant traditions that celebrate physical strength and yet does not repudiate the claim of Hindu "spirituality" and "tolerance." In their view, there is no contradiction—and I think they are right, when we read "tolerance" in the way I have proposed above. The construction of "tolerance" as the essence of "Hindu spirituality" should thus be understood as a discourse intended not only to unite competing Hindu groups but also as an avenue of complaint about the intolerance of those who do not wish to be included, such as Muslims.[84]

Sikh Reform

In our discussion of the Sikhs we have seen how a religious movement, which was similar to many other Hindu movements, gradually developed a brotherhood (*khalsa*) with a discursive tradition of militancy and a clear set of symbolic identity markers. The formation of this religious community was further helped by its connection to the Punjab and to the Jats, the dominant peasant group in the region. After an initial setback when the British annexed the Punjab, this collective identity was furthered by the British through their agrarian development schemes as well as their military recruitment policies. The development of religious nationalism among the Sikhs cannot, however, be understood without taking into account the major role played by the reform movement, the Singh

Sabha. The first Singh Sabha was established in 1873 and preached the purification of the Khalsa from "Hindu" practices. One of the key issues was thus the assertion of boundaries between Hindus and Sikhs, clearly in reaction to reformist activities on the part of the Arya Samaj. A major victory for the Singh Sabha movement occurred in 1905, when Hindu images were removed from the Golden Temple in Amritsar, the main center of worship for Sikhs.

In the early decades of the twentieth century Sikh reformists increasingly turned their attention to the management of Sikh temples, *gurdwaras*. These temples were the property of priestly families whose moral and ritual behavior did not conform to the purist standards of certain reformists who originated in the Singh Sabha movement but came to call themselves Akalis ("followers of the timeless"). The most important campaign of the Akalis was a struggle for the control over the temples. In 1925 the agitation succeeded in placing the temples in the Punjab under the authority of the Shiromani Gurdwara Parbandhak Committee, a representative body of the Khalsa, the Sikh brotherhood. Since then the control of this committee has become the most coveted prize in Sikh politics.

The slogan of the Singh Sabha movement was that Sikhs were not Hindus. The boundary between members of the brotherhood and other Sikhs was thereby transformed into a fundamental distinction between Sikhs (namely, members of the brotherhood) and the "others," Hindus and Muslims. Religious groups such as the Nanakpanthis and the Nirankaris and Namdharis, who followed the Sikh teachings but did not accept the brotherhood, had to declare that they were not Sikhs, but Hindus. In particular, the brotherhood's control over Sikh temples and the founding of a Sikh political party (the Akali Dal) based on the temple committee has greatly enhanced religious state formation.

Nevertheless, the process of homogenization of a religious community of Khalsa Sikhs has remained partial and fragmented. First of all, despite the abolishment of personal leadership there always remained gurus who claimed to speak for the whole Sikh community and were able to upset the authority of the temple committee. Some of these remained largely outside the fold of the brotherhood and formed their own religious communities, despite resistance from the brotherhood. Others tried to reform the brotherhood from within. The most radical example of this is the late Jarnail Singh

Bhindranwale (1947–1984), a *sant* who was connected to a Sikh seminary. He became the leader of the group who, early in the 1980s, began to demand the formation of Khalistan, a separate Sikh state. It is important to note that this group first directed its terrorist attacks against the Nirankaris, a movement that had originated within the Sikh community but had remained outside of the brotherhood. Probably most of the killings today continue to be of "heretical" Sikhs. Only later did much of the struggle among factions in the Sikh community focus on control over the traditional sources of political power, the Sikh temples, the most important of which is the Golden Temple in Amritsar. This struggle is to be interpreted not only as a battle for control over material resources, though indeed temple resources are very important, but also over the symbolic foci of Sikh identity. Therefore the attack by Indian troops in 1984 on the Bhindranwale group that had taken control over the Golden Temple was felt as an attack on the personal integrity even of those Sikhs who were against the Bhindranwale group. Second, to the present day it has been a common practice among Punjabi families to initiate one son into the brotherhood, while the rest of the family followed Sikh or other teachings as it saw fit. Extremists within the brotherhood have made such an attitude increasingly difficult to maintain, but it continues to exist.

In the Sikh case, then, we see that the early emphasis on access to the ultimate truth, unmediated by living gurus, led to the formation of a brotherhood, the Khalsa, which, as a whole, had authority over religious and worldly matters. This "protestant" notion of the authority of the community has been crucial for the logic of Sikh reformism. While it originated as an attempt to purify religious practice, its main target soon became the priestly ownership and management of centers of religious communication, such as *gurdwaras*. Control had to be given to the brotherhood. Reform had in this case direct implications for the formation of a Sikh political party and ultimately for the issue of separatism.

The communication of identity has always been a key issue for the Sikh brotherhood. While it is often difficult to discern the doctrinal differences between members of the brotherhood and followers of other Sikh teachings, the hair and dress of a "real" Sikh maintain the boundary perfectly. A relatively open boundary between Sikhs and others is felt as a direct threat to the constituency of the brotherhood, in which priests have turned politicians and politicians priests.

In sum, it is argued here that in the study of the relation between religion and nationalism too much emphasis has been given to the scripturalist, fundamentalist, and middle-class aspects of reform movements, while the continuity of religious organization and discourse has been neglected. There is no doubt that reform movements have had a major impact on religious discourse, but they have not replaced "traditional" religion by a "modern," middle-class form of religion. The reform movements in Islam, Hinduism, and Sikhism have transformed established forms of religious organization and communication, even though in some cases, such as that of the Arya Samaj, they have remained marginal in terms of their direct constituency.

A master narrative linking reform and modernity in a simple way is not helpful. The discursive traditions of Islam, Hinduism, and Sikhism, in which "reform" had to position itself, were different. Despite significant similarities in the relation of these discursive traditions to Western discourses, the reform occurred within the context of these different indigenous traditions and thus its impact varied in all three cases.

In the case of Islam, nineteenth-century reform continues an old debate about the place of Sufi saints in Islam, but it transforms this debate by bringing it to the masses. In this way it also creates a mass community for Muslim nationalism. The reformist argument about the "Hindu" character of Sufi worship is obviously directly related to the demarcation of boundaries between the two communities. This argument was, however, muted among Indian Muslims in the aftermath of partition, and it is no longer relevant in Pakistan, where the anti-Sufi argument has come to be entrenched in a radical Muslim nationalist movement. In the case of Hinduism, reform has created a discourse on "tolerance," "spirituality," and "nonviolence" that continues an older ideological pattern of "inclusivism" in Hinduism but relates it to modern nationalism. While this discourse is found in the mainstream of Indian nationalism, it is also present in extremist organizations like the VHP and the RSS. Sikhism has witnessed a reform that directly opposed the "inclusivistic" tendencies of Hindu ideological movements. It continued the eighteenth-century formation of the Khalsa, a brotherhood that was clearly demarcated from the rest of society. More successfully than any other reform movement, it was able to take control over major sources of political and religious power, the *gurdwaras*. This formed the basis of a religious nationalism, which uses the old idiom of resistance against "the rulers in Delhi."

All three case studies ended in a discussion of the most extreme variant of religious nationalism: the Jamaʿat-i-Islami, the RSS, and the Bhindranwale group. It is good to recognize that these extremist groups have relatively small constituencies. Nevertheless, because of their extremism, they manifest some of the tendencies within mainstream religious nationalism most clearly, which also explains their relative success. My argument is not that these movements "represent" Muslims, Hindus, or Sikhs, but that they show us some of the more general discursive grounds on which nationalists in South Asia operate. In the next chapter I will try to provide concrete examples for Islam and Hinduism of the way discursive traditions were transformed in the colonial and postcolonial periods and of the role reformist movements have played in that transformation.

Chapter Three

Ritual Communication

Modes of Communication

If we accept the view that India has its own historical development, which is contemporary to that of the West but occupies a different geographical space, we have to look for some long-term patterns that may help us to account for the specific characteristics of Indian nationalism. One of the most important developments seems to be the way in which precolonial modes of communication were transformed in the colonial and postcolonial periods. In this context it is crucial to acknowledge that innovations were introduced in the colonial period but to avoid subordinating the entire discussion to the traditional-modern dichotomy.

Of great interest here is Benedict Anderson's discussion of the convergence of print technology and capitalism in what he calls "print-capitalism."[1] In his view, language is the primary basis of community, and a nation is essentially a community of people who communicate through the same "print-language." We can extend that view by arguing that systems of communication, such as language, but also pilgrimage and other ritual actions, also provide the basis for communities. The introduction of innovations such as print, and later radio, television, and film, in the colonial and postcolonial periods is important in the development of these systems as well, and thus in the creation of Indian nationalism. These innovations, which make increasingly rapid communication possible, do not, in contrast to what Anderson argues, erode the sacred languages and the communities they made possible but in fact reinforce the importance of at least some of these languages as the basis of religious communities. This is surely the case with Arabic, but I would argue that the growing importance of Hindi as language for Hindus and Urdu as language for Muslims is also an instance of the use of language to create religious nations.

Moreover, the spread of Hindu civilization in India has been aptly called Sanskritization, because that civilization (*sanskriti*) is founded on a textual tradition in Sanskrit. While Sanskritization is a long-term historical process, it is much enhanced by improved communications. As Jonathan Parry argues, "modern communications are—in the medium term at least—just as likely to reinforce 'traditional' religious values, to lend a helping hand to the 'civilizing' process of Sanskritization, as to contribute to a process of secularization."[2] Indeed, although the technological improvement of communications may have an impact on the message communicated, this transformation is not in any way connected with a change from religious culture to secular culture. The idea that technological transformation does entail such a change depends on the assumption not only that "print-capitalism" makes the idea of the nation possible but also that there is an essential cognitive difference between those who live in societies with print and those who live in "pre-print" societies.

The idea that "the technology of the intellect" has the potential to transform social and mental life is developed cogently by Jack Goody in his work on the impact of literacy.[3] But it is important to see that the ubiquitous traditional-modern dichotomy is here found at the level of modes of thought. The traditional mode of thought is religious, not skeptical, and absolutist, not allowing change, while the modern cognitive mode is the reverse. Literacy marks the transition from the traditional to the modern. Goody, however, also acknowledges the existence of a restricted literacy, which confines literacy to the religious use of the literati, who guard the orthodoxy of the Book. In the course of modernization, this restriction is finally removed.

Parry has demonstrated convincingly that in India the use of the literate Sanskrit tradition does not have any of the characteristics that Goody and others assume to be inherent in literacy. In my view the same pertains to the use of the literate Arabic and Persian traditions. But what about print? Much of the revolutionary impact of literacy has, in turn, also been claimed for printing. However, the implications of print technology largely depend on the institutional context, so there is no reason to assume any antithesis between the types of rationality found in print and pre-print cultures. The larger context in which print technology was received in Western Europe was marked by the emergence of Protestantism, which seems to have favored empirical observation and scientific inquiry. Likewise, the impact of "print-capitalism" in India depends on the Indian context in which print technology and other improvements in communication were received and used.

This has cleared the way for a discussion of the relation between religious nationalism and religious modes of communication. Religious nationalism equates the religious community with the nation and thus builds on a previously constructed religious identity. Let us therefore look at the role of communication in the construction of identity. While the development of a religious organization is crucial for the construction of religious communities, the decisive factor remains the ritual communication of identity. "Who am I?" and "What should I do?" are two central questions in a person's quest for identity. Belonging to a community can help to provide an answer to these questions and motivate people as agents in shaping their life. A sense of belonging and the feelings of honor and shame connected to it are felt bodily as natural emotions, but they depend on webs of social signification. The construction of a person, with specific feelings of anger, desire, love, and shame, depends on discourse in public space. Charles Taylor emphasizes that self-awareness, which is central to being a person, is bound up with language and that language creates public space.[4] His analysis of discourse focuses on conversation, discussion, and debate. It is certainly a vital insight that who we think we are can depend crucially on our conversations with others. Our feelings are shaped by language. Taylor recognizes, moreover, that in some (what he calls "earlier") societies this conversation may include extrahuman interlocutors and be carried on in sacred space. I would like to draw attention to the specific features of ritual communication and to ritual space as a locus for self-awareness.

Ritual is a special form of communication. Although there is no universal criterion for separating ritual from nonritual, most societies do demarcate ritual from other social action. In an important article, Stanley Tambiah gives a working definition: "Ritual is a culturally constructed system of symbolic communication. It is constituted of patterned and ordered sequences of words and acts, often expressed in multiple media, whose content and arrangement are characterized in varying degree by formality (conventionality), stereotypy (rigidity), condensation (fusion), and redundancy (repetition)."[5] Tambiah argues persuasively that the cultural content of ritual is grounded in particular cosmological and ideological constructs. Ritual's efficacy depends on the dynamic nexus between these cultural constructs and ritual's formality and rigidity. Tambiah emphasizes that ritual, as conventional action, distances participants with their private emotions and motivations from the ritual enactment. While it is certainly true that the meaning and efficacy of ritual cannot be explained by the intentions of the actors, however, these intentions are not utterly irrelevant to ritual action. It is not that intentional behavior is entirely opposite to conventional behavior, as Tambiah argues, but that intentions are interpreted and molded in the ritual process.

A distinction between "in-order-to" motives and "because" motives, made by Bruce Kapferer following Alfred Schutz, is useful here.[6] "In-order-to" motives are subjective and future-oriented. A process of objectification relates the subjective motives an actor has for a given action with the conscious reflection on that act by the actor and others. "Because" motives thus constitute the objective meaning of an act as it is interpreted in the context of social practice. "In-order-to" motives have to be converted into "because" motives in order for the action of a person to make sense to that person and in order for others to understand the actor's concerns and perspectives. This approach implies that action, ritual and otherwise, is rooted in the objective world as actors intersubjectively construct it. However, the element of distancing remains of crucial importance in the construction of the ritual actor and his motives.

Ritual action distances itself from historical events by offering its construction of the world and of history through the performative media of singing, dancing, and the manipulation of material objects. This explains why the symbolic forms of ritual and its construction of reality remain relatively unchanged, even though its societal context may have changed considerably. In a recent study, Maurice Bloch tries to show that the symbolic content of the Merina circumcision ritual did not change over the course of two centuries, despite considerable societal transformations in Madagascar.[7] He explains this by arguing that the ritual refers to the otherworldly, which is removed from historical events, and that its form of discourse (singing, dancing, the use of material objects—activities that have no ordinary referential meaning) also distances it from the everyday. The ritual provides an ideology in which this world is replaced with the other world. Whoever seizes the position of intermediary between this and the other world achieves an unquestionable authority.

Bloch's argument is certainly important, but I do not accept his assumption that a ritual has a definite, limited number of meanings (preferably reducible to one master meaning) and that this can be retrieved by a type of analysis that treats the ritual as a text. This approach isolates performance from the flow of events and conflicting interpretations in which it is embedded and, by so doing, arrives at what it argues is the essence of ritual discourse. Although I agree with Bloch that ritual form is very resistant to change, I would argue that transformations in the scale of performance as well as in the larger political arena in which the performance takes place result in changes in what that performance means to the participants. What I would like to call the constituency of participants in ritual, as well as the place of particular performances in a ritual repertoire, may change significantly.

A good example of this is the ritual performance of pilgrimage. The improvements in roads and railways in India during the last century have made pilgrimage a more readily available mode of religious communication for a growing group of people. The sheer growth in numbers has dramatically changed the whole organization of this type of ritual action.[8] While particular ritual sequences in Hindu pilgrimage, such as the giving of gifts to Brahman priests, may display a great continuity, they are embedded in a flow of experiences and actions that undergoes important transformation. In my view it is hardly possible to give a precise account of the change in the symbolic content of pilgrimage over a period of time, since this would entail arranging a series of essential meanings in a historical succession. However, it is possible to delineate changes in the arena in which certain interpretations are made authoritative. The search for essential meanings is in that way replaced by a description and analysis of the social construction of meanings over time.

While rituals remain relatively constant in form but change in what they mean or do—performatively—to participants, they are used in a restrictive manner in political ceremonies. The construction of their symbolic form, as well as the message these ceremonies are intended to convey, can be directly traced to the "agency" of religious movements. Hindu nationalism offers a number of good examples, such as the Cow Protection Movement and the "sacrifice for unity," both of which I will discuss in detail later.

I fully agree with Bloch's important point that ritual legitimates in its authoritative discourse several types of domination: gender hierarchy as well as state domination. These patterns of domination are realized in the ritual construction of personhood. Much of the persuasiveness and efficacy of ritual derives from the fact that it deals with mortality and illness. It is an antagonistic discourse, which works by violently conquering and subjugating death and, by extension, whatever is "demonic," "other," "weak," and so on. Since ritual creates domination, powerful groups and movements try to seize control over it and use it for their purposes. This explains the continuous struggle over sites of ritual communication, be they Sufi shrines, Sikh *gurdwaras*, or Hindu temples.

However, what Bloch neglects in his study is that what on one level is the creation of domination is on another level resistance against encapsulating forms of colonial domination.[9] Religious discourse and practice can thus simultaneously establish the authority of religious elites and resist missionary and colonizing efforts. We have to recognize the importance of the struggle against Christian missionary attacks for the formation of contemporary Hinduism and Islam in India. Later on, religious defiance pits itself against the secularism of the bourgeois elites of the nation-state. This element of resistance and protest is, for example, very strong in Iranian Shi'ism as well as in Indian Sikhism. In many cases, then, resistance and domination work together in a dialectical process.

A direct relation among the ritual communication of personhood, nationalist discourse, and violence on the part of the state has been established by Kapferer in a stimulating discussion of Sinhalese nationalism.[10] Kapferer tries to show how in sorcery rituals the order of the body is identified with the order of the state. Evil threatens the order of the body and the body politic, and violence is seen as an appropriate means to expunge evil. According to Kapferer, nationalist ideology interprets the hierarchical argument inherent in Buddhist cosmology within a coherent scheme that comes to define the Sinhalese experience of the world. In other words, Sinhalese nationalism realizes a potential that is contained within the logic of Buddhist cosmology. By engaging people's consciousness of their world and their personhood, nationalist ideology attains motivating power. The only difficulty with Kapferer's analysis is that he reifies Buddhist cosmology by making it a system of orientations that entirely governs cognition, while neglecting the ways these orientations are produced and contested. However, his point that the passions and violence of nationalism are integral to definitions of personhood is well taken.

Ritual can thus be seen as a form of communication through which a person discovers his identity and the significance of his actions. It works largely by defining not only the "self" but also the "other," whether outside or within the self, and by subjugating the "other" through symbolic violence. A good example of this process seems to be the logic of conversion and reform. Hindu and Muslim rituals aim at the transformation of the self by conquering lusts and passions. The imagery is that of violence: the Hindu god who kills the demon, the Sufi saint who destroys his enemies. The community of true believers can only exist by overcoming the internal and external forces that threaten personal and cosmic harmony. Movements, groups, can seize control over ritual discourse to communicate their ideology. What seems to happen in religious nationalism is that ideological movements give a new interpretation to the cosmological understandings communicated in religious ritual. The nation is presented as an extension of the self and nationalism as part of religion, dealing with the shame and honor, the illness and death, of the person.

It should be reasonably obvious that, as Anderson argues, nations are "imagined communities." Religion provides particular imaginations of the world and particular (ritual) ways of communicating them. While according to religious ideology these imaginations are "natural," "given," and "unchanging," they are actually produced in social arenas. The production of religious meaning and practice as part of a historical construction of nationalist identities is one of my main concerns. And although writing and print are important vehicles for communication in India and elsewhere, I would argue that ritual takes pride of place in the communication of the idea of a religious nation.

In the next section I want to demonstrate how in two specific cases—the Hindu veneration of the cow and the Muslim institution of purdah—the ritual communication of identity is appropriated by religious nationalism.

Body, Gender, and the Nation

Political analysts sometimes wonder how nationalism can be so emotionally demanding and yet at the same time so satisfying. People seem to be ready to feel pride or exasperation and even to kill or to die for their nation, as if it were their own family. In fact, the sense that the nation is one's own family writ large appears to be exactly what nationalism attempts to foster. This can be successfully done because nationalist discourse refers to a commonality of experience that generates similar habitual dispositions. It is not only the mystique of blood but also that of "belonging" that creates the emotional force of nationalism. Nationalist ideology reinterprets the ideas, feelings, and practices that constitute and orient routine social life.[11] It uses the idiom of family ties to express the loyalties, rights, and obligations, as well as the ambiguous passions, involved in belonging to a nation.

In this section I want to examine how ritual communication has linked nationalist discourse on nation and state and religious discourse on the family in South Asia. As I will argue, the theme of the management of desire is crucial in linking these discourses. This theme is treated differently in Hindu and Muslim discursive traditions, although there are also important similarities. At a very general level, the management of desire concerns the control of female sexuality by men exercising patriarchal power. This observation is indeed so general that one author has argued that any sociology of the body will ultimately hinge on it.[12] The honor of the family and, by extension, the nation depends on the integrity, modesty, and submissiveness of the female body.

The nation is often imagined as a brotherhood of men protecting their womenfolk. Men are portrayed as strong and powerful; women as weak and powerless. But protection also implies the exertion of male authority, to which women have to submit. The state represents male authority as if it were the father of the nation. While I will argue that this general picture applies to both Hindu and Muslim nationalism, I would also contend that the complexities and ambiguities of religious discourse on femininity and the female body must be taken into account. I will try to do so in dealing with two different instances of religious nationalism in South Asia, the Hindu Cow Protection Movement that took place in North India between 1880 and 1920 and the Islamization program of the late 1970s and early 1980s under Zia ul Haq's regime in Pakistan.

The Cow as Mother of the Hindu Nation

Protection of *gau mata* (mother cow) became one of the most important issues of an incipient Hindu nationalism between 1880 and 1920. The Cow Protection Movement demanded that the colonial government ban cow slaughter. When that failed, it attempted physically to prohibit the slaughter and sacrifice of cows. The movement created a rift not only between Hindus and the British but also between Hindus and Muslims, since the latter acted as butchers and also used the cow as sacrificial victim in their celebration of Bakr-Id, a festival commemorating Abraham's offering of Ishmael. The organizational aspects of the movement as well as the violent agitation and riots connected with it, to which I will return later, have been very well studied by historians. Much less attention has been given to the Hindu love for mother cow and the protection of her body. Modern historians do not go as far as the colonial observers of the movement by assuming that religion is only the smoke screen for political agitation, but the emphasis on organization does imply an assumption that mother cow is simply a rallying symbol for the mobilization of the Hindu community—something that serves the struggle for independence, even if it has the rather unfortunate side effect of alienating the Muslim population. What is left to be (at least partly) understood is why people would want to die and kill for the protection of cows. Much of the research begs the question of what the cow's body meant to the Hindu protectionist.

When we turn to anthropology for interpretations of the prohibition against cow slaughter, we encounter a most curious discussion that was initiated by Marvin Harris.[13] In Harris's view the sanctity of the cow is a rational taboo, a cultural mechanism, protecting a low-energy, small-scale, animal-based ecosystem. He focuses on the traction provided by bulls and the use of manure as fertilizer and cooking fuel, arguing that the sanctity of the cow serves its functional purpose well. Furthermore, he claims that the taboo arose at a time of immense ecological pressures on human and cattle populations alike. Much of the ensuing discussion has shown that Harris's ecological and functional approach is highly speculative and at some points demonstrably false.[14] Most authors now accept that the sanctity of the cow has instead to be understood in terms of Hindu religious tradition, but unfortunately not much progress has been made in interpreting that tradition.

My argument is that the sanctity of the cow's body and the prohibition against killing her and eating her flesh is made real for Hindus in crucial ritual performances that communicate a great variety of cosmological constructs. I would further suggest that these constructs mainly concern images of femininity and the female body. In the North Indian region in which the Cow Protection Movement was most successful in the nineteenth and twentieth centuries, two connected strands of Hindu discourse and ritual practice were most influential: Brahmanical ritual concerning death, pollution, and sin, and devotional worship of gods and goddesses.

The central notion in the Brahmanical worship of the cow is that a human being depends entirely on the cow in life as well as in death, as a child depends on his mother. The cow is, in Brahmanical theology, often used as a symbol of the earth, the nourisher. She is the mother of life, the substance of all things. She is a goddess who fulfills every wish (*kamadhenu*). She is the symbol of wealth and good fortune (*lakshmi*). A ritual sequence whereby one worships the cow by circumambulating it clockwise (*parikrama*) and respectfully touching its four feet with one's forehead is part of a great many Brahmanical rituals. There is, however, a special ritual that connects the cow to death. In this, the Vaitarani ritual, a cow is first worshiped and then its tail grasped with both hands. This is in preparation for that terrible event after death in which the dead have to cross the fetid river of death to arrive at the opposite bank, on which the kingdom of the dead is found.

Not only is the body of the cow sacred but also its products. Cow milk is seen as a life-giving substance, with the result that dairy products are the most highly valued sources of nourishment for

Hindus. There is a directly felt relation between the drinking of milk and one's bodily well-being. To eat a vegetarian meal prepared in ghee (clarified butter) and with milk products makes a person *sattvik* (pure, of the highest quality). Clarified butter, considered the purest fluid possible, is extensively used in Brahmanical sacrifice and as a cooking medium at feasts. A mixture of the five products of the cow (*pancagavya*)—milk, curds, butter, urine, and dung—is consumed in Brahmanical rituals of expiation. The mixture is also used to purify the body of pollution. For example, it is smeared on ulcers. The purity of cow dung is evident from the fact that food is cooked on it and that nobody would hesitate to touch food after touching the dried dung. Lakshmi, the goddess of wealth, is thought to reside in cow dung.

The other context in which we encounter the symbolism of the cow as a protecting and wish-fulfilling mother is that of devotional religion. Especially rituals and myths centering on Krishna—one of the most popular gods in Hindu India, at least since the composition of the *Bhagavata Purana* in the ninth or early tenth century—are saturated with this symbolism. Krishna's life story, which is celebrated in numerous rituals, is that of a god who grows up in pastoral surroundings among cowherds. As we noted earlier, there are two phases in that story, the first focusing on the relation between Krishna and his mother, and the second on the amorous relations between Krishna and the cowherdesses. It is primarily in the first phase that we encounter the symbolism of the cow and of milk. One of the best-known stories about Krishna's childhood is that he repeatedly steals butter and curds from his mother. Hindu interpretations of Krishna, the butter thief, make much of milk as a symbol of motherly love. The child has an endless appetite for milk and a boundless love for his mother who provides it, just as a cow is always ready to suckle her calf.

There can be no doubt that the construction of the cow as a nurturing mother goddess is very strong in Hinduism. However, the benevolent cow is not the only image of the female. The illness goddesses, such as that of smallpox, are called "mother," but they are feared and propitiated. Patients are said to be the vehicle of the goddess, and she is politely asked to leave. It is often remarked that these fierce, aggressive goddesses are overheated, since they are alone, without husbands. This also extends to women who, when they die unmarried and/or without children, can turn into wandering witches who threaten those who are happy. A goddess is only benevolent as long as she is married and a "satisfied" mother. During the Cow Protection Movement Kali, the dark goddess, or Durga, who rides a tiger, were often invoked in mass meetings. They are fierce, bloodthirsty mothers who destroy evil and protect their worshipers. When the order of Hindu society is threatened the goddess assumes her aggressive aspect. No doubt, the peaceful, vegetarian cow is one side of the mother image, while the illness goddesses and Kali and Durga, who accept blood sacrifices, are the other side. Killing the cow calls for the action of Durga, who rides a tiger. The iconography of Hindu nationalism makes abundant use of the two images of the mother: the nurturing cow and the dangerous Durga on her tiger.

Very important in images of the female is their relation with the construction of patriarchy. The most influential discourse on the family in Hindu North India is to be found in the myths and practices celebrating the marriage between the god Rama and the goddess Sita. Rama is the virtuous king (*dharmaraja*). Theologically, he is conceived as the "lord of propriety" (*maryada purushottam*). A striking aspect of his character is his detachment. The story of Rama's life is essentially a cautionary tale about the disruptive effects of sexual desire. It shows that the only way to control disruptive passion lies in a properly "detached" marriage. As we saw earlier, Rama is the ideal, detached husband who is the guardian of the order of society and of the family, while Sita is the ideal, submissive wife who shows unquestioning loyalty to her husband. She is called *pativrata*, someone who observes a vow tying her to her husband in perfect fidelity and who serves her husband as a god. This term is also encountered in descriptions of the disputed practice of "widow burning," *sati*. If a woman's husband, her god on earth, dies before her, she proves that she is true (*sati*) to her vow by immolating herself on his pyre. As a *sati* the wife will help her deceased husband reach "the other side," just as the cow does in the Vaitarani ritual.[15] The concepts of *pativrata* and *sati* imply a special form of holiness for women that lies in selfless surrender to the husband-god.[16] There is a strong belief among Hindus that the wife is responsible for the well-being of the husband. If he dies before her, she "has eaten her husband," as the Hindi expression goes. But the husband can only survive when he resists the attractions of the female body through detachment. It is his duty to love his wife with detachment and to preserve order in the family by his male authority.

As mother cow, then, the female is a protectress of men, a nurturer of the family. Married and a mother she is submissive and treats her husband like a god. Alone and without children, however, she is only called "mother" to pacify her, since she is dangerous and powerful. The image of the male is as complex as that of the female, combining as it does the image of Krishna as a child, depending on his mother, and that of Rama as a man, ruling his wife and his kingdom. A third image connects a man directly with the image of mother cow: that of the god Shiva. Shiva, the independent, self-sufficient male, is symbolized by the bull who, as an act of worship, is set free by its owners and may roam the Indian streets unmolested. Religious discourse on both Shiva and Rama focus on ascetic detachment. A man not only is a person of authority but is also detached and devoted to "higher goals." In that sense he has to realize the power of detachment and devotion within himself. And that power is unanimously seen as feminine in Hinduism.[17]

Mother cow is thus only one image in a repertoire of images concerning the female body and the interplay of femininity and masculinity. However, it is a crucial image, since as a mother the cow signifies the family and the community at large. She depends on the authority and protection of the male of the family. While mother cow refers to family and nation alike, her protection refers to patriarchal authority and to the Hindu state, the rightful kingdom of Rama (*ramrajya*). It is within the logic of religious discourse that the protection of the cow became the foremost symbol of the Hindu nation-state. Sacrifice of the cow signified simultaneously the illegitimacy of British rule and an insult to Hindu patriarchy.

There can be little doubt that protection of the cow already had a political significance before the British period. Foreigners who traveled to India in the sixteenth century report the worship and protection of the cow.[18] There is evidence of institutions to look after old and infirm cattle (*goshalas*) from the same period. Some Muslim rulers, like Babar and Akbar, seem to have imposed a ban on cow slaughter. During the mutiny of 1857–58 the king of Delhi banned cow slaughter in Delhi to forge unity between Hindus and Muslims. Both Maratha and Sikh rulers defined their kingship in terms of the protection of the cow. It is therefore not surprising that the first agitation against cow slaughter under colonial rule took place in the Punjab after the British victory over the Sikhs. Cow slaughter had been a capital offense in the Sikh kingdom, and the Namdharis or Kukas, founded by Bhai Bhalak Singh (1799–1862), started to agitate for cow protection. This Sikh reform movement related the British victory to the decline of Sikhism. Reform implied violent resistance to the rule of those "unclean butchers from London," as a popular song had it.[19] In 1871 Namdharis killed Muslim butchers in Amritsar and Ludhiana, while they declared Sikh rule in a village in Ferozepur. The growing militancy of the Namdharis led to the violent repression of the sect by the British. It is important to note that from the start cow protection challenged the legitimacy of British rule, although the immediate violence was directed at Muslims who killed cows.[20] Cow protection was clearly a sign of the moral quality of the state.

The role of North India's foremost Hindu reform movement, the Arya Samaj, in making cow protection a Hindu cause in large parts of North India is not to be underestimated. In 1881 Swami Dayananda Saraswati, founder of the Arya Samaj, published a treatise with the title *Gokarunanidhi* (Ocean of mercy to the cow). In this treatise he firmly opposed the slaughter of mother cow as an anti-Hindu act. In 1882, together with "orthodox" Hindu leaders who had been his opponents on other occasions, he founded a committee for the protection of cows. In the following decade the Arya Samaj played an important role in the establishment of cow protection societies in different parts of British India. These societies were particularly successful in the Northwestern Provinces and in Oudh, Bihar, and the Central Provinces.

As we saw in the previous chapter, the Arya Samaj propounded the idea that Hindus had to return to the ancient religion of the Vedas and abolish all later accretions, which had debased their religion. Dayananda's movement had important doctrinal similarities with Sikhism in its rejection of image worship and of the ritual superiority of the Brahman priest, which may partly account for its success in the Punjab as compared to other regions. However, Dayananda's arguments struck a familiar chord not only with the Sikhs but also with "orthodox" Hindus. It is a peculiar feature of the Arya Samaj that, while it attacks the ritual superiority of the

Brahman priest, it has an orthodox, Brahmanical theology and accepts some crucial features of Brahmanical ritual, such as the worship of mother cow. Dayananda's championing of Hindu and Sanskrit, as well as his efforts to ban cow slaughter, found wide support beyond the circle of his followers. In my view one of his greatest contributions was that he used the peripatetic nature of Hindu asceticism in order to disseminate "causes" or "issues" that were central in Hindu identity formation. Dayananda and his fellow preachers traveled all over India, giving lectures and founding societies. Improved communications by train, bus, and rail meant that messages traveled much faster than before. Also, the Aryas made good use of printing presses to spread their ideas in pamphlets and daily newspapers. In this way the notion of cow protection could become an issue that was not limited to one particular region.

Typically, it was British colonial policy that gave the movement a major impetus. In 1888 the Northwestern Provincial High Court at Allahabad ruled that a cow was not a sacred "object" as defined in section 295 of the Indian Penal Code, and that Muslims who slaughtered them could not be held to have insulted the religion of the Hindus—an offense that could be punished with imprisonment.[21] Following this ruling police had to protect Muslims who wanted to slaughter cows. Consequently, the British and the Muslims came to be seen as allied beef-eating barbarians determined to insult the deepest religious sentiments of the Hindus. Cow slaughter was also an excellent symbolic issue, given that Muslims used to sacrifice cows during the Bakr-Id festival. While goats could also be slaughtered at that festival, it became imperative for Muslims not to bow down to Hindu encroachments on their "ancient" right to sacrifice cows on Bakr-Id. Time and place were thus set for violent encounter.

While all such conflicts—then and now—have to be understood in the local context, I do not agree with Gyanendra Pandey, who argues that these conflicts are only connected by a colonial narrative of communalism.[22] They also form configurations that resemble one another, whatever the local differences. An important element was the inadequacy of the British response to these conflicts, as for example, in Azamgarh in 1893.[23] Here the British even played the role of catalyst in the disturbances. The local magistrate had directed that Muslims who wanted to sacrifice on Bakr-Id should register. He wanted this information in order to pinpoint possible areas of trouble, but his orders were interpreted as promising protection to all Muslims who wanted to sacrifice—and even to those who never had done so in the past. This ill-advised action on the part of the magistrate of Azamgarh created a discourse on "established custom," which had a Hindu and a Muslim version, that made "custom" itself the battleground. The action of the British seemed to indicate that they did not even want to refer to what was negotiated as "custom." The British interference can plausibly be interpreted as the immediate cause of widespread violence in the district.

The networks built by the Arya Samaj and by "orthodox" ascetics were now increasingly used for the "defense of the cow" against barbarian aggression. However, not only did *sadhus* travel around to spread the message but, as research on pilgrimage shows, there was an increase in the number of pilgrims visiting pilgrimage centers where they could be informed about the movement.[24] Donations to support the movement were solicited from every household. Chain letters were circulated to mobilize support when cow sacrifice or the transport of cows to government pounds had to be stopped.[25]

It seems that every Hindu, from high to low, had to become part of the national family. The cow societies were supported by the "little kings" (*rajas*) of the Indian countryside. The rajas had been transformed in the colonial system from rulers of land cum population to large landlords subsumed under British tenure systems, or, in Thomas Metcalf's apt phrase, from lords of the land to landlords. As is clear from several accounts, the protection offered by the British to this ruling elite enabled them to invest considerable amounts of money in religious causes such as the building of temples and the beautification of pilgrimage centers.[26] Although they had to remain somewhat in the background of the movement because of their special relations with the British, there is no doubt that they supported it wholeheartedly. The direct organization of the movement was, however, left to the service classes in the cities and petty landholders and schoolmasters in the rural areas. Through measures like caste excommunication, boycotting, and fines, Hindus who had sold cows to butchers were forced to buy the cattle back. Itinerant groups that were engaged in cattle transport, such as the Nats and Banjaras, were obliged to fall in line with what increasingly became a "Hindu nation" fighting for one and the same cause. This seems to be the case when at the Bakr-Id festival of 1893 riots broke out over a large region in Bihar and the eastern parts of the Northwestern Provinces and Oudh. Large groups of people were mobilized through existing marketing structures.[27] Thousands of people attacked Muslims in districts like Azamgarh, where the British lost control completely for several days. Perhaps the most striking feature of the riots was that the entire Hindu population of villages was involved, not just Hindus of a certain economic and social status.[28]

The riots of 1893 signaled the end of the first phase of the Cow Protection Movement. But its significance can hardly be overestimated. As the lieutenant-governor of the Punjab put it in 1894: "The cow-killing question is the question of all others, which, at least for the last 20 years, has been regarded by us all as the gravest danger that threatens us in India."[29] A second phase began after the Durbar of 1911; tension rose again with riots in the Hindu sacred center Ayodhya. This was followed by a number of disturbances involving the cow protection issue until, in the 1920s, it appears that the Khilafat movement created a temporary truce between Muslims and Hindus. In the decades of struggle for independence that followed, the great ideologue of Indian nationalism, Mahatma Gandhi, continued to use the love for mother cow in his imagined vision of the Indian nation, although he tried, at the same time, to include Muslims in the national family. Gandhi exemplifies in many ways the linking of devotional discourse on gender and the transformation of the self to nationalist discourse on the Indian nation.

Mahatma Gandhi

In Mohandas K. Gandhi's emergence as the Hindu leader of the nationalist struggle against the British in the 1920s we can see an important step in the construction of a "moderate," pluralist version of Hindu nationalism. Gandhi's success as a nationalist leader and cult figure depended on his use of Hindu devotional discourse.[30] In this respect, Gandhi was certainly not an isolated figure. He had his predecessors in Hindu saints like Vivekananda and Aurobindo and his successors in persons like Vinoba Bhave and Jayaprakash Narayan. Gandhi called himself a *sanatani* (orthodox) Hindu who believed that Hindu scriptures such as the Vedas sprang from the same ultimate divine inspiration as the Bible, the Qur'an, and the Zend Avesta. He saw a universal, essential morality in these scriptures. That is why Hinduism, in his view, was not an exclusive religion but accepted all ways to God. This interpretation of Hinduism as "universal religion" derives from orientalism but has been incorporated in Hindu reform, as we discussed in the previous chapter. We see here a "pluralist" Gandhi who proclaimed an all-embracing Indian spirituality as a defining characteristic of the nation. However, since his discourse and practice were recognizably Hindu, they did not fail to alienate Muslims, who had their own discourse on universal religion.

Muslims had no difficulty in perceiving a hidden message in Gandhi's universalism. According to Gandhi, Hinduism can be distinguished from other religions by its love and protection of mother cow, which he saw as the central fact of Hinduism. However, the Cow Protection Movement was particularly directed at defining the Hindu community against Muslim sacrificers and British rulers. Muslims bore the brunt of the ensuing violence and reacted by asserting their own identity in distinction from that of Hindus. Gandhi attempted to reconcile the two communities constructed by the Cow Protection Movement. He argued that "the present-day 'Cow Protection' had degenerated into a perpetual feud with the Musalmans, whereas true cow protection means conquering the Musalmans by our love."[31] In that way he tried to make cow protection a movement that would not alienate Muslims but instead win them over to the devotional path of love. Thus did Gandhi attempt to include Muslims in his version of a pluralist nationalism.

However, we cannot fail to notice that Gandhi's pluralist nationalism retains a Hindu character, inasmuch as it emphasizes the spiritual superiority of the protection of one's mother in comparison to her sacrifice. Despite all the talk of tolerance, the Muslim sacrifice of a cow was thereby seen as an objectionable act. Gandhi's pluralism therefore did not make much sense from the point of view of many Muslims. In fact, Gandhi's attitude toward Muslims can be compared to his attitude toward untouchables. He argued that untouchables were *harijans*, children of Hari (Vishnu), who should be incorporated into the Hindu nation through purification and moral uplift. In espousing that view Gandhi aligned himself with a long tradition of Hindu expansion that operates through hierarchical incorporation and assimilation but has, in the end, little to do with a pluralist acceptance of the equality of different traditions.

Gandhi was certainly a shrewd politician. He projected a saintly image on the scene of nationalist politics, and, when he toured through the country, people made great efforts to gain his *darshan*.[32] In the tradition of Hindu saints Gandhi showed that his powers were attained through spiritual exercise, or, as he calls it himself, "experiments with truth" (*satyagraha*). These experiments dealt with all the minutiae of life but find their apogee in celibacy. According to Gandhi, Hinduism is a religion of renunciation of the flesh. He saw marriage as a "fall." After having fathered five children, he took a vow of celibacy at the age of thirty-six. Gandhi's celibacy recapitulates a dominant theme of Hindu asceticism: retention of semen bestows supernatural power (*shakti*). As a leader of the nationalist struggle he showed himself and his Hindu followers that his powers were acquired through disciplining the body. While this theme glorifies the self-sufficient male, Gandhi's *satyagraha* also exemplifies another important theme of Hindu devotionalism, namely, that true selfless devotion is feminine. His program of action focused on "nonviolence" or "passive resistance," for which he thought women were much better qualified than men.

Gandhi's political articulation of this theme brought him into conflict with other Hindu nationalists at the height of Hindu-Muslim conflict during partition. His assassin, Nathuram Godse, a Brahman from Maharashtra, declared in his trial that "I firmly believed that the teachings of absolute ahimsa as advocated by Gandhiji would ultimately result in the emasculation of the Hindu Community and thus make the community incapable of resisting the aggression or inroads of other communities, especially the Muslims."[33] This statement is quite interesting, given the fact that Gandhi had always argued that nonviolence (*ahimsa*) was the solution to the emasculation of the Hindu nation under colonial rule. Nonviolence was, in his view, a product of "fearlessness" (*abhaya*), which could only be gained through chastity.[34] It should be clear from our discussion of wrestling in the previous chapter that Gandhi drew here from a considerable tradition regarding power (*shakti*) and bodily strength (*bal*), but that he transformed it by connecting it to a notion of nonviolence that derived from a rather different sphere, namely, that of sacrifice. His assassin, as well as other members of the RSS, came from a background of Maratha militancy that did not allow the discursive shift Gandhi was trying to accomplish.

The dialectical tension between femininity and masculinity in Hindu devotional practice is carried over into Hindu nationalism, as has been eloquently argued by the Rudolphs. On the one hand, there is the idea that Hindus are like women, since they have been conquered, raped, and enslaved—first by Muslims and then by the British. On the other hand, there is the idea that one can sublimate one's femininity, bring it to a higher plane by the retention of semen, and thereby attain supernatural power, which is seen as feminine. This is exemplified in Gandhi's program of nationalism based on spiritual transformation.

Gandhi took this program very seriously. Not only did he take the vow of celibacy and regular vows of fasting but in the midst of his struggle to stem the tide of Hindu-Muslim violence during the partition of India he tried to increase his powers by taking naked young women to bed with him in order to test his detachment. He seems to have started this "experiment" after his wife's death on 22 February 1944.[35] It led to great unrest among his followers, who managed to persuade him to stop it. However, in 1946 he resumed the "experiment" with his grandniece Manu. He did so because of the enormous increase in Hindu-Muslim violence in India just before partition, especially in the predominantly Muslim district of Noakhali in Bengal, an area that Gandhi toured on foot to spread his message of nonviolence. As he put it himself: "Ever since my coming to Noakhali, I have been asking myself the question 'What is it that is choking the action of my *ahimsa* [nonviolence]? Why does not the spell work? May it not be because I have temporised in the matter of *brahmacharya* [celibacy]?'"[36]

Again, Gandhi's idea that his asceticism (*tapas*) and his celibacy (*brahmacharya*) would give him power (*shakti*) that could be used to control not only the microcosm of the body but also the macrocosm came from an established Hindu discursive tradition. To use female bodies as instruments to gain a higher self, however defined, had also a considerable pedigree in so-called left-hand Tantrik traditions that had never become part of a "respectable" mainstream. Nevertheless, to combine this Tantrik use of the female body to transform the self with a puritanical attempt to banish all unchaste feelings is again an idiosyncratic transformation of the tradition.

That his actions were greeted by considerable social opprobrium cannot have taken Gandhi by surprise, but, in my estimation, Gandhi could not have cared less, considering what in his view was at stake. He felt that his spiritual ability to control himself would enable him to save the nation.

Gandhi also demanded from his group of followers that they take the vow of celibacy, which he saw as a prerequisite for a total devotion to the national cause. It is clear that, for these followers, Gandhi was a saint. His behavior was conspicuously that of a Hindu saint, in that he derived his powers from sexual abstinence, diets, and fasts—in short, from the perfection of body and mind. However, it is important to see what kind of saint Gandhi was. He broke away from established channels of saintly power to become a new phenomenon, the individual saint of Hindu nationalism. It is crucial that he did not attempt to root his sainthood in a spiritual pedigree by taking a guru. Moreover, despite having all the trappings of a guru, he remained a layman, formulating a political philosophy based upon an orientalist reading of Hindu scripture, combined with the contemporary Western utopian visions of Ruskin and Tolstoy. He invented a political style that has since become the style of all Indian politicians, regardless of their persuasion. Again, it is important to note that this "laicization" and "ethicization" of religious communication has taken place almost entirely outside of the established religious communities, which only seem to come into their own with the founding of the Vishva Hindu Parishad. While politicians have for decades used a saintly facade, only now have saints come to reveal themselves openly as politicians.

Gandhi's message was that of a "spiritual Hinduism" that would include other religions, albeit given the common acceptance of such cherished Hindu notions as cow worship and vegetarianism. The steps he took to transform Hindu discourse and practice were considerable, but, in the final analysis, have to be understood from within that tradition. Despite his attempts to formulate a message of tolerance and pluralism, his idiom remained Hindu and has thus contributed substantially to Hindu nationalism. Moreover, the old issues continued to exist. In the postcolonial context cow protection remained a source of conflict between Hindus and Muslims. Hindu nationalism continued to fight a secular state and to seek an ideal

Hindu state (*ramrajya*) that would protect the body of the cow as the mother of the Hindu nation.

Covering the Female Body
in Muslim Nationalism

Islam does not, in general, use the ritual worship of sacred icons, animate or inanimate, to convey its message. Few beliefs and practices could thus be more alien to Muslims than the Hindu worship of the cow as mother of the community of believers. Islam focuses on moral behavior in public space, as exemplified by the life of the Prophet. It defines what humans ought to be and do by its codification of the practice of the Prophet, who realized perfectly in his life the revealed truth of the Qur'an.[37] Movements that seek to construct an ideal Muslim society, a "house of Islam," have to refer to the example of the Prophet. No doubt, however, interpretations of that example differ as much as the blueprints of an ideal society. Confronted with the Muslim League's demand for the creation of Pakistan many religious leaders declared themselves against a Muslim nation-state. Some of them argued that, as a universal religion, Islam could not form the basis for a narrow nationalism.

Nevertheless, when Pakistan emerged from the independence struggle, it was declared to be an Islamic state. What I want to argue here is that one of the key images of the nation-state became that of patriarchal power (authority and protection) exercised over female bodies. As in the Hindu case, however, this image was complicated by the dialectic of femininity and masculinity. It is the institution of female seclusion and veiling (*purdah*) that, as a ritual system of communication, becomes the sign of a society ordered by Islam.

Purdah exists among both Muslims and Hindus in South Asia but operates entirely differently among them. While Hindu purdah is related to relations of respect between affines, Muslim purdah is related to the unity of the kindred vis-à-vis the outside, nonkindred world.[38] Different ideologies of the family appear to account for these differences in purdah. Since purdah in the Muslim case involves seclusion from the public sphere, it is closely bound up with the status of the family, which Hindu purdah is not. Families that can afford to keep women in seclusion, and thus uninvolved in economic activity outside the home, have a relatively high status. As Patricia Jeffery expresses it, the seclusion of women is a function of a family's worth, in an economic sense, but also becomes indicative of their social worth, of their honor.[39] At the same time there are also important similarities between Hindu and Muslim purdah. Purdah is a means to protect women against their own sexual desires and against sexual advances by outsiders. The connected concepts of honor (*izzat*) and shame or modesty (*sharam*) are relevant here.

Body concealment is the major idiom through which modest women can communicate the honor of the family. The minimum requirement is baggy trousers and loose dresses, worn with a shawl (*dupatta*) that covers the head and the top half of the body. For leaving the home a long cape with cap and veil (*burqa*), which conceals the entire body, is appropriate for women who observe purdah. This is, however, worn exclusively by Muslim women. The *burqa* has become a crucial sign of Islamic strictness in South Asia. Among those who try to establish this strictness, the sari, which is worn with a short-sleeved blouse that exposes the midriff, is regarded as shameless (*be-sharam*). However, modesty is communicated not only by garments that cover and conceal the body but also by bodily movement. Marcel Mauss's remark that he could recognize a girl who had been raised in a convent because she will walk with her fists closed would easily be understood by both Hindus and Muslims.[40] In particular, manipulating the shawl and casting the eyes down are signs of modesty, although clearly there is a whole repertoire of behavior.

Given that the Prophet is the model of behavior in Islam, Muslims have to turn to the traditions concerning the relations between the Prophet and his wives as well as the teachings of the Prophet himself for the legitimation of purdah. Of course, as always, the interpretation of these traditions forms a battleground for different groups, all of whom claim authority. One authoritative statement for Indian Muslims emerged from the Deobandi school, still one of India's most influential Islamic seminaries. It is contained in the *Bihisti Zewar* (Jewelry of paradise) by Ashraf Ali Thanawi, published in 1906 and widely available even today.

The *Bihisti Zewar* takes purdah for granted and concerns itself with the proper place of women in the family and in society at large.

This encyclopedic work of over one thousand pages was meant for women, which in itself signifies that women were to some extent included in the educated public. It deals with the transformation of the self ("the greater *jihad*") by teaching behavioral propriety (*adab*). By rational understanding of the law and habitual conformity to it, the lower self (*nafs*) is brought onto a higher plane. It is important to note that the book assumes that women have the same potential for that transformation as men, and perhaps even more so. In her discussion Barbara Metcalf argues that the ideal person, as portrayed in the book, has the following characteristics. She is "soft, deferential, given to silence, meek in the face of dispute. In a short biography the ideal is described: a person warm, generous, troublesome to no one, humble, never talkative, eyes lowered in modesty, grateful for even the smallest blessing, accustomed to work with one's own hands—milking goats, washing clothes. But this is a portrait of none other than the Prophet of Islam himself, for the religious ideal, reinforced in the woman's case by the requirements of her role, turns out to be the feminine ideal intended for all."[41] The female role, however, requires that she relate to her husband as to God, with obedience and gratitude.

It is striking how much of the discussion in this treatise reminds one of the dialectics of femininity and masculinity in Hindu devotionalism and nationalism, discussed above. We should, of course, be wary of taking this particular text to represent South Asian Muslim discourse on women, irrespective of time, place, and social context. Nevertheless, I do see purdah as a crucial element in that discourse over a longer time and in many places. The *Bihisti Zewar* is a reformist treatise that deals with the education of women in the household without questioning purdah as an Islamic fact for the elite and an ideal for the rest of the community. There is no attempt to make purdah a sign of the Muslim nation, but it was a sign of "correct conduct" (*adab*) that could be adopted in the discourse of religious nationalism.

It was only after the emergence of Pakistan, and especially in the last two decades, that religious nationalists tried to use purdah as a discursive tool to define the Islamic nature of Pakistan. In that context it also became an issue of state policy. Using the idiom of the family, nationalism makes the modesty (*sharam*) of women come to signify the honor (*izzat*) of the nation, safeguarded by a patriarchal state. While Muslim nationalism has been an important factor from the beginning in Pakistan, it asserted itself strongly in the 1970s and 1980s. In 1977 agitation by religious parties against the so-called Islamic socialist government of Bhutto led to a state of emergency and a military coup by Zia ul Haq, who promised to introduce an Islamic system of government (*nizam-i-islam*). Maududi's Jama'at-i-Islami came to exert considerable influence on Zia's Islamization program, not because it had gained large support among the population or formed the link between military and civil society, but because it provided the Zia regime with an ideological orientation. Moreover, as I argued in the previous chapter, movements like the RSS and the Jama'at-i-Islami present the clearest articulation of a religious nationalist discourse that is, to an important extent, shared by those movements that espouse "socialism" and/or "secularism." It was Bhutto who came up with the idea of calling his socialism Islamic.

In Maududi's view the ideal Muslim society should be ordered according to the example of the Prophet and the ordinance of the law. Such an enterprise would require an authoritarian, centralized state to guide the people along the right path. According to Maududi, an ordered society can only be maintained if there are safeguards preventing the arousal of sexual urges, except between a married couple. Therefore, purdah is an Islamic way of ordering social life.[42] Within purdah, women's role is an inferior one: "Islam effects a functional distribution of the sexes and sets different spheres of activity for both of them. Women should in the main devote themselves to their household duties in their homes and men should attend to their jobs in the socio-economic spheres."[43] Sayyid Asad Gilani, chairman of the Lahore branch of the Jama'at, made the point very clearly in a 1983 pamphlet entitled *Three Women, Three Cultures*: "1. There is no mixed society. 2. Women avoid going out of the home. 3. If they need to go out, they do not adorn themselves and use a veil. 4. They avoid conversation with men who are not related to them. 5. If they must speak, they speak briefly and directly, not gently and sweetly."[44]

Zia's Islamization program was to a large extent cosmetic. It intended to use the discourse of movements like the Jama'at-i-Islami without actually changing much in the society. One of the issues that attracted a great deal of attention was the position of women in public life. A good example was the proposed prohibition of women athletes from competing publicly. More fundamental were some attempts at legal reform with respect to the position of women. Potentially most significant was the new Islamic Law of Evidence, which ruled that the testimony of two women is only equal to that of one man in financial cases. A great number of other discriminatory proposals were put forward, although little appears to have been effected.[45] However, it is not the efficacy of state interference that is the major issue here but the prevalence of discourse on women in the construction of an Islamic nation-state.

Not only in Pakistan but also in India the legal position of Muslim women has become an issue around which the nature of Muslim community can be asserted. In 1985 the Supreme Court of India passed a judgment in favor of Shah Banu, forcing her former husband to pay alimony. This judgment caused an enormous outcry among Muslim politicians and religious leaders, who interpreted it as an attack on Islamic law and the Muslim way of life in Indian society. The agitation led to the passing of a "Muslim Women's (Protection of Rights on Divorce) Bill" in 1986, which made it impossible for other Muslim women to follow Shah Banu's example. What happened in the Shah Banu case is that the Supreme Court acknowledged an appeal to secular law, namely, the Criminal Procedure Code, which concerns the maintenance of wives, children, and parents and had been applied since 1872.[46] In this way the judgment appeared to ignore the principle that Muslims in India are governed by Muslim religious laws in matters relating to the family. (Incidentally, one of the ironies of the case is that Muslim personal law, which is defended as if it were the never-changing *shari'at*, is largely an orientalist construction of the British period.)

Muslim nationalist discourse in India and Pakistan concerning women uses an idiom of shame and honor, operative at the level of the family, to express the notion that an Islamic state has to "protect" women. This is precisely the subject of Salman Rushdie's novel *Shame* (1983), which is simultaneously a family chronicle and a national history. The theme of honor and shame (*izzat* and *sharam*), which together result in the subordination of women and the suppression of sexuality, holds both histories together. If one can speak of an argument in a novel, it is Rushdie's argument that the repression of women in Pakistan engenders other types of political repression. However, he believes that this attempt at repression will never succeed in the end. "It is commonly and, I believe, accurately said of Pakistan that her women are much more impressive than her men . . . their chains, nevertheless, are no fictions. They exist. And they are getting heavier. If you hold down one thing, you hold down the adjoining. In the end, though, it all blows up in your face."[47] In *The Satanic Verses* (1988) Rushdie went one step further by exploring the ideological legitimation of female seclusion and subordination in the exemplary life of the Prophet. Given the logic of Muslim nationalist discourse, it was to be expected that such an exploration—which, as I have argued elsewhere, touches the core of Muslim identity—would cause a great uproar among Indian Muslims.[48]

Patriarchal Control and Antagonistic Nations

Nationalist discourse on the nation and the state in South Asia depends, to a large extent, on religious discourse and ritual practice concerning the relation between men and women in the family. The similarities between Hindu and Muslim discursive traditions are considerable. Patriarchal control over the female body is a general theme in both traditions. Women are sacred objects that have to be "protected" against outsiders as well as against their own desires. This protection is offered by their husbands and male relatives at the level of the family and by the state at the level of the nation. In a complex and ambiguous manner this theme is interwoven with that of the transformation of the self by the conquest of desire. The male body is not "naturally" the source of power and authority but has to be disciplined to become that. Through moral discipline it conforms to the feminine ideal of detached devotion to god. While women are transformed by the devotion to the husband-god within the family, men have to discipline themselves in public life.

Despite these similarities, Muslim and Hindu nationalisms construct antagonistic nations. In the Cow Protection Movement mother cow is protected against Muslim butchers, while sacrifice of the cow at Bakr-Id becomes the inalienable privilege of the Muslim community. In the Shah Banu case the Muslim "minority" feel that their religious rights have to be defended against attacks from the Hindu "majority," while Hindu activists claim that they are protecting destitute Muslim women against Muslim men. Here we see the confirmation of Bloch's (and also Rushdie's) point that ritual legitimates both gender hierarchy as well as state domination. These patterns of domination are realized in the ritual construction of personhood. It is an antagonistic discourse that works by violent conquest of both the "self" and the "other."

Nationalist discourse emerges in a colonialist and orientalist context. The extent to which legal discourse determines the logic of nationalist movements is striking. The British codified Hindu and Muslim law so as to provide themselves with instruments for ruling India. In so doing, they also defined the arena of cultural debate. In the case of the Cow Protection Movement the decision of the Allahabad court that a cow was not a "sacred object" elicited a violent response. British decisions regarding "customary rights" played a significant role in the ensuing riots. In Muslim debates on Islamic law the British codification of that law plays a major role. The legal orientalism of the colonial state challenges the ambiguous boundaries of Muslim and Hindu communities. A multiple response to that challenge is given by reform movements and "orthodox" movements. It is a creative reinterpretation of precolonial religious discourse on body and gender.

Not only are these nationalisms externally antagonistic but they are also internally homogenizing. Nationalism is a selective, homogenizing discourse that tends to demarcate social boundaries sharply and to narrow down the diversity and ambiguity of everyday life. One wonders, for example, which sections of the "Hindu nation" suffered as a result of the Cow Protection Movement. Poor Hindu peasants who had sold their cattle to Muslim butchers were forced to buy it back. Nats and Banjaras, involved in cattle trade and transport, were attacked. Islamization in Pakistan during the Zia regime was inspired by a movement that had very little support as a political party in free elections. Moreover, the Jama'at-i-Islami's interpretation of Islamic tradition is contested by many other Islamic movements as well as by women's organizations in Pakistan. It is important to note that the Hindu or Muslim nations are not the products of transhistorical religious sentiments but of specific discourses, which do not go uncontested.

Chapter Four

Peregrinations

Introduction

In the previous chapter we saw the extent to which nationalist discourse makes use of the ritual construction of the "self" and the "other." In this chapter I want to explore the construction of territory in nationalist discourse in a rather similar way. The concept of "territory" is crucial in nationalism and in the nation-state. A nation-state is a spatial unity lying between borders that it must defend. This is the sacred "Father-land" about which the Hindu nationalist V. D. Savarkar speaks in his definition of the Hindu.[1] Territory is also, as Louis Dumont argues, a continuous tract of country that symbolizes the unity of individuals who own parts of the country. When the nation is "a collection of individuals and their properties," territory is the total of the properties belonging to that collection of individuals, known as the nation.[2]

Despite this emphasis on the boundedness of the national territory, it is a truism that nationalism transcends local boundaries. Sandria Freitag sees two important elements in the European shift from the local community to that of the nation-state: "(1) participation in collective rituals informed by an ideological framework that came to equate 'community' and 'nation'; and (2) creation of a 'public sphere' which citizens of the nation helped shape through the exercise of informed public opinion."[3] It is indeed important to see that nationalism does not mean a replacement of one frame of reference by another but the equation of the local community with the nation. The national identification becomes gradually more

106

important. The "public sphere" in India may escape our attention, not because it does not exist, but because its channels of expression are often different than those in Europe. In the colonial period the authorities allowed only certain forms of expression and tried to suppress others. However, it is clear that, for example, the cow protection societies or the Singh Sabhas, as well as the several movements in favor of regional languages, belong to what can be called "the public sphere."

As usual, there is a tendency in some of the literature to see the spheres of the nation and of the local community as mutually exclusive and as opposite in nature. This is, for example, the case in Ferdinand Tönnies's opposition of *Gemeinschaft* and *Gesellschaft*. The first is essentially the local community of premodern society, while the second term refers to modern society, in which ties of blood and geographical belonging are replaced by functional ties between individuals.[4] Nationalism, however, does not fit into this modernization scheme since, rather than replacing the bonds of local kinship, it expands them so as to include larger populations in the nation, which thereby becomes "a family writ large." This is often seen as the Janus-face quality of nationalism.

Whereas the move toward a larger identification in nationalism is thus often seen as a move toward modernity and universality from the confines of the traditional, parochial community, it is often not recognized as a discursive move, no doubt supported by changing material structures of communication. The "local community" is a trope within the discourse of modernity. This community is imagined as entirely different and thus either better or worse than the one we live in now.

I want to show in this chapter, first, that larger frameworks of reference were already available to people before colonialism brought nationalism to India, and second, that nationalism builds on these earlier conceptions and transforms them. It is in two types of movement beyond the boundaries of local communities that I see these conceptions of a larger world emerge: migration and pilgrimage. In neither of these forms of movement do people leave their homes in order to get lost in the wider world. Instead, there is a constant circulation of persons, goods, and information that connects specific communities with the larger world and is thus crucial in constructing both the local and the wider community. In a very real sense this creates "world-views" that recognize boundaries but are much less "local" than the discourse of modernity would have them be.

Although it might seem that migration and pilgrimage are two entirely different kinds of movement, the one "secular" and the other "sacred," this impression is not correct. Pilgrimage has always been closely linked to long-distance trading, to networks of commerce and finance, and therefore to political regimes. Migration, while governed by the rules of supply and demand in a labor market, is intimately connected to holy wars and other forms of religious expansion, to the spread of ideas (for example, in colonialism), and, most significantly, to the construction of a "public sphere" outside the homeland in which new forms of national and religious identity are imagined.

Some of the points I will try to make in this chapter about the relation between migration and pilgrimage, on the one hand, and nationalism, on the other, can be illustrated by transnational religious movements. At the end of the chapter I will discuss an important Muslim movement, the Tablighi Jamaʿat, which operates transnationally by sending groups of lay Muslims around the world to call their fellow Muslims to their religious duties. Here nationalism is rejected by an Islamic universalism, but this rejection has political consequences for the nationalist projects of the countries in which these Muslim migrants live. Finally, I will discuss at some length the Vishva Hindu Parishad, an organization we have already encountered several times. The VHP exemplifies the transformation of earlier rituals of pilgrimage in nationalist rituals of integration. It also operates transnationally in its attempts to create a "world Hinduism," which reveal an interesting dialectic between nationalism and transnationalism.

Migration

An important colonial and nationalist myth has long been that "traditional" Indian society consisted of "autarkic villages." Essentially, the myth says that Indians lived in independent, self-governing "village republics." The traditional state is portrayed as an usurping entity, which siphoned off part of the wealth of the villages in the form of taxation and gave precious little in return. The British, however, removed these state structures to allow the villages to develop and prosper—to enter history, in short. This myth was not confined to colonialist rhetoric but was also taken over by Marx in his critique of British colonialism. It was further developed by Wittfogel in an argument on the "Asiatic mode of production."[5] More generally, the idea of village autarky is an essential element in the anthropological interpretation of India's so-called traditional economy, the jajmani system (see chapter 1).

Evidence of considerable constant migration from one part of India to another, and from India to other parts of the world, flies in the face of this notion of an independent, autarkic village community. Also, the evidence of large cities, *qasbas* (market towns), and regional markets—all connected by networks of commerce and migration—cannot be accommodated in the mythology of modernity, which needs its quintessential "other." Moreover, at the discursive level, Indian society abounds with stories of migration. The story of the Hindu nation begins with the "Aryan migration." The story of the Muslim nation begins with the notion of *hijra*, the forced emigration of the Prophet and the establishment of the first Muslim community. It continues with the spread of Islam, resulting in the migration of Muslims from the Arab heartland of Islam, and from Turkestan, Iran, and elsewhere, to India. Often these stories of migration are remembered in family names, such as Afghani or Ardebili, as well as all the names relating to early Islam, such as Sayyid, Sheikh, or Ansari. The force of this discourse on origins was brought home to me, when, years ago, I spent some time in a London hotel owned by a Muslim from Hyderabad. Despite the fact that his family had lived there for centuries, he would not identify himself with India but told me that he was an Irani. The discourse on the history of the most powerful groups in North India, such as the Rajputs and Jats, is likewise that of migration.

In fact, that manpower went where it was in demand is not a modern phenomenon. And, as Dirk Kolff has argued persuasively, manpower was, at least from the medieval period, one of the most important resources of India.[6] Kolff shows that a large portion of the income of the state was distributed to the military work force of India. He is not only referring to armies here but also to the dependents of that work force. Kolff sketches a fascinating picture of an unruly Indian countryside, populated by millions of peasants, armed to the teeth. Rulers—both Mughals and others—tried to subjugate the rebellious peasantry by forced migration, deportation, and enslavement. Another, more important, course of action, as Kolff suggests, was to pacify the countryside by enlisting the armed peasants as foot soldiers. To a significant degree, this must have been seasonal labor, governed by the agricultural cycle, with peasants enlisting to survive the slack seasons.

One of the most important areas of recruitment from at least the fifteenth century onward was eastern Hindustan (present-day eastern Uttar Pradesh and the Bhojpuri-speaking part of Bihar). Baksar, a pilgrimage center on the Ganges, was a central market where the Mughals recruited soldiers, who became known as Baksariyas. They were the main matchlockmen who fought in Gujarat and in South India on the side of the Mughal armies and, in the eighteenth century, were employed by the British East India Company in Bengal. It is important to see here that these mercenary soldiers maintained ties with their homeland through land and marriage. Their folk songs dwell on the celebrated Indian theme of *viraha*, love in separation. They remained peasant-soldiers, alternating farming and service (*naukari*). The British empire inherited this tradition, but gaining monopoly over military violence in the nineteenth century it severed its ties with it after the mutiny in 1857. Kolff suggests that the closing of this avenue of labor opportunity might be an important factor both in the continued labor migration to other parts of India and other colonies as well as in the deepening poverty of the area over the last hundred years.

An important aspect of soldiering in India was its relation to peripatetic asceticism.[7] To become an ascetic is also a choice that allows for considerable mobility. Especially before the nineteenth century the ascetic path was an avenue of access to the combined resources of pilgrimage, trade, finance, and soldiering. While Kolff shows the importance of the ascetic as a model for the peasant-soldier, he was not only a model. As we saw earlier, Hindu ascetics were the actual soldiers in many of the armies of Rajasthan and formed the major part of the army of the Shiʿa nawabs of Awadh in the eighteenth century. As in the case of *naukari*, peasant-soldier-ing, the British brought an end to these ascetic activities in the late eighteenth and early nineteenth centuries. This meant again a blow to labor opportunities outside of farming, especially in Hindustan.

The end of the tradition of soldiering in Hindustan may have influenced the extent to which people in the area were willing to listen to jobbers recruiting for indentured labor in the Caribbean. The indenture system, which functioned between 1834 and 1917, succeeded slavery, which was abolished throughout the British empire by the Act of Emancipation of 1834. Under the system, 1.5 million people, a large number of them from Hindustan, migrated to colonies as far apart as Mauritius, Fiji, and Guyana. Only about a third of them chose to return after their five- or ten-year contract expired.[8] Unlike the earlier *naukari*, this type of migration prevented many migrants from maintaining ties with the homeland, which became, as a result, a fairyland. At the same time, it is striking to what extent Indian affairs in these faraway colonies continued to be influenced by developments in India, as well as the other way around. Much of the internal conflict within the overseas community focused on Hindu-Muslim tensions and, within the Hindu majority, on tensions caused by the success of Arya Samaji missionaries from the 1910s onward. Missionaries from the Ahmadiyya reform movement were likewise relatively successful among indentured Muslims, leading to Sunni-Ahmadiyya tensions that still persist today.

Clearly, indentured labor was not the only motive for the emigration of Indians. A much longer history connects Gujarati merchants with the Gulf and with East Africa and Tamil merchants with Burma, Malaysia, and the rest of Southeast Asia. Clifford Geertz argues that the "Indic" civilization found in nineteenth century Bali had existed in much of the rest of Southeast Asia before the Muslim expansion in the fourteenth century.[9] The Gujarati migration is one of the oldest Indian migrations outside of India, and it continues to be one of the most important. Gujarati merchants (*banias*) lived in Aden and Zanzibar from at least the fifteenth century.

The colonial expansion in East Africa created opportunities for other Gujarati communities, such as the Patidar, the Hindu Patels. The typical story is of brothers who migrate and brothers who remain on the ancestral lands. Remitting the bulk of their earnings, successful migrants could eventually return to their villages to live in the relative splendor of brick (*pakka*) houses. After setting up shop in East Africa—notably Tanzania, Kenya, and Uganda—as well as in South Africa, these migrants have also spread to England, the

United States, and Canada, partly forced out by the Africanization
policies of dictators like Idi Amin. Religious organizations, notably
that of the Swaminarayanis, which were important among the Patels, followed the migration patterns of their lay followers. The
success of the Patels, despite considerable setbacks, is remarkable.
The American expression "Patel Motel" refers to the fact that the
Gujarati Patels are among that country's most important motel
entrepreneurs. Of course, not all is rosy. There are great differences
in wealth and education among Patels, and not everyone who joins
the emigration boom is a successful entrepreneur. Patels also dominate New York's newspaper kiosks—a tricky business even in the
best of times. In *So Far from India* (1982) the filmmaker Mira Nair
shows us a Gujarati migrant, living on his own in New York without
the means to bring his wife and child to America. She also shows
us his wife, back home with her in-laws in Ahmedabad. It is a
fractured life, full of loneliness and hardship, of defeat as much as
success.[10]

Another migrant group with far-reaching networks is formed by
the Punjabis—Muslim, Sikh, and Hindu, and both Pakistani and
Indian. The Sikhs are almost the paradigmatic migrants. A third of
the world's some 13 to 16 million Sikhs live outside of the Punjab,
and over a million live outside India. The Sikh taxi driver or me-
chanic as well as the Sikh merchant can be seen anywhere in India,
but also in cities like London and New York. Here, as in the case
of Hindustan, migration was strongly stimulated by military recruitment, this time on the part of the British army. Military service
opened a window to the subcontinent, to the British empire, and
then to the world at large.

The Persian Gulf has been an area of South Asian migration for
centuries, but it has become more important since the 1960s. Although the numbers involved are small compared to South Asia's
enormous population, they are large in comparison to the native
population of the Gulf states. Moreover, the contributions of these
migrants to India's economy is significant. In 1979 they were $1.6
billion—half of the total of remittances from migrants abroad. The
impact on India's trade balance is also considerable. Moreover,
states like Kerala, which have a high share in Gulf employment,
depend economically on this source of revenue.[11] The impact on
Pakistan's economy is even larger, since the number of Pakistanis

employed in the Gulf is greater still. Besides its economic significance, labor migration to the Gulf also affects Hindu-Muslim relations in India. The oil wealth of the Arab countries and their occasional support of missionary activities in other countries has led to
the persistent myth of mass-scale conversions of Hindu untouchables induced by oil money. Especially following the Meenakshipuram case of 1981, discussed in chapter 2, this myth has been used
repeatedly to prove that the Hindu nation is under threat. Evidence
for the myth is provided by the new wealth of the migrant workers
and their families, observed with jealousy by all others. Although
the two are totally unconnected, migrant wealth feeds into the story
of conversion by petro-dollars—despite the fact that Indian Muslims
who work in the Gulf are often very negative about the way they
are treated by their employers, their fellow Muslims, so that the
pan-Islamic effect of the migration is very doubtful. Hindu migrants
are also not likely to be converted in countries whose policies focus
on maintaining strict boundaries between immigrants and natives.

The importance of migration for the construction of nationalism
is considerable. As John Kelly shows in a meticulous discussion of
Fijian material, the sexual situation of "coolie" women under the
indenture system becomes one of the main issues in Indian politics
in the 1910s. The debate about how Indian women can retain their
virtue under the conditions of indenture, which raged in the Indian
newspapers, was taken up by the nationalists in order to demonstrate the morally corrupt nature of colonialism. Their agitation led
to the abolition of indenture in 1918. The issue illustrates nicely
our argument in the previous chapter that nationalist discourse
connects the control over the female body with the honor of the
nation.[12]

In the development of Hinduism among the formerly indentured
Indian population in the Caribbean it is striking that the competition
between the reformist Arya Samaj and the "conservative," Brahman-
led Sanatan Dharm (literally, "orthodox religion") movement has
resulted in a standardization and homogenization of religious practice. In turn, that practice has come to be regarded by both Hindus
and non-Hindus in the Caribbean, as well as in other parts of the
world such as Britain, as a visible marker of group identity and
collective purpose. An ethnicized Hinduism or Hindu nationalism
in the Caribbean has led to the formation of Hindu political parties.

Perhaps, despite all the differences, this ethnicization of Caribbean Hinduism also suggests the potential of Hinduism in India.[13] For example, this ethnicization of "Hinduism abroad" might at least partly explain why the VHP has been able to gain massive support for Hindu nationalism among expatriate communities, as we will see later in this chapter.

The case of the Sikhs also displays interesting features of the connection between migration and nationalism. In the period from 1880 to 1920 Sikhs went first to Southeast Asia as free laborers and later to Australia, Canada, or the United States, all countries that rapidly began to regulate nonwhite immigration. In 1910 the Canadian government severely restricted the immigration of Asians, and specifically of Indians (largely Sikhs). In the United States an Asian Exclusion League was formed in 1908. The experience of discrimination led to an interesting reaction in both the United States and India. In the United States a fringe organization, the Hindustani Workers of the Pacific Coast, was formed in 1913 and began to publish a weekly paper called *Ghadr* (Revolution), which stated its objectives in the following manner: "Today there begins in foreign lands, but in our country's language, a war against the British Raj. What is our name? Ghadr. What is our work? Ghadr. Where will Ghadr break out? In India. The time will soon come when rifles and blood will take the place of pen and ink."[14]

The interesting thing here is that the experience of discrimination in North America led to nationalist activity that centered on India. Moreover, these feelings were not limited to migrant circles but had an important impact on movements within India. In fact, the discrimination that migrants faced in Canada and California was widely publicized in India. An Indian journal in the Punjab quoted an extract from a Canadian newspaper, which stated: "The smoke-coloured Hindu, exotic, unmixable, picturesque, a languid worker and a refuge for fleas, we will always have with us, but we don't want any more of him. We don't want any Hindu women. We don't want any Hindu children. It's nonsense to talk about Hindu assimilation. The Sikh may be of Aryan stock, [but] I always thought he was of Jewish extraction. He may be near-white though he does not look like it. British Columbia cannot allow any more of the dark meat of the world to come to this province."[15]

A very important incident occurred in 1914 when the Canadians

sent a ship that contained mostly Sikh immigrants back to India.
The bitter and violently disaffected passengers, who were rumored
to have smuggled weapons on board, were met at Budge-Budge,
near Calcutta, by a strong police force. A fracas ensued in which
eighteen men were killed by police fire. The rest were sent to prison
in the Punjab. This created widespread protest in the Punjab and
great support for Sikh nationalism in the first decades of this century.[16] The Sikh diaspora continues to be a prime example of the
influence of a worldwide, transnational community on religious
nationalism in South Asia. The Khalistan movement of today, for
example, receives much more support among migrant circles in
England and Canada than among Sikhs in the Punjab. One of the
amusing touches in Rushdie's *Satanic Verses* is that the Sikh hijack-
ers of an Indian airplane speak Punjabi with a Canadian accent. A
more sober literary comment is Bharati Mukherjee's short story
"The Management of Grief," in which an Indian plane is blown up
by Canadian Sikhs.

For Indian Muslims contacts with the larger Islamic world were
and are a matter of course. Notions of center and periphery have
of course shifted over time, but the Hijaz (Mecca-Medina) has
certainly always been central in the Muslim imagination. We do
not speak only of the hajj here, though. Travel to Islamic centers of
learning (*rihla*), such as Cairo, has always been very important for
Muslim scholars and Sufis. Moreover, such travel does not only
mean excursions but often also migration for longer or shorter
terms.

An example of the existence of Muslim networks throughout the
Muslim world and the Indian subcontinent can be found in the
career of Sayyid Ahmad of Rai Bareilly (1786–1831). In 1865 Maulvi
Ahmadullah of Patna, a follower of Sayyid Ahmad, was tried and
convicted of conspiracy by the British, who viewed the Wahhabi
reform movement as a threat to British rule. In an analysis of the
trial papers of Maulvi Ahmadullah, Peter Robb suggests that the
message of the Wahhabi reformists was taken from Mecca by Sayyid
Ahmad and spread by traveling preachers across the continent. In
addition, long-distance contacts of commerce and trade, reinforced
by all-India marriage networks, helped to spread the Wahhabi message. Sayyid Ahmad's own career is illuminating: "He began in the
service of a celebrated Pindari (freebooter), became a disciple of

Shah Abdul Aziz (a leading scholar in Delhi), preached among the Pathans of Rampur (the Rohilla state), then across British India concentrating on Bengal (remaining some time in Patna). He launched his religious war against the 'tribes of Sikhs' from border regions of non-British Punjab beyond Peshawar, until the Pathans rebelled against his rule."[17] One might suggest here that the transnational character of Islamic movements, such as the Muslim brotherhood, heavily influenced by Maulana Maududi, continues a long Islamic tradition and has only come to be called transnational in the context of nationalism. Islamic discourse and practice, while accepting the reality of nation-states, also transcends it.

Besides these networks of Sufis and 'ulama' and their followers, connected by travel to centers of learning, there is an important general model of migration available in Islam in the *hijra* of the Prophet and the first Muslim community from Mecca to Medina. Here we have a doctrinal obligation to emigrate as an expression of the identity of the Muslim community.[18] It depends on the distinction of a *dar al-Islam* ("house of Islam") and a *dar al-harb* ("house of War") against which Muslims had to wage a jihad, a holy war. This distinction was of prime importance in the Muslim reaction to colonial expansion. In India, Muslim discourse centered on the question of whether British India was *dar al-harb* and thus necessitated both emigration and war. Sayyid Ahmad's answer to this question was clearly in the affirmative, but it was only one of the possible answers.[19] It is in this discursive tradition that at least some Indian Muslims who migrated during and after partition perceived their emigration. They were called "refugees," *muhajirs*, a term with strong religious connotations since it referred to the *hijra* of the Prophet. Although those connotations have weakened, the *muhajir* identity has gradually become a definite identity for the Urduspeaking immigrant population in Pakistan. The *muhajirs* have thus remained distinct from other groups in Pakistan, such as the Punjabis and Sindhis, despite their Muslim commonality. They have not followed the model set by the Prophet, in which the *muhajirs* formed a new brotherhood with the *ansaris*, the inhabitants of Medina. Nevertheless, the religious connotations of the term *muhajir* have been revived by a political party, the Muhajir Qaumi party, which attributes a kind of moral leadership to the *muhajirs*, inasmuch as they created Pakistan.[20]

The importance of migration for the construction of nationalism is peculiar neither to India nor to religious nationalism. Eric Hobsbawm emphasizes the importance of mass emigration in the emergence of the later phase of European nationalism (which he calls "right-wing," in that it replaced the liberating legacy of the French Revolution). The half-century before 1914 witnessed the greatest international migration in history. This migration produced nationalism in two ways. It created xenophobia among the people already well established, both the middle and working classes, in the countries of immigration. This led to forms of nationalism that emphasized the "defense of the nation" against the threatening immigrant. We can see something similar happening today in France and England. And, on a smaller scale, we can see it in the rhetoric of the Maratha Shiv Sena in Bombay, which in the 1960s focused chiefly on Tamil immigrant laborers but nowadays has shifted its attention to Muslims.

The imposition, through xenophobia, of a negative identity certainly also enhanced nationalist sentiment among migrants. More generally, the migratory experience led to more embracing identifications on the margins of the host society. Those who had not thought of themselves as "Indians" before migration became "Indians" in the diaspora. The element of romanticization that is present in every nationalism is even stronger among nostalgic migrants, who often form a very rosy picture of the country they have left. It is thus not only "colonial" nationalism that is formulated abroad, but many others also. Hobsbawm gives as an example the fact that Thomas Masaryk signed an agreement in Pittsburgh to form the state uniting Czechs and Slovaks, since at that time Slovak nationalism was more alive in Pennsylvania than in Slovakia.[21]

The significance of migration can be seen not only on the group level but also on the level of individual nationalist leaders. As we have seen, the system of indentured labor ended in 1917 under pressure from the Indian National Congress. The agitation was led by Gandhi, who had seen the depressing conditions of this "new system of slavery" during his stay in South Africa. Arguably, Gandhi's stay in England and South Africa opened his eyes to the nationalist cause. He not only was able directly to acquaint himself with the discriminatory treatment of Indians as "British subjects" under South African racial laws but also learned to see Indians as an ethnic group, a "nation." The marginal position of the migrant and the special qualities of group formation among exiles seem in general to play a significant role in the formulation of nationalist discourse. While this may already be the case with the "Westernized" intellectual who becomes marginal to both his own culture and the colonial culture, it is even stronger when such a Western-educated person has a vivid migrant experience. To see one's society from the outside with the eyes of the "other," but to be not at all assimilated, still experiencing a marginality and strangeness enhanced by colonial discrimination, leads to bold personal transformations that may have paradigmatic significance for the larger society.

The experience of migration is thus not by accident formative in the nationalist career of Mahatma Gandhi. But it also plays a crucial role in the construction of Hindu nationalism in general. Swami Vivekananda, initially a struggling monk in India, became famous thanks to his attendance at the World Parliament of Religions in Chicago in 1893 as a "representative of Brahmin sannyasins."[22] He systematized his construction of the "ancient system of yoga" for classes he gave for Americans in Brooklyn. This was one of the first and most important steps in systematizing "Indian spirituality" as a discipline healthy for body and spirit, which has become so important in transnational spiritual movements of Indian origin. Vivekananda's success in the United States did not go unnoticed in India. He returned as a certified saint. He went on to found the Ramakrishna Mission to spread the message of Hinduism, the "eternal religion" (*sanatana dharma*), but died soon after. As I argued in chapter 2, Vivekananda's writings and the activities of his transnational Ramakrishna Mission have been fundamental for the creation of a nationalist neo-Hinduism. I see the VHP, in some respects, as the successor of the Ramakrishna Mission.

One of the best examples of the impact of travel on religious nationalism is found outside of India in the career of a Sinhalese Buddhist monk, Anagarika Dharmapala (1864–1933). In a fascinating argument Gananath Obeyesekere shows that an identity crisis in Dharmapala's youth was symptomatic of a nationalist identity crisis facing the Sinhalese in general.[23] Dharmapala was born in Colombo into a family of farmers that had migrated from the south of Ceylon. Though his father had made a fortune, the family was not accepted in Colombo's Westernized and Protestant elite society.

Dharmapala thus faced an early conflict between a Buddhist upbringing at home and the Christianity taught in the Catholic mission school he attended. The adolescent boy came under the influence of Buddhist monks who engaged in religious debates with Christians. In 1884, when he was twenty, the theosophists Madame Blavatsky and Colonel H. S. Olcott took him with them to their headquarters in Madras. According to Obeyesekere the trip to Madras was a rite de passage from confused adolescence to a mature adulthood. The young man cut his ties with his family, shed his Western name David, and became Anagarika ("homeless"). The stay with the Theosophists convinced him of the decline of Buddhism and the need to revitalize it. So he replaced his family name with Dharmapala, "protector of the doctrine." The stay in Madras and a consequent trip through Ceylon with Olcott and Charles Leadbeater made him look with new eyes at Sinhalese culture and made him a leader of Sinhalese-Buddhist nationalism.

The cases of Vivekananda and Dharmapala show (again) the importance of direct contact with Western orientalist scholarship at the level of individual leadership. The mass migration of Indians to the West in the postcolonial period is obviously a rather different matter, giving a new twist to religious discourse. Religious organization is one of the few forms of collective life among migrants, so that, paradoxically, migration to the lands of unbelievers strengthens the religious commitment of the migrants. Mosques, temples, and *gurdwaras* are central symbols of pride and cultural resistance against racist denigration. A striking fact about migrant life in the West is its institutional completeness, from mosques to groceries and banks. This gives migrant communities a political strength, which they can bring to bear on the politics of their country of origin as well as in the country of immigration. It is this dialectics of nationalism and transnationalism that we will explore later in this chapter and in our discussion of the Rushdie affair in chapter 6.

Pilgrimage

The distinction between the local community and a larger, more embracing world is encountered not only in general sociological theory but also in ritual studies. Ever since Durkheim (or Fustel de Coulanges), anthropologists have been concerned with the ritual construction of social (group) identity. Rituals have been classified according to whether they work on the individual level or on the level of the community at large. In community rituals, which are performed in public space, a distinction is sometimes made between rituals relating to community in the narrow sense (household, family, village) and those relating to community in a wider sense (nation, community of believers). Rituals like ancestor worship are placed in the first category, while a ritual like pilgrimage seems to belong in the second one. This distinction in types of ritual can be interpreted as reflecting different levels of integration in society.

Pilgrimage reinforces "the larger moral community of the civilization."[24] A classical statement of this function occurs in an article by Eric Wolf on the Virgin of Guadelupe in Mexico, whose cult "links together family, politics and religion; colonial past and independent present; Indian and Mexican. . . . It is, ultimately, a way of talking about Mexico: a collective representation of Mexican society."[25] In a similar vein M. N. Srinivas writes about Hindu sacred centers as the places in which the Sanskritic tradition is transmitted to the peasants of the region: "Every great temple and pilgrim centre was a source of Sanskritization, and the periodic festivals or other occasions when pilgrims gathered together at the centre provided opportunities for the spread of Sanskritic ideas and beliefs."[26] Whereas Srinivas's analysis refers to the integration of a civilization, David Mandelbaum makes a somewhat different, although related, analytical move by arguing that pilgrimage acts to create national identification and thus plays a role in nation building: "There is a traditional basis for the larger national identification. It is the idea, mainly engendered by Hindu religion but shared by those of other religions as well, that there is an entity of India to which all inhabitants belong. The Hindu epics and legends, in their manifold versions, teach that the stage for the gods was nothing less than the entire land and that the land remains one religious setting for those who dwell in it. That sense was and is continually confirmed through the common practice of pilgrimage."[27]

That pilgrimage is always a ritual of the wider community is in some sense a truism. By definition, it involves a journey from one's village or town to a sacred center and back, and its performance appears to reinforce the notion of a wider community of believers. This ritual thus seems to lend itself to be linked up with the discourses and ritual practices of religious nationalism. In a recent book on the emergence of communalism in North India, Sandria Freitag emphasizes the importance of collective, symbolic activities in public spaces. Freitag sees these activities as belonging to a realm of "public arenas" that in the nineteenth century "became an alternative world to that structured by the imperial regime, providing legitimacy and recognition to a range of actors and values denied place in the imperial order."[28] Although pilgrimage is one of the most important collective activities through which community in India expresses and redefines itself, Freitag has nothing to say on the subject, probably because, although she is interested in collective rituals that bridge the local and the wider community (the nation), her analysis remains largely confined to rituals of the local community. What we might consider is the possibility that pilgrimage in India, based on linkages between distant regions, provided notions of religious community long before the British entered the scene. Information and ideas went from one part of India to another and, in case of the Muslims, even from Mecca to India and vice versa.

Pilgrimage (*tirtha-yatra*) is a practice frequently enjoined in Hindu discursive traditions. A large part of the subcontinent is interconnected by clusters of pilgrimage centers. There is a verse in many Sanskrit texts enumerating "seven cities that grant release": Banaras, Kanti, Hardwar, Ayodhya, Dwarka, Mathura, and Ujjain. Banaras, Hardwar, Ayodhya, and Mathura are in northern India, Ujjain in the middle, Dwarka in the western part, and Kanti is in most texts identified with Kanchipuram in South India. A *tirtha* is a crossing place on a river and therefore, metaphorically, a place to cross to "the other side," to the "other world" of ancestors and gods. Pilgrimage is undertaken in connection with rites of passage, especially cremation, but also, more generally, for the worship of gods and ancestors. Special clusters of pilgrimage centers are connected to the main Hindu gods, Vishnu and Shiva. The incarnation (*avatara*) doctrine is especially relevant to the centers connected with Vishnu. Rama, an incarnation of Vishnu, has as his centers of worship his birthplace, Ayodhya; the birthplace of his wife, Sita, Janakpur in the Nepalese Terai; Chitrakut, his place of exile, in Madhya Pradesh; and Rameshwaram, the place where he worshiped Shiva before attacking the demon Ravana, in Tamil Nadu. The birthplace of Krishna, the other major incarnation of Vishnu, is Mathura, the place of his youthful adventures with cowherd girls is Brindavan, and the place where he ruled is Dwarka in Gujarat. Shiva is represented by an aniconic phallic form and there are several important of these so-called *lingas* in different places in India: Kedarnath in the Himalayas, Vaidyanath (Baijnath) in Bihar, and Somanatha in Kathiawar, as well as several places in the south. Besides these well-known centers, which are quite significantly regarded as all-India places, there are numerous other places of regional and/or sectarian importance.

While the tendency of mostly middle-class Hindus to make an all-India pilgrimage in special buses and trains is probably rather recent, there are well-established pilgrimage routes that connect places like Hardwar in the north, Banaras and Gaya in the Gangetic plain, and Puri in the east. Moreover, there is little doubt that some pilgrimage centers have been visited by fairly large groups of people from large "catchment areas" that existed before the colonial expansion. Places like Banaras and Gaya, and to a lesser extent Hardwar and Puri, belong to that category. Coupled with trade and migration, pilgrimage must have contributed to a precolonial sense of the "sacred geography" of Hindu India.

It is, at the same time, true that for an increasing number of Hindus the significance of pilgrimage has grown considerably in the colonial and postcolonial periods. The eighteenth and nineteenth centuries brought great transformations to Indian society, which were reflected in the public arena of pilgrimage. Especially the improvement of the infrastructure enabled more and more people to perform pilgrimage. Also, the emergence of a relatively secure class of landowners and bureaucrats resulted in a greatly expanded patronage of religious institutions, such as pilgrimage centers.[29] Finally, Western discourse on the nation as a territorially based community colluded with religious discourse on sacred space. The importance of pilgrimage and sacred centers in the (re)definition of community in India becomes clear when we consider the various struggles for control in these arenas. In some cases these are struggles primarily within a religious community, such as the Singh Sabha movement among the Sikhs in the 1920s, which tried to reallocate control over Sikh temples. In other cases these are struggles between the state and religious elites, such as the struggle for control over Hindu temples in South India. And again there are struggles between communities over the control of sacred space, such as in the Mahabali affair, a dispute between Hindus and Jains over a shrine in Maharashtra, and in the Ayodhya dispute between Hindus and Muslims.

The emphasis on (national) integration in the anthropological study of pilgrimage is clearly exaggerated. It should be recalled from our earlier discussion of ritual that the ritual construction of community often implies violence and antagonism. Its efficacy depends on the construction of an arena in which the "self" is opposed to the "other," which is demonized and violently conquered. As always, antagonism is one of the most important mechanisms of integration. While some of the violence is directed inward to discipline the members of a community, part of it may be directed outward to members of other communities in the form of "riots." This is immediately evident when large groups of people jointly go on a pilgrimage in procession, which is a physical assertion of control over space. It is thus not strange that movement in processions, locally and in the context of pilgrimage, often leads in India to communal violence.

This can be illustrated on the symbolic and practical level by looking at the relation between the Rama cult and the Ayodhya affair. Pilgrimage is a major ritual performance in the Rama cult, and it integrates performers into a wider community of believers. In the discourse of the Rama cult, Vishnu takes incarnation (*avatara*) as Rama, the son of Ayodhya's king, to save the world from the growing power of demons. He travels throughout India to Lanka in exile, which turns into a tour of royal conquest. It is this freedom of movement—the removal of every obstacle to motion—that symbolizes Hindu notions of sovereignty. Finally, Rama launches with his army of monkeys an attack on Lanka and slays all the demons. Returning to Ayodhya he becomes the paradigmatic just king (*dharmaraja*) who preserves the purity of the caste order and the chastity of women. His rule (*ramrajya*) serves as an ideal in Hindu political thought.

While this discourse clearly links movement to sovereignty and to the assertion of community, the definition of this community and of the "others" from which it must differentiate itself depends on the historical context. Whereas until the nineteenth century the

Rama cult had to be violently defended against Shaivite Hindus, in the nineteenth and twentieth centuries it is linked to the discourse of Hindu nationalism, which defines Muslims as the enemy. In the current politics of India the *yatra*, pilgrimage in procession, is used by Hindu nationalists to express this discourse of Hindu nationalism. In this case it is possible to analyze the nationalist transformation of a ritual repertoire in some detail.

The VHP experimented on a large scale with the ritual procession in what it called a "sacrifice for unity" (*ekatmatayajna*) in 1983. Sacrifice in this case referred to an extremely complex and well-organized cluster of processions that reached, according to the VHP estimate, some 60 million people.[30] Three large processions (*yatra*) traversed India in November and December 1983. The first started on 16 November in Hardwar in the north and reached Kanyakumari (India's southernmost point) on 20 December. The second, inaugurated by the king of Nepal, started in Kathmandu on 26 October and reached Rameshwaram in Tamil Nadu on 16 December. The third started on 15 November in Gangasagar and reached Somanatha on 17 December. Significantly, the three processions crossed in the middle of the country, in Nagpur, which is not a pilgrimage center but the headquarters of the RSS. This meeting in Nagpur was duly compared with the *triveni*, the confluence of three holy rivers (*sangam*) in Prayag (Allahabad), one of India's most sacred spots. The RSS clearly played a major role in organizing this manifestation of Hindu nationalism. In each sacred place that one of the processions visited, however, it was welcomed and blessed by local religious leaders, without RSS symbolism overshadowing the whole enterprise.

At least forty-seven smaller processions (*upayatras*) of five days' duration traversed other parts of the country, connecting up at appointed meeting places with one of the three larger processions. The processions followed well-known pilgrimage routes that link major religious centers, suggesting the geographical unity of India (*bharatvarsha*) as a sacred area (*kshetra*) of Hindus. In this way, pilgrimage was effectively transformed into a ritual of national integration. Processions of temple chariots (*rathas*) are an important part of temple festivals in India. An image of the god is taken for a ride in his domain, during which he confirms his territorial sovereignty and extends his blessings. The processions of the VHP made use of *rathas* in the form of brand-new trucks. Each of the three main processions was named after its "chariot": Mahadevaratha, Pashupatiratha, and Kapilaratha, names that refer to gods and saints worshiped in the places from which the processions started out. The symbolism of the temple chariot was thereby perpetuated—but also the militant symbolism of the war chariot of Arjuna in the *Bhagavad Gita*. The *Bhagavad Gita*, which was made into the fundamental text of Hinduism first in the nineteenth century and later by Gandhi, emphasizes the duty of the warrior to fight when war is inevitable. In the pamphlets of the VHP Arjuna's chariot is a recurring symbol.

The "chariots" of the VHP also carried an image of Bharat Mata, Mother India. The mother goddess is worshiped in many forms in India, some of which are relatively new. Santoshi Mata, "Satisfying Mother," for example, conquered India in the 1960s under the influence of a very successful movie. The political use of mother symbolism is also nothing new in India. In Andhra Pradesh the regional party Telugu Desam introduced a Telugu mother goddess, and the late Indira Gandhi tried to use the symbolism of the goddess for her own glorification. The connection between the worship of the mother goddess and Mother India has been most forcefully laid in Bengal where the cult of the goddess is exceptionally strong. The Indian National Congress has chosen "Bande Mataram" (Hail mother), a poem by the nineteenth-century Bengali nationalist Bankim Chandra Chatterjee, as the national anthem, despite the poem's strong Hindu emphasis. In carrying images of Bharat Mata around the country, the VHP made its own contribution to this nationalist tradition.

The chariots also carried an enormous waterpot (*kalasha*) filled with water from the Ganges and a smaller waterpot filled with local sacred water. The chariots were each followed by a truck that sold Ganges water in small bottles. The Ganges is seen as a deity, and her water contains the power to purify from sin and to grant salvation. All the sacred water in the rest of India is ultimately derived from the Ganges. In this way all rivers and temple tanks are symbolically connected with the Ganges as the unifying symbol of Hindu India. The *kalasha* is one of the most important objects in Hindu ritual. It symbolizes power and auspiciousness. The processions of the "sacrifice for unity" made very effective use of an existing ritual repertoire on the mother goddess, on the sacredness of Ganges

water, and on Lord Rama, transforming this repertoire to communicate the message of Hindu unity. This message could only be
conveyed by a ritual repertoire that engages generally accepted
Hindu conceptions without running into conflict with specific doc-
trines espoused by one of the many religious movements represented in the VHP. It was also perfectly clear that those who did
not participate in this Hindu ritual could not be seen as part of the
nation. Effectively, the message was as much about Hindu unity as
about the Muslim "other." Striking is the comment by Acharya
Giraraj Kishan, organizer of the sacrifice for unity: "In many parts
of the country the Christian and Muslim friends too extend their
co-operation and proved that irrespective of their mode of worship
all of them are Hindus culturally and nationally."[31] The ritual also
publicly rejected a major threat to unity among Hindus: untouchability. Rituals were sometimes performed by untouchables or
members of so-called backward castes.

The processions garnered enormous publicity and enabled the
VHP to start local branches in all parts of the country. VHP documents stress the international participation in the ritual. Nepal sent
one of the *rathas*, thereby conspicuously confirming its claim to be
a Hindu nation-state. A delegation from Burma, bearing water from
their holy river Irrawadi, joined the Kapilaratha in Calcutta. A
"tributary" procession (*upayatra*) from Bhutan also joined one of
the main processions. All this led the organizer of the sacrifice for
unity to comment: "It proved that Nepal, Bhutan and Burma may
be politically separate from Bharat but the cultural soul of all these
countries is one within."[32] Water from a holy site on Mauritius,
Ramsar, was brought by a former minister from Mauritius, and
sacred water was also brought from Pakistan and Bangladesh.

Hajj, pilgrimage to Mecca, is one of the five "pillars" of the
Muslim faith. There is an element of duty to it but also an element
of choice, the expenses of the journey providing a readily available
excuse. One who has returned from pilgrimage to Mecca is respectfully called *hajji*, and the pilgrimage is, from the social point of
view, a clear rite of passage to a higher status. The pilgrimage should
also mark a certain personal change, a shift in priorities to the things
of the afterlife. As part of the pilgrimage ritual the pilgrim dresses
in a shroud and is thus symbolically dead. His return to normal
society can thus be interpreted as an extra lease on life, after which

mundane matters become somewhat less relevant. The *hajji* is thus seen in Muslim society as an older man whose wise council is sought after. At the same time, one could argue that the title *hajji* is a marker of middle-class status and financial stability.

As in the case of Hindu pilgrimage there is in the hajj a sense of a sacred geography long predating colonial expansion. There is also a dramatic increase in the numbers of pilgrims involved in the hajj from the nineteenth century onward. On the one hand, in this period the hajj increasingly became a conduit for Wahhabi influence on Muslim views of correct Islamic conduct in South and Southeast Asia.[33] On the other hand, while this may be seen as a transnational, pan-Islamic influence, the organization of the hajj has come more and more into the hands of the nation-states from which the pilgrims depart. Whereas before the twentieth century the hajj was a privately organized affair, the British colonial authorities moved toward controlling it, overtly expressing concern about sanitation problems, although they were secretly concerned about anticolonial Islamic politics as well. This role of control and surveillance has been taken over by the post-Independence nation-states. Now the hajj has become a system of national pilgrimage to a transnational site. National contingents, whose number, finances, duration of stay, and transport are regulated by state institutions, have taken the place of individual or group pilgrimage. As a result, the hajj has come to reflect internal political arrangements. The Pakistani decision to declare Ahmadiyyas, a politically important minority group in Pakistan, non-Muslims made it very difficult for them to continue to go on the hajj. The hajj has also become a site of international conflict, such as that between the Shi'ite pilgrims from Khomeini's Iran and the Sunni rulers of Saudi Arabia.

Although it is the most important, the hajj is not the only form of pilgrimage among Muslims. In India more Muslims probably go—and more often—on pilgrimage (*ziyara*) to shrines in which Sufi saints are buried (*dargah*) than they go on the hajj. These shrines compare very well to Hindu centers of pilgrimage. While many of them belong to regional networks and thus contribute to regional identities, some are of all-India importance. The best example of such a shrine is that of Mu'in al-din Chishti in Ajmer (see chapter 2). Historically, the shrine has been given large endowments by the Mughals and by Hindu rajas. Hundreds of thousands of pilgrims visit Mu'in al-din's shrine each year, especially at the celebration of the *'urs*, the festivities on the anniversary of the saint's death. Not only is the pilgrimage an all-India one but Muslims who have emigrated to Pakistan, South Africa, Canada, Yemen, and the United Kingdom still come to visit the shrine. P. M. Currie reports that Indian Muslims living in Wembley, London, celebrate a local *'urs* for those who cannot travel to Ajmer.[34] Such celebrations and pilgrimages surely emphasize the "Indianness" of the Muslims of the subcontinent, since the Ajmer cult is very much tied to South Asian Islam.

Transnational Movements

In this section I want to discuss a Hindu transnational movement and an Indo-Muslim transnational movement, both of which combine an interest in migrants and an interest in the ritual possibilities of processions and movement in groups. The Hindu movement is the Vishva Hindu Parishad; the Muslim movement is the Tablighi Jama'at. In the case of the VHP transnationalism is an aspect of a fiercely political, nationalist movement. In the case of the Tablighi Jama'at transnationalism is antinationalist and strongly apolitical in orientation. As I will argue, though, this orientation has political consequences. The two examples indicate two opposite directions in which the dialectics of nationalism and transnationalism can develop. I will begin with the Tablighi Jama'at.

The Tablighi Jama'at

The Tablighi Jama'at was founded in 1927 by Mawlana Muhammad Ilyas (1886–1944), a religious teacher who lived near the great Sufi shrine of Nizamuddin in Delhi and belonged to the Chishti brotherhood of Sufism.[35] In 1934 he started a great revivalist campaign among Muslims of Mewat. Going from person to person he called upon them to follow their Muslim duties, such as praying in the mosque. Gradually he formed groups of laymen (*jama'at*) who went for fixed periods to invite (*tabligh*) their fellow Muslims to perform their duties. This created a snowball effect whereby more and more people became involved in this activity. In an interesting way the action of "going in *jama'at*" transforms both those who devote their time to this pursuit and those they visit. The emphasis on movement in groups reminds one strongly of Sufism, and I would suggest that the Tablighis to some extent replace Sufis by adopting their techniques, if not their spiritual message. The groups went around first in Mewat, then also in other parts of India, and, finally, in the early fifties abroad to places like Nigeria and England, wherever Muslims were to be found. The movement thus spread from South Asians to others and is now the most successful movement among Muslims in the world.

Ilyas's ideas do not differ much from those of the Deobandi school and are not very elaborate. In fact, the simplicity of the message contained in the Tablighi Jama'at cannot be surpassed. It asks simply for the performance of duties that every Muslim already knows. It further stresses at its mass gatherings ('*ijtima*) the example of the Prophet. Ilyas's major achievement lies in bypassing the '*ulama*' to create a strong organization of laymen. This is not to suggest that the movement opposes the '*ulama*'. On the contrary, it pays respect to them and is backed by the internationally oriented Nadwat-al-ulama, based in Lucknow. However, it stresses the equality of the participants in the *jama'at*, and it avoids theological debate.

The movement has a strong transnational character and has therefore been very successful among migrants.[36] As in South Asia they are not concerned with proselytizing among non-Muslims. Rather, they fit in perfectly with the tendency of migrant communities to form a closed society. In that sense they also form a perfect defense against assimilation. In Western Europe this tendency is fostered by discrimination in the work place and a resulting mass unemployment among migrants. The movement gives unemployed men a new sense of purpose in that they can devote their time to *tabligh*. It also helps family men to deal with the great problems of educating their children in an alien, non-Muslim environment.

Despite its importance, the Jama'at is not well known among non-Muslims in immigrant countries. This ignorance is enhanced by the strong apolitical stance of the movement. The idea is that wordly affairs do not matter: one should try to be a good Muslim simply by fulfilling one's duties. When every Muslim does so, this will have an exemplary effect and turn the whole world into a world of believers. It is therefore not the state that has to be changed but society. However, this program does have political consequences.

It requires that Muslim girls to go to school with their heads covered, which has led to great problems in France. It fosters an attitude of intransigence as far as Islamic duties, such as prayer and fasting, are concerned. It contributes to the Islamization of the whole question of assimilation, race, and ethnicity in the immigrant countries. It also emphasizes Islamic education, which brings it into conflict with state-organized education. In all these instances the apolitical stance of the Jama'at leads to confrontation with the state. However, there is little indication that these confrontations feed into a religious nationalism focused on effecting changes in the migrants' countries of origin, as in Maududi's Jama'at-i-Islami.

The Vishva Hindu Parishad

The Vishva Hindu Parishad was founded in Bombay on an auspicious day, the birthday of Lord Krishna, 29 August 1964. One hundred and fifty religious leaders were invited to Sandeepany Sadhanalaya, the center of a Hindu missionary movement headed by Swami Chinmayananda. The host had been instrumental in organizing the conference and became its president. Shivram Shankar Apte, a worker of the Rashtriya Swayamsevak Sangh, was elected as its general secretary. In the meeting it was decided that the organization would have the following objectives:

(1) To take steps to arouse consciousness, to consolidate and strengthen the Hindu Society. (2) To protect, develop and spread the Hindu values of life—ethical and spiritual. (3) To establish and reinforce contacts with and help all Hindus living abroad. (4) To welcome back all who had gone out of the Hindu fold and to rehabilitate them as part and parcel of the Universal Hindu Society. (5) To render social services to humanity at large. It has initiated Welfare Projects for the 170 million downtrodden brethren, who have been suffering for centuries. These projects include Schools, Hospitals, Libraries, etc. (6) Vishva Hindu Parishad, the World Organisation of six hundred million at present residing in 80 countries aspire [*sic*] to revitalise the eternal Hindu Society by rearranging the code of conduct of our age-old Dharma to meet the needs of the changed times. (7) To eradicate the concept of untouchability from the Hindu Society.[37]

The transnational character of the VHP was stressed by the presence of representatives from Trinidad and Kenya. It was also emphasized in the following definition of the Hindu, given in one of the VHP's publications: "The term 'Hindu' embraces all people who believe in, respect or follow the eternal values of life—ethical and spiritual—that have evolved in Bharat [India]." As the publication goes on to explain: "From this definition it is clear that a person is not debarred from calling himself a Hindu—in the most universal application of the word—just because he might have been born in, or might be living in, countries other than Bharat."[38]

The founding conference also decided to have a World Hindu Convention on the occasion of the *kumbh mela* festival on 22 January 1966 in Allahabad. *Kumbh* and *magh melas* are important bathing festivals held at regular intervals in holy places. Millions of Hindus attend these festivals, which thus provide a crucial opportunity for the laity to meet mendicant monks (*sadhus*). A second World Hindu Convention was held in 1979, also in Allahabad. A meeting of important religious leaders on 20 June 1982 in Delhi gave the VHP organization its final shape. It was to have two levels: an assembly of religion (*dharmsansad*) as a central body, and on the state level, "advisory committees" (*margdarshak mandals*) made up of leaders of the various participating religious communities.

It has recently been argued that the VHP was founded on the initiative of the leader of the RSS, M. S. Golwalkar, in order to give the RSS an opportunity to work with leaders of Hindu religious movements.[39] There is probably a good deal of truth in this argument. As we will see later in this chapter there is no doubt that the extremely well-organized RSS was actively involved in the organization of the political rituals staged by the VHP in the 1980s. However, to see the VHP simply as an instrument of the RSS, part of the so-called RSS family of organizations—as is routinely done in India—is to underestimate the extent to which the VHP goes beyond the RSS in its articulation of what I will call "modern Hinduism." Religious ritual and doctrine are kept to an absolute minimum in the RSS (see the discussion in chapter 2), whereas the VHP is an organization in which religious leaders play a major role.

These religious leaders are united in their wish to promote a certain kind of "spiritual" Hinduism through ritual propaganda, but, for the rest, have their own followers and agendas. Hinduism does not have a central authority or a churchlike organization. Thus, it is almost miraculous to see the extent to which the VHP is able to keep all these independent leaders on one platform without major conflicts and breakups. An example of the tensions involved here can be found in the action of one religious leader, the Shankaracharya of Dwarka, who is alleged to have ties with the Congress (I) party. In May 1990 he started a campaign independent of the VHP because of a disagreement on astrological issues. By seeking an authoritative statement from Brahman scholars on the issues in question, the VHP contained the possible damage of this action. Its ability to do so resulted from two factors: the extent to which the discourse of modern Hinduism has come to be shared by all these leaders and the extent to which the VHP has been able to focus on issues that have a great unifying potential.

In my opinion, these differences in organizational structure and discursive style between RSS and VHP are not only very important but explain, at least partly, the very success of the VHP in comparison to what the RSS has been able to accomplish. However, it is very difficult to go beyond what the religious leaders themselves have to say when it comes to assessing the VHP's following among the general population. What I would suggest is that the following is as broad as that of the constituent religious communities, which is primarily a very broad cross-section of the urbanized middle class and the middle peasants, with the notable exclusion of tribals and untouchables. It is to the latter two groups that the VHP tries to reach out. In the 1970s the VHP focused on missionary work in tribal areas and on organizing Hindus overseas. In 1982 it claimed to have 302 district units, under which there were 2,700 branches. Outside of India it claimed to have 3,000 branches in twenty-three countries. Its total membership at that point was 118,522, including 233 full-time workers.[40] There can be little doubt that the organization has grown considerably since then, because only in the eighties did it gain prominence on the Indian political scene. As we saw in the previous section, this was achieved by the creative use of political ritual on a grand scale.

However, we have to get some idea of what the VHP's ideology is before we are able fully to grasp what this ritual is intended to communicate. My argument here will be that the VHP tries to create a modern Hinduism as the national religion of India. In this way nationalism embraces religion as the defining characteristic of the nation. The VHP is certainly not an "antimodernist" movement.

In fact, if nationalism is the discourse of modernity, the VHP's project is fundamentally modernist. As I have argued earlier, Hindu nationalism articulates certain long-term transformations in Hindu discourse and practice that feed upon orientalist understandings of India and are as such deeply enmeshed in Western conceptions of modernity.

The influence of orientalism is obviously a large subject, studied in greater depth elsewhere.[41] Let me make just a few points here. Inspired by the Enlightenment, orientalists brought modern phil-ological methods and concepts to bear on India's past. By producing critical editions of Hindu scriptures they replaced a largely frag-mented, oral tradition with an unchanging, homogenized written one. In that way a "history," as established by modern science, came to replace a traditional "past." They also canonized certain scrip-tures, such as the *Bhagavad Gita*, which prepared the ground for Mahatma Gandhi to make this Sanskrit work into a fundamental scripture of modern Hinduism. By looking for the roots of Western (Aryan) civilization in Vedic and later Hindu scriptures, they created an image of the decline of Hindu society after "the Muslim inva-sions." This in turn laid the foundation for a Hindu nationalist (communalist) interpretation of Indian history. The impact of ori-entalism on modern Indian thought is thus immense, but we should be wary of essentializing it. In the first place, the orientalists were involved in debates amongst themselves and with their opponents, the utilitarians. Second, contrary to what Edward Said proposes in his ground-breaking *Orientalism*, there was not a one-way imposi- tion of orientalist discourse on Asian realities but rather an intense intellectual interaction between orientalists and Indian scholars. Instead of rejecting capitalist development, science, and technol-ogy, the VHP attempts to nationalize these signs of modernity. What it does reject is the secular state, but its argument is based upon the modern democratic principle of "majority rule."[42] It argues that the "majority community" should rule the country, while the "mi-nority communities," such as Muslims and Christians, should accept that as a political reality.

I want to suggest that if we take fundamentalism as antimodern, as Bruce Lawrence does in a recent book, we lose sight of the fact that many fundamentalist movements are not only enmeshed in modernity as a material structure (that is, by providing material goods and services), but that as a "countertext," to use Lawrence's term, fundamentalism may share some basic discursive premises with the modernist text.[43] In other words, fundamentalism as an argument in a cultural debate presupposes some of the modernist assumptions, such as the importance of scientifically established "facts"—at least it does so in the case of the VHP. What we might consider are the ways in which indigenous discursive traditions are transformed through their encounter with colonizing discourses from the West.

Modern Hinduism, as defined by the VHP, is the religion of the Indian nation. As we have seen, in the VHP definition the term *Hindu* "embraces all people who believe in, respect or follow the eternal values of life—ethical and spiritual—that have evolved in Bharat." This is remarkably similar to Robert Frykenberg's definition of Hinduism as "Nativism," and it reveals the collusion of the VHP's definition of Hinduism with scholarly discourse that portrays Hinduism as a civilization rather than as a religion.[44] It is also a very broad definition that transcends internal differences of a doctrinal, organizational, or regional nature. While it might appear that even Indian Islam and Christianity could be included in such a definition, it is one of the key themes of the VHP that Hindu society is threatened by Islam and Christianity, which are forces of disintegration. Hindu civilization is seen as originating on Indian soil, while Islam and Christianity are "foreign" despite their long presence in India. Muslims and Christians can redeem themselves only when they realize that they are in fact converted Hindus and return to the Hindu fold.

As we noted in chapter 2, a recurring theme in such reform movements is that of Hindu weakness. Hindu society is weakened both "externally," by conversions to "foreign" religions, and "internally," by differences and conflicts among Hindus. Unity is the remedy for weakness, and unity is accomplished through the rhetoric of "nativism." However, this quest for unity does not to exclude nonresident Indians. On the contrary. By now the VHP is probably the strongest transnational movement among Hindus all over the world. There is, then, an interesting interplay of "foreignness" and "nativeness," of "nationalism" and "transnationalism" here. I would suggest that the marginality felt by migrants in other parts of the world makes them into important agents of innovation at home.

The VHP is not a scripturalist movement. It avoids disputes about "fundamental scriptures," since its aim is to reconcile reformism and "orthodoxy" (sometimes called *sanatana dharma*) in all its manifold forms. It even wants to include Jainism, Buddhism, and Sikhism by defining them as part and parcel of an all-embracing Hindu civilization, in which "Hindu" refers to the sacred soil from which all these religions spring. This strategy is often presented as part of the "tolerance" that characterizes Hinduism in the eyes of both Hindus and outsiders. However, as I tried to demonstrate in chapter 2, this characterization has a specific orientalist history.

The "mainstreaming" of India will not be without its problems and contradictions. Inclusion and exclusion are aspects of historical processes of identity formation, which have to be understood in terms of their internal dynamics as well as of changing context. The Sikhs are an interesting case here. One of their important leaders in the early sixties, Tara Singh, as well as Ghyani Bhupendra Singh (president of the Akali Dal), was among the founders of the VHP. Tara Singh addressed the 1964 conference of the VHP in Bombay as follows: "I am confident that if once the Hindus and Sikhs embrace each other, it will send a new current of revitalization all over the country and the movement shall flood the hearts of even those who live abroad."[45] This was not exactly what would happen in the eighties. Clearly, separatism has a greater importance on the Sikh agenda today than unity with the Hindus.

Another important example of the politics of inclusion, rather than the "tolerance" of difference, is the VHP's program to draw tribals and untouchables into the Hindu fold. The VHP has been consistently at work to bring these groups within the Hindu nation, since their marginality, socially and specially, makes them in the VHP's view easy victims of "foreign" conversion by Christian and Muslim missions. These communities are beyond the pale in the traditional Hindu view, but the mere fact that they live on "Hindu" territory means in the logic of nationalism that they should be part of the Hindu nation. The rhetoric is simultaneously that of Gandhian development ideology (the so-called uplift of the tribals) and of battle against competing missionary efforts. On the one hand, VHP discourse feeds upon Gandhian concepts of social reform in its attacks on the "evils of caste society."[46] On the other hand, the missionary activities of the VHP among tribals can be interpreted as a continuation of the expansion of Hindu monastic groups in frontier areas (see the discussion in Chapter 2). This long-term expansion has been reframed in terms of social welfare and nation building. The VHP has blamed conversion to Christianity in the northeastern parts of India for the separatist movements in those areas. Their activities among untouchables stepped up in 1981 after an untouchable subcaste in the village of Meenakshipuram in Tamil Nadu converted en masse to Islam. As we saw earlier, "petro-dollars" became the master trope not only to make Muslim missionary efforts suspect but to demonstrate that the Hindu nation was threatened by world Islam. The Meenakshipuram conversions have been the most publicized issue in the VHP's "defense of Hinduism." The VHP's propaganda about the "Islamic threat" rapidly led to the organization of the sacrifice for unity in 1983 and to the movement for liberating Hindu sites in 1984.

In short, what the VHP tries to do is to formulate a modern Hinduism that can serve as the basis of a Hindu nation. This brings it into conflict with the self-proclaimed secularism of the Indian state and with Muslims and Christians, who cannot be included in its idea of the nation. In my view it is clear that the VHP's ideas are directly derived from the discourse of modern, spiritual Hinduism. In other words, the VHP takes a kind of "oriental spiritualism" that was offered as a package to Western audiences and brings it back to India. On the level of discourse there is very little difference between VHP propaganda and the sayings of the founder of the Ramakrishna Mission, Swami Vivekananda. Moreover, Vivekananda had the same audience as the VHP. The difference lies in the historical development of that audience, the modern middle class.

What I find striking in the VHP is the extent to which the leadership of a modern guru like Chinmayananda, who has a following among middle-class Indians in urban India and in the United States, has become more generally accepted. As a disciple of Shivananda, the founder of the Divine Life Society, and a codisciple of Chidananda, Shivananda's successor, he belongs squarely to modern Hinduism. After spending a period in the Himalayas with his second guru, Tapovanam, Chinmayananda started in the 1950s to give lectures that he called "sacrifices of learning" (*jnanayajna*). At that time he was very much opposed by the "orthodox" because of his opposition to caste and gender differentiation in spiritual education.[47] Gradually, though, he made his way up and now has a schedule that includes every year places in India, Malaysia, Africa, and even summer camps in the United States.

His movement is very similar to the Ramakrishna Mission, and one can see a direct link between the teachings of Vivekananda and those of Chinmayananda. What I see as very important is the extent to which this kind of teaching has moved from the margin to the center of "monastic" Hinduism. Even gurus with a much longer pedigree and a firm footing in established high-caste communities, like some of the Shankaracharyas, have started to use the discourse of modern Hinduism. For example, the influential Shankaracharya of Kanchipuram in Tamil Nadu makes extensive tours throughout India to express the need for the renewal of the Hindu spirit, which he feels is threatened from all sides. He is involved in the "uplift" of untouchables and in the construction of Hindu mission hospitals—social matters that were of no concern at all to his immediate predecessor.[48] Moreover, all modern religious leaders seem to follow Chinmayananda's lead in being interested in the overseas Indian communities.

This might suggest that, in terms of life-style, an important constituency in India, the middle class, has caught up with its expatriate counterparts in the West and that, as such, modern Hinduism caters to similar needs, here and there. This is reflected in VHP discourse on "individual growth," "social concerns," and religion as "a code of conduct" whereby every man can make a success of life, which sounds like the credo of the success-oriented Western middle class. If there is a "mainstream" constituency for the VHP's discourse on spiritual Hinduism as India's "national identity," then it is the middle class, together with those who aspire to that status.

Chapter Five

Conceptions of Time

Introduction

Nationalism has a contradictory need to demonstrate empirically its ideological claim that the nation it wishes to create has always existed. It demands that archeology, philology, and history deliver the "facts" to "prove" that the imagined nation exists both in and beyond history. In this chapter I want to take up the important issue of the link between the nationalist interpretation of history and religious discourse on change and time. As I noted earlier, religious discourse tends either to deny historical change altogether or else to show its ultimate irrelevance. It is my argument that Hindu nationalism combines this antihistorical feature of religious discourse with an empiricist search for "facts" that has been highly influenced by orientalism. To illustrate this argument, I will discuss two campaigns to "rebuild" temples allegedly destroyed by Muslim rulers: Somanatha in the early 1950s and Ayodhya in the 1980s. While the construction of the past is crucial to all nationalisms, the discussion in this chapter is limited to the Hindu nationalist construction of history because of its immediate relevance to the Ayodhya issue, which is obviously still very much alive.

A common assumption about India and, specifically, its Hindu civilization is that it lacks a sense of history. In a very negative appraisal, *An Area of Darkness* (1968), V. S. Naipaul speaks of India as a "land of ruins." "A people with a sense of history might have ordered things differently. But this is precisely the saddening element in Indian history: this absence of growth and development. It is a history whose only lesson is that life goes on. There is only a series of beginnings, no final creation."[1] It is clear from this book that, at the time, Naipaul blamed traditional civilization for this lack of a creative, historical sense.

In a recent lecture for the Manhattan Institute Naipaul made a somewhat similar point about Muslims. "Despite the history we had in common, I had traveled a different way. Starting with the Hindu background of the instinctive, ritualized life; growing up in the unpromising conditions of colonial Trinidad; I had gone through many stages of knowledge and self-knowledge. I had been granted the ideas of inquiry and the tools of scholarship. I could carry four or five or six different cultural ideas in my head. Now, I was traveling among a colonized people who had been stripped by their faith of all that expanding cultural and historical knowledge of the world that I had been growing into on the other side of the world." Here it is faith, religion, that prevents people from pursuing knowledge. The alternative Naipaul proposes is what he calls "universal civilization," born in Europe but now truly universal, stripped of its racial taints. At the heart of this civilization is the idea of the pursuit of happiness, which contains "the idea of the individual, responsibility, choice, the life of the intellect, the idea of vocation and perfectibility and achievement. It is an immense human idea. It cannot be reduced to a fixed system. It cannot generate fanaticism. But it is known to exist, and because of that, other more rigid systems in the end blow away."[2]

Naipaul expresses in the clearest possible terms the modern ideals of the Enlightenment and distinguishes them from those of religious civilizations, which have faith instead of knowledge, tradition instead of history. Given his personal biography of migration and achievement, Naipaul may be a greater believer in the "universal civilization" than most, but I think he expresses a very common line of thought. We see here again the pervasive dichotomy of "traditional" and "modern" in relation to conceptions of time, as expressed in Lévi-Strauss's famous metaphor of "hot" (modern) and "cold" (traditional) societies. Interestingly, Lévi-Strauss stresses the ideological nature of these conceptions of time. While he acknowledges that every society participates in a history that goes back to the beginning of humanity, he argues that "cold" societies ignore change and social difference whereas "hot" societies focus on them to stimulate development.[3]

Development is the key term in modern historical discourse. After the demise of colonialism after the Second World War, developed nations are distinguished from underdeveloped ones, which have to catch up through modernization programs sponsored by the developed countries. The world is divided in three: a "first world" of capitalist development, a "second world" of communist development, and a "third world" of underdevelopment. Modernization and development are thus intimately connected to the competition between capitalism and communism. The intellectual critique of the modernization paradigm remains within the discourse of development in its focus on the "development of underdevelopment."[4] It argues that the world's core regions create and sustain underdevelopment in the periphery of the "third world." This critique was also a major element in the "economic nationalism" of (ex)-colonized countries like India.[5] The argument was that Britain had caused the "underdevelopment" of India and that left to itself it would have done much better. Since Independence, the idea of development has continued to be a major element in India's planning rhetoric and apparatus, put in place by Jawaharlal Nehru. There is a strong belief in "the making of society" through modernization, planned and executed by the state. The Indian nation-state is in that respect very much the inheritor of the colonial state. While there are differences among businessmen, politicians, and intellectuals about the policies to be followed, there is no challenge to the discourse of development as such. Nationalism and development are intimately connected in the notion of the "growth of the nation," as if it referred to an individual biography. As in Naipaul's argument, religious tradition is often seen as an impediment to development, since it does not value change and lacks a modern sense of history. In these terms, what modernization is up against is India's religious lack of historical sense. And, indeed, Nehru thought that economic development, engineered by a secular state, would solve that problem.

On the face of it the whole notion that Indians lack a sense of history seems ridiculous. Nevertheless, it is repeated again and again, especially by Indological experts on the Hindu civilization.[6] The most frequent observation is that Hindus have a cyclical conception of time in which the passing of time is viewed negatively. Humanity now lives in the worst of times, and times can only become worse still until the end of this world period, the terrible *kaliyuga*. Moreover, an individual biography is unreal since it is only one link in a chain of existences (*samsara*). Individual existence becomes real only thanks to transcendental knowledge (*jnana*), which liberates the soul from transmigration. It does not derive reality and meaning from history. In fact, history is illusory.[7] This negative valuation is taken to explain the lack of interest Hindus presumably have in the recording of historical facts. Another argument is not that Hindus lack a sense of history but that history is occluded in Sanskrit discourse, since historical referentiality implies a lower truth value. Sanskrit literature does have historical writing (*itihasa*), but even this is "Vedicized," made to conform to the notion that all "knowledge" derives from the Vedas, which transcend time and history.[8]

That Hindu discourse often tries to avoid historical referentiality is certainly true. Religious shrines are, for example, believed to be beyond time and history. This is well expressed by Sitaram, a Hindu writer on Ayodhya:

People keep saying that what was built in this town in modern times is new. And there is a grain of truth in that; but on the other hand no one doubts that the pure stream of the Sarayu and the land of Ayodhya, founded by the first man, are without beginning. . . . We should accept that Indian time is without beginning and end and goes beyond counting. To call one thing present and another thing past is against the idea that all is permeated by the One. Small and great are equal. What we call one moment is in fact indestructible time and when we cut it into small parts, then there is no end to our cutting. We can only see the divine setting of Ayodhya with an Indian eye. The knowledge of Europe is of no avail to reach the depth of ancient India.[9]

This line of argument is perfectly acceptable to the priests and pilgrims in Ayodhya. On this level the "real" Ayodhya can only be experienced through meditation, and the things one actually sees nowadays in a visit to Ayodhya are merely instruments to attain that vision (*darshan*). This attitude is not an example of a lack of historical awareness in the Hindu tradition, but it does indeed entail a clear devaluation of history.

Sitaram's effort to suppress evidence of historical change is not exclusive to Hindu discourse. It is found in discourse on religion, politics, and kinship in every society. The claim that some instituted practice goes back to "time immemorial" or to the Vedas or to the Prophet or to the "Founding Fathers" is intended to make a given practice seem legitimate and correct.[10] As a representation of the past it may be assailed by those who have other claims. It may also be disputed by those who do not accept the discursive premises of the claim because, for example, they view them as "traditional" and "backward." The point to be made, though, is that the valuation of time and historical change, whether negative or positive, is a discursive strategy of the present.

It should be clear that in India, as elsewhere, religious discourse exists alongside other discourses and that religious discourse is not monolithic. In hagiographical traditions there is simultaneously an attempt to narrate sequences of historical events and to make this narration suit contemporary ideological purposes.[11] This typically results in conflicting versions of the same story. To produce from an outsider's perspective a historical narrative that makes sense of these conflicting narrations one has to go beyond the ideological purposes of these hagiographies while at the same time remaining open to their meaning.[12] An important tool for historians is always to confront the religious tradition with other historical sources, relating to such mundane matters as taxation, for example. This already implies that there are other discourses available with which one can compare the religious narrative.

However, it would be fallacious to argue, as positivist historians might want to do, that there is a sharp boundary between "religious fiction" and "material facts" in the representation of the past. Political and economic sources are not neutral compilations of facts but discourses of state power, which are often enmeshed with religious legitimations of political rule. Contrary to what is often believed, this picture does not change structurally in the colonial period. What is striking in the British historiography of India is its "orientalist empiricism," to employ a term coined by David Ludden.[13] Instead of occluding the "facts," it celebrates them to the extent that the narrative framework almost disappears. In the early period of British expansion in India (before the nineteenth century) the gathering of knowledge about the subcontinent and its population was largely in the hands of a few individual entrepreneurs who made knowledge their trade. In the later phase the gathering of knowledge becomes a massive state project designed to produce discourses to facilitate the rule of India. The facts are woven into narratives about the essential differences between Hindus and Muslims, the internal caste differences among Hindus, the rigidity and backwardness of Indian society, and so on—all pointing to the need for enlightened colonial rule. Needless to say, these narratives are not homogeneous, nor do they remain in place for the entire period of colonial rule. They are also not entirely produced by the British but are the product of the collaboration of Indian informants, translators, spokesmen, and British officials. However, if a generalization might be allowed, the colonial discourse relates, in one way or another, to the master narrative of progress and modernity, while the indigenous discourses relate to master narratives of salvation.

From the nineteenth century onward, Indian and Western discourses interacted to the extent that they are sometimes difficult to separate. This is especially clear in the nationalist interpretation of Indian history, which is heavily influenced by orientalist historiography. Orientalists had glorified India's ancient past, before the "Muslim invasions," and Sir William Jones had discovered the commonality between Greek, Latin, and Sanskrit. In the orientalist view, that "Aryan" civilization declined in what was called the "Muslim period," but the British had brought that period to an end, thereby introducing backward India to the modern world.[14] These perspectives were adopted by the nationalists with the added t‚ist that the British in fact impeded access to the modern world and should quit India. This nationalist view is clearly a Hindu one. On the Muslim side it is complemented by a view that focuses on the achievements of the Mughals and on the decline of India after the British ascendancy.

The search for and glorification of the past of the nation belongs squarely to all nationalist discourse. In the Indian case both the facts and their interpretation were delivered by orientalist research. The empiricist emphasis on "fact finding" was also inherited by nationalist historians. At the same time, the nationalist narrative is deeply rooted in religious discourse, which also relates the present to a glorified past. The religious argument aims at the construction of a community of believers and, as always in identity formation, draws a boundary between believers and others. It relates the community to sacred space, a network of sacred sites, and sacred time, the period of revelation. The nationalist argument does very much the same. In the case of Hindu nationalism, it identifies the nation with the community of believers, sacred space with national territory, and sacred history with national history.[15]

We can see here a collusion of religious and nationalist discourse. On one level there is a denial of history. The nation is seen as beyond time and history. It is involved in a perennial struggle with "barbaric outsiders" (*mlecchas*), first Muslims, then the British. In the end, though, the Hindus will carry the victory, just as the gods always prevail over the demons. In the Hindu nationalist view, Hindus prospered before the Muslim invasions in the eleventh to twelfth centuries. This "golden age" is epitomized by the period of the Gupta empire (320–540 A.D.). Since then Hindus have lived through increasingly dark ages. Even Independence has not brought them total victory, since "secularists" with their "Westernized minds" continued to colonize the nation. However, there is no doubt that in the end the Hindu nation will be victorious, since that is given in the order of things (*dharma*).

On another level there is a major shift in the approach to "facts," to "historical referentiality." Facts are no longer something irrelevant sub specie aeternitatis, as in prenationalist religious discourse, but are important evidence of the eternal existence of the nation. The orientalist master narrative of the necessity of colonial rule has been replaced by the nationalist teleology of the ultimate victory of the nation. The emphasis on "facts" implies a literal reading of religious sources. It also implies a combination of the historical study of literary sources and archeological research on material remains, the "hard facts." But all these "facts" have to fit the predetermined narrative.

Archeological excavations were performed at sites described in the two great Sanskrit epics, the *Mahabharata* and the *Ramayana*. Pottery called Painted Grey Ware was found at the *Mahabharata* sites and used to date events and dynasties mentioned in this epic. Excavations at *Ramayana* sites, such as Ayodhya, revealed that these sites were younger than the *Mahabharata* ones, which posed a certain problem. Even though, as could be expected, other traditions could be found to support the archeological finding that Rama of the *Ramayana* is later than Krishna of the *Mahabharata*, in the main these findings conflicted with a tradition almost universally accepted by Hindus that Rama should come before Krishna. As one archeologist commented, however, "we will strive and strive with success to make Archaeology and Tradition about Rama and Krishna meet on the same plane of time."[16] In the meantime it must be observed that this is a case in which the regime of archeological facts forces researchers to reject part of religious discourse, without, however, challenging this discourse as such. Archeological facts remain a technical matter for specialists; they do not enter the public arena nor do they challenge authoritative arguments in that arena. Nevertheless, the discovery of such facts allows archeologists and historians to believe that they are not simply following religious dogma but are in pursuit of pure scientific knowledge. B. B. Lal, a former director-general of the Indian Archaeological Survey, thus sees his project on the historicity of the Hindu epics as a "test on the touchstone of archaeology."[17]

The metaphor often used by archeologists is that they deal with the terra firma. However, as Romila Thapar argues, there is nothing firm here: "In the absence of contemporary written records or deciphered scripts, any attempt to correlate archaeological material with traditional accounts of the past becomes a venture into speculation. This is particularly so as the literary sources represent accretions over a period of many centuries and the archaeological evidence is partial, supported more by exploration than excavation and ultimately based on vertical rather than horizontal excavation."[18] Thapar pleads for more intensive excavation before attempting to link archeological information with historical tradition.[19] A project such as B. B. Lal's goes against the grain of such a plea, though. The sites are chosen on the basis of the literary tradition, and the narrative frame of the tradition is accepted and filled up with archeological findings. Moreover, the point Thapar makes about "accretions" is highly significant. The Sanskrit epics and Puranas are not unified, homogeneous texts but compilations of disparate, often conflicting, regionally diverse oral and written traditions, in which one version often presupposes another.[20] The entire notion of a homogeneous literary tradition is the result of hard, orientalist labor in the production of "critical editions." The critical editions of the *Mahabharata* and the *Ramayana*, as well as ongoing Purana projects, symbolize very well the process of selection and unification that is essential to the nationalist project. Archeology and textual research thus play a crucial role in the nationalist appropriation of history, as will be demonstrated in the two cases discussed below.

Ayodhya and Somanatha:
Eternal Shrines, Contested Histories

Sacred sites—such as the shrines of Rama in Ayodhya and of Shiva at Somanatha—are contested not only as markers of space but also as markers of time.[21] They are the physical evidence of the perennial existence of the religious community and, by nationalist extension, of the nation. I use the term "evidence" deliberately here, since archeological and historical research is used to come up with positive proof for religious history. The history of shrines, as told in religious tales and established by archeological evidence, is the history of the nation.

As we saw earlier, the Vishva Hindu Parishad started a campaign in 1984 to remove a mosque in Ayodhya built in 1528 on a spot held to be the birthplace of the Hindu god Rama and to replace it by a temple. The historical argument put forward by the VHP was that the mosque had replaced a temple that was demolished by a general of Babar, the first Mughal emperor. The VHP often cites as a precedent for the Ayodhya case another case in which a Hindu temple destroyed by a Muslim ruler was reconstructed in independent India. This is the temple of Somanatha in Saurashtra.

Somanatha: The Shrine Eternal

K. M. Munshi was an important freedom fighter and Congress leader who, after Independence, went on to become union minister in a cabinet led by Nehru.[22] In December 1922 he visited Junagadh, a princely state in Saurashtra (Gujarat) ruled by Muslim nawabs. During this trip, he went to see the ruins of the ancient temple of Somanatha on the seashore at Prabhasa Patan. "Somanatha" is one of the names of the god Shiva. The site is not only connected to the mythology of Shiva, however, but also to that of Krishna, who is thought to have abandoned his human incarnation (*dehotsarga*) here. Munshi's recollections are telling:

My heart was full of veneration and shame. Millions have worshipped, and worship today, Shri Krishna as "God Himself." Thousands, in every generation, had gained prestige or made money in His name or as His representatives on earth. But the nation had fallen low; none dared to raise his voice to rescue the sacred spot where once His mortal remains had been consigned to flames. I left Dehotsarga with bitter humiliation in my heart. In 1937, at Pahlgam in Kashmir, I wrote my novel *Jaya Somanatha*, with my eye "in fine frenzy rolling." I saw its grandeur as in A.D. 1024. I saw its ghastly destruction and I visualised its reconstruction under victorious king Bhimadeva. Reconstruction of Somanatha was then but the nebulous dream of a habitual dreamer.[23]

In this passage reference is made to the destruction of the temple by Muslims, to the decline of the Hindu nation, to the current suppression of the Hindu population under the nawabs of Junagadh, and to a dream of reconstruction.

This dream was soon to be fulfilled. At Independence the nawab of Junagadh attempted to have his territory included in Pakistan, although Hindus formed 82 percent of Junagadh's population. The National Congress reacted by forming a parallel government and led an uprising against the nawab, who fled to Pakistan. The dewan of the nawab invited the Indian army into Junagadh and handed the administration over to the Indian Union. Sardar Vallabhai Patel, India's home minister and a Gujarati politician whose stature in Congress was almost equal to that of Nehru, visited Junagadh on 12 November 1947, the day of the Hindu festival of Diwali. At a huge public meeting he announced the following: "On this auspicious day of the New Year, we have decided that Somanatha should be reconstructed. You, People of Saurashtra, should do your best. This is a holy task in which all should participate."[24] On 11 May 1950 the foundation stone was laid for a new temple, and on 19 October the ruins of the old temple were pulled down. These events led Munshi to the following ruminations: "An ancient race subconsciously felt that it was Somanatha which connected it with the past and the present; it was the eternal symbol of its faith in itself and its future. As often as the shrine was destroyed, the urge to restore it sprang up more vividly in the heart. . . . That is why for a thousand years Mahmud's destruction of the shrine has been burnt into the Collective Sub-conscious of the race as an unforgettable national disaster."[25]

Munshi's nationalist dream had come true, but not without opposition. Some of the opposition came from archeologists who opposed the removal of the ruins. As Munshi himself writes: "In the beginning, some persons, more fond of dead stones than live values, pressed the point of view that the ruins of the old temple should be maintained as an ancient monument. We were, however, firm in our view that the temple of Somanatha was not an ancient monument; it lived in the sentiment of the whole nation and its reconstruction was a national pledge. Its preservation should not be a mere matter of historical curiosity. Some of my scholar friends had hard things to say about me for my 'vandalism.' They forgot that I am fond of history, but fonder still of creative values." When the question was pressed by the Department of Archaeology, Sardar Patel expressed his views as follows: "The Hindu sentiment in regard to this temple is both strong and widespread. In the present conditions, it is unlikely that that sentiment will be satisfied by mere restoration of the temple or by prolonging its life. The restoration of the idol would be a point of honour and sentiment with the Hindu public."[26]

It is clear that two perspectives on history clashed here. Professional historians and archeologists wanted to protect the site as an "ancient monument." However, in an interesting move Munshi pointed out that in British India Governor-General Lord Curzon had already named the shrine an "ancient monument," implying that these scholars were simply perpetuating a colonial view of the site. His view, like that of Sardar Patel, was that the ruined temple was not an "ancient monument" but a place of worship in a living tradition of the "Hindu nation," which had now liberated itself from foreign rule, both Muslim and British. The latter perspective, with its strong political backing, won the day.

Later, after the death of Sardar Patel, another kind of opposition was voiced against the reconstruction. According to Munshi, the Jam Saheb of Nawanagar, a local dignitary and trustee of the Somanatha Trust, had written to Indian diplomats "to send a pinch of soil, a few drops of water and twigs, from the respective countries to which they were accredited, so that the reinstallation of the idol might symbolise the unity of the world and the brotherhood of men. At least one of the diplomats felt that his secularism was in danger of being misunderstood and complained about it to the Prime Minister."[27] The matter was discussed at meetings of the cabinet, and Nehru, the prime minister, wrote Munshi about it.

In his reply on 24 April 1951 Munshi points out to Nehru that Patel had been firmly behind the scheme and would have performed the inaugural ceremony himself, had he not died in the meantime. Munshi also reminded Nehru that Mahatma Gandhi had discussed the scheme with Patel and had not only agreed with it but had stipulated that the funds necessary for the reconstruction of the temple should come from the public, not from the government of India. This was a characteristically shrewd move of the Mahatma, and the proposal was accepted by Patel and the trustees. One passage in Munshi's letter is particularly revealing: "I can assure you that the 'Collective Sub-conscious' of India today is happier with the scheme of reconstruction of Somanatha sponsored by the Government of India than with many other things that we have done and are doing. Yesterday you referred to 'Hindu Revivalism.' I know your views on the subject; I have always done justice to them; I hope you will equally do justice to mine. Many have been the customs which I have defied in personal life from my boyhood. I have laboured in my humble way through literary and social work to shape or reintegrate some aspects of Hinduism, in the conviction that that alone will make India an advanced and vigorous nation under modern conditions."[28] Munshi must have been able to allay Nehru's worries, since the installation ceremony for the temple on 11 May 1950 was performed by the president of the Republic of India, Dr. Rajendra Prasad.

Although money had indeed not been spent directly by the government of India, there is no doubt about the support the project received from state institutions. The government of India and the Saurashtra government each had two representatives on the board of trustees. An advisory committee was set up, with Munshi as chairman and the director-general of archeology as convener. The use of archeology is of particular interest here. In 1950, during the one and a half months immediately prior to the demolition of the temple, B. K. Thapar of the Department of Archaeology was deputed to conduct excavations. In his account of the excavations he begins with the historical background. According to Thapar, the earliest historical reference to the temple relates to the visit of a Hindu ruler, who came to worship sometime between 942 and 997. Thapar then continues: "In A.D. 1026 Sultan Mahmud of Ghazni, having heard the stories circulated by the Hindus that the invader

could have destroyed no idol in India, had the idol of Somanatha
been pleased with them, descended upon the temple with his
iconoclastic zeal to dispel the false belief of the Hindus. After
capturing the temple he ordered the linga to be disfigured and
broken into pieces and thereafter the whole of the temple to be
burnt to the ground. The Sultan did not stay there for more than a
fortnight. According to the official (contemporary) historians, he
turned away in haste since Paramadev, the great ruler of the Hindus,
was advancing with a force to block the Sultan's way of retreat."[29]
The temple was rebuilt by Hindu kings but was again desecrated
in 1297 when Alaf Khan, a general of the Khilji rulers of Delhi,
marched on it. The next destruction of the temple was in 1394 by
Muzaffar Khan, a governor of Gujarat. In 1413 and in 1459 Muslims
again destroyed the temple. After 1459 the area was entirely under
Muslim rule, but the temple continued to function until it was again
demolished in 1669 by the Mughal emperor Aurangzeb. In 1706
the shrine was converted into a mosque, but it seems not to have
functioned as such very long. After Aurangzeb's death in 1707 the
Marathas started to challenge the authority of the Mughals in the
area. In 1783 the Maratha queen Ahalyabai, a famous builder of
Hindu shrines all over northern and western India, erected a shrine
for Somanatha, a little distance away from the ruins of the old one.
In 1812 the shrine came under the control of the rulers of Baroda
under the terms of an agreement with the nawabs of Junagadh.
Finally, in 1922 K. M. Munshi visited the shrine and had his dream.

The account of the excavations furnishes a lot of details about the
architecture of the temple. Its main function, however, seems to
be to provide archeological evidence that the present site is the site
of the "original temple" and that the other temples were built on
top of it, proving, as Thapar says, "the Hindu tradition that the
place of linga installation should remain the same irrespective of
the reconstructions."[30] This statement is of obvious importance for
the reconstruction. For the rest, the archeological account simply
supports the historical one. For example, Thapar argues that some
portions of the temple show "signs of deliberate breakage which
could, on some plausibility, be attributed to Sultan Mahmud of
Ghazni."[31]

What the Department of Archaeology of the government of India
does in this case is to use the tools and vocabulary of modern

empirical science to fill in some lacunae in a story already well established. But the story remains the same, and it is the story of perennial enmity between Muslim iconoclasts and Hindu idol worshipers. As Thapar aptly puts it, the "stable element" in the story of the temple is "the strong determination on the part of the local populace to keep the temple alive and to restore its glory even in the face of devastating raids which had become more or less regular after the great expedition led against it by Emperor Mahmud of Ghazni in A.D. 1026. The result was that after each invasion some reconstruction or rehabilitation in the structure was inevitable."[32]

What the reconstruction of Somanatha, firmly supported by the state, did was not only to build a Hindu place of worship but to make a statement on the national past. Somanatha is a monument of the Hindu nation that has finally won its continuous struggle against "foreign" oppression. Mahmud of Ghazni and Aurangzeb, the first and last Muslim destroyers of Somanatha, were presented as enemies of the Hindu nation, and their final defeat was celebrated in the reconstruction.[33] Although Munshi had a dream, the story of Somanatha was not a figment of his imagination. It was firmly supported by historical and archeological research. Indeed, a remarkable reverence for the "historical facts" is evident in the entire reconstruction project. From the early days of the East India Company British orientalists had been engaged in the reconstruction of India's past. With the firm establishment of British rule in the nineteenth century an enormous effort was launched to find facts in order to "rule by records."[34] Facts, though, do not speak for themselves. It is the historian who makes a story out of them. One of the most important master narratives of colonial orientalism in India dealt with the inimical relations between two nations, Hindu and Muslim. The nature of these relations formed a powerful legitimation for the presence of the British as an "enlightened" race of rulers.

No doubt, there are "facts," such as the demolition of Hindu temples by Muslim rulers or taxes on infidels as well as Hindu resistance against such things, that could be used to support the master narrative. But there are also other facts, such as patronage of Hindu shrines by Muslim rulers or vice versa, that problematize the story. More important, though, is the essentialism inherent in the Hindu versus Muslim version of Indian history. This version divides Indian history into a Hindu period (1000 B.C. to A.D. 1200) and a Muslim period (A.D. 1200–1800) on the basis of the religion of some of the ruling dynasties. It brackets together Arabs, Turks, and Persians under the term "Muslims," even though that term is rarely used in contemporary sources before the thirteenth century.[35] It uses the term "Hindu" as if it describes a unified religious community, despite the fact that the term is not found in pre-Islamic sources. (It was first used by Arabs and later by others to refer to the inhabitants of the area near the river Sind, or the Indus.) Basically, it is an ahistorical view of the past in its denial of discontinuity and its assertion of essentialized categories.

Munshi's dream and its realization can thus be understood in the context of the construction of a nation of Hindus. Durkheim's view that, in religion, the community worships itself is nowhere as firmly shown as in religious nationalism.

Ayodhya: Rama's Eternal Shrine

The reconstruction of Somanatha encountered some marginal opposition from secular nationalists, but not from Muslims. It is unclear to what extent Hindus of the area were still interested in the shrine before the reconstruction movement, but Muslim interest appears to have been entirely absent. With the demise of nawabi rule in Junagadh the temple had lost whatever political significance it might have had for the Muslim elite of the area. Although Aurangzeb is said to have converted part of the demolished temple into a mosque, this did not lead to it being taken into use as such.[36] In short, the ruins of Somanatha were not seen as a sacred place by Muslims and the reconstruction of the temple therefore not as a reason for opposition. The situation is entirely different in what has over the last few years become one of the most explosive issues in Indian politics: the dispute over Babar's mosque in Ayodhya, Uttar Pradesh. Just as Munshi and Patel planned the reconstruction of Somanatha, Hindus in Ayodhya planned the installation of the god Rama's idol in a mosque built in 1528 by Mir Baqi, a general of Babar, that, according to local tradition, replaced a demolished temple marking the birthplace of Rama. Operating in a frame of mind seemingly very similar to that of Patel and Munshi, Hindus of the area wanted to redress the historical oppression of the Hindu nation by reclaiming this sacred site.

The context in which Hindu nationalists had to operate in Ayodhya was fundamentally different, however, since the mosque had been in use until recently. Moreover, it had been the site of a violent dispute, recorded in both colonial and Persian sources, between Hindus and Muslims for well over a century. According to the first district commissioner of Faizabad, Patrick Carnegy, in 1855 agitation on the part of militant Sunni Muslims about a mosque alleged to exist in Hanumangarhi, a Hindu temple compound in Ayodhya, led to an assault on the Babari mosque by Hindu ascetics, who took the place. About the Babari mosque, Carnegy commented: "It is said that up to that time the Hindus and Mahomedans alike used to worship in the mosque-temple. Since British rule a railing has been put up to prevent disputes, within which in the mosque the Mahomedans pray, while outside the fence the Hindus have raised a platform on which they make their offerings."[37] In this account, then, there was a dispute about a mosque before the British took over the region, but this mosque was not the Babari Masjid. Rather, it was a mosque that allegedly occupied the same spot as the most important Hindu temple in Ayodhya, Hanumangarhi. The conflict led, however, to a Hindu assault on what must have been the most important mosque near Hanumangarhi, which is now universally known as the Babari Masjid, although it might then have been known simply as the Jama Masjid.[38]

The 1855 dispute is confusing for those interested in the current Babari Masjid conflict. Most commentators today take it for granted that the 1855 dispute had been about the Babari Masjid in the first place. One can understand the confusion. Whereas today all attention is given to a conflict about a mosque that occupies the place of a temple, the conflict in 1855 was about a temple occupying the place of a mosque. The situation has even befuddled a careful historian like Michael Fisher, who ignores the evidence that the Hindu temple Hanumangarhi might have been the first bone of contention and that the dispute gradually shifted its focus to the mosque.[39] Indeed, no party in the conflict nowadays even mentions a disputed site in Hanumangarhi, and given the beleaguered situation of the Muslim minority today it seems difficult to imagine a bunch of Muslim militants launching an attack on Hanumangarhi, a fortified temple, with the belief that they should repossess their sacred space. Nevertheless, there is good reason to accept that this was indeed the case in the mid-nineteenth century. The god worshiped in Hanumangarhi is Hanuman, who appears in the *Ramayana* as Rama's devoted monkey friend and is now unequivocally the property of the Rama cult. But this was not always the case. Local tradition has it that the god worshiped on the hill on which the Ramanandis built Hanumangarhi was indeed Hanuman, who was worshiped by both Shaivite ascetics and Sufi fakirs under the name Hathile.[40] The devotees of Rama, the Ramanandis, had to chase these competitors away before they could claim the place. This struggle is recounted in local tradition. I would suggest that the belief of Muslims in the nineteenth century that within the precincts of Hanumangarhi a sacred place could be located that belonged to them was based on this tradition.

That Muslim militants could launch an attack on such a well-entrenched Hindu bulwark as Hanumangarhi has to be understood in its broader political context. The attackers were Sunnis under the leadership of Shah Gulam Husayn, a religious scholar (*maulvi*). Ayodhya was located in Awadh, a regional realm that had been governed by Shi'ite rulers since the beginning of the eighteenth century. The massacre of the Muslim militants by Hindu *sadhus* (and their supporters, local landowners) compromised the Islamic legitimacy of Shi'ite rule, which was, in any case, always under threat of being rejected by the Sunnis, who form the majority of the Muslim population. The predicament of Wajid Ali Shah, the ruler of Awadh, was, however, worsened by the fact that he not only had to avoid hurting Sunni feelings but also was effectively dependent on the political support and consent of the British resident in Lucknow, who took to the defense of the Hindus. A government commission was formed, which concluded that no mosque existed in Hanumangarhi. This led to violent remonstrations among Muslims. A Sunni leader, Maulvi Amir Ali Amethavi, called for a holy war and organized an army to march on Ayodhya. Now, however, the chief Shi'ite religious official declared that such an attack on the infidel was forbidden when it was not supported by the state. In effect, he ruled against any popular action on the part of Sunnis within a Shi'ite state. The Shi'ite ruler had the prerogative to protect the Islamic law. When the holy warrriors decided to ignore the warnings of the Shi'ite government and marched on Ayodhya, they were confronted by government troops and massacred. Soon after these events the British decided to take over the administration of Awadh by making it a province of British India.

The 1855 dispute throws light on a complex configuration. No doubt, there was a communal conflict between Hindus and Muslims about sacred space. However, this conflict also involved the complex relations of Shi'as and Sunnis to the Hindu population. Disenfranchised Sunnis wanted to take political action against Hindus when they felt that the Shi'ite state was not protecting Muslims or advancing Islam. The capability of the Shi'ite state to do so was, however, limited by its dependence on the British. Moreover, the Shi'ite rulers of Awadh had always depended on support from Hindu elites, whom they wished to avoid alienating. In fact, many of Ayodhya's temples, including Hanumangarhi, had been built with the money of Hindu officials serving in Awadh's Shi'ite government.

In a way, the British interference caused the collapse of the delicate balance the Shi'ite rulers had to maintain. When they finally moved in in 1856, the British understood that it was their foremost task to police and control communal relations. Since the Hanumangarhi issue had effectively dissolved, they focused on the other potential site of conflict, the Babari Masjid. By placing a railing, they materially and symbolically divided the worshipers in the Babari Masjid compound. As we saw earlier, this arrangement seems to have been more or less sufficient until gradually deteriorating communal relations led to a new Hindu assault on the mosque. In 1934, when cow slaughter at the Muslim festival of Bakr-Id in nearby Shahjahanpur led to riots, the mosque was attacked and a number of Muslims killed. A punitive tax was levied on the Hindus of Ayodhya and damage to the mosque repaired. After Independence, though, the mosque had to be protected by a police picket because Hindus had started agitation in front of the mosque.

Despite this precaution Hindus entered the mosque on the night of 22 December 1949 and effectively converted it into a temple by installing an image of Rama. The following morning large crowds, believing that Rama had appeared, assembled in front of the mosque and tried to force entry. However, the gate was locked, and the police force had been strengthened. Nehru was disturbed by the potential implications of these events and wrote the chief minister of Uttar Pradesh, Govind Ballabh Pant, that he should interest himself personally in the matter.[41] Sardar Patel, the deputy prime minister, whose support had been crucial in the case of Somanatha, was opposed to the action of the Ayodhya Hindus, perhaps not in principle but on practical grounds. In a letter of 9 January 1950 to the Uttar Pradesh chief minister he wrote: "I feel that the controversy has been raised at a most inopportune time both from the point of view of the country at large and of your province in particular. . . . It would be most unfortunate if we allowed any group advantage to be made on this issue. . . . Such matters can only be resolved peacefully if we take the willing consent of the Muslim community with us."[42]

However, the district magistrate, K. K. K. Nayar, refused to remove the image, despite instructions from the chief secretary of Uttar Pradesh and the inspector general of police. In a letter of 27 December to the chief secretary Nayar wrote: "I could, if the government decided to remove the idol at any cost, request that I be relieved and replaced by an officer who may be able to see in that solution a merit which I cannot discern. For my part I cannot in my discretion, which is the only legal sanction behind my action in this matter, essay to enforce such a solution as I am fully aware of the widespread suffering which it will entail to many innocent lives."[43] Nayar's view was supported by the divisional commissioner, who proposed keeping the site under police control but allowing a priest to perform the necessary worship until the excitement had worn off and a plan could be made with leaders of both the Hindu and Muslim community. Something similar was indeed done. A committee of respectable Hindus of Ayodhya was allowed to enter the temple and worship the image every year on 22 December, although the site remained closed to the general public. In the meantime civil suits were filed by both Hindus and Muslims concerning the exclusive right to worship.

There is some noteworthy ambivalence in the actions of the state. A forceful conversion of Babar's mosque into Rama's temple was stopped by the police who closed the gate, and the restricted access to the image limited the success of the Hindu activists considerably. Nevertheless, the people who had placed the image in the mosque were never caught or tried—although, in an interview in the *New York Times* on Sunday, 22 December 1991, Abbot Ram Chander

Das Paramahams declared openly that he was the one who had put the image inside the mosque.[44] Moreover, the image was not removed nor was Hindu worship completely stopped. This implies that the mosque had de facto been converted into a temple, since Hindu worship had replaced Muslim worship. Among the higher levels of the administration there had been a strong feeling that the image had to be removed, but District Magistrate Nayar, under whose responsibility the idol had been surreptitiously installed, had been totally uncooperative.[45] Letting the courts decide implied a political strategy of pacification by infinite delay and indecision. In the political context of the eighties, which is very different from that of the fifties, this strategy would no longer work and, in fact, would result in another political use of the legal system.

The very fact of Hindu worship in the mosque naturally left the issue wide open for further action. However, after the frenzy of the years following partition no further initiative was taken on the local level. This can be explained by the fear felt by local religious leaders that a temple on Rama's birthplace would provide too much competition for existing religious attractions in Ayodhya. The action had to come from outside, and it only came in 1984 with the VHP's campaign, described earlier. What concerns us in this chapter, though, is the historical argument in Hindu nationalism. Instead of simply claiming as a matter of religious belief that the mosque occupies the spot on which Rama was born, the VHP goes further by claiming that a temple on the birthplace was demolished by Muslims and replaced by a mosque.

For this further claim evidence has to be provided in the form of historical and archeological "facts." However, in this case the government has not allowed the Department of Archaeology to provide evidence. It has thus fallen to B. B. Lal to do so. As we know, Lal is the leading Indian archeologist who seeks to test the historicity of the *Mahabharata* and the *Ramayana* on, as he says, "the touchstone of archaeology." Between 1975 and 1980 he headed a team that excavated several sites in Ayodhya. These excavations took place under the auspices of a national archeological project, called "Archaeology of the Ramayana Sites," which aimed at the rediscovery of the places connected with that epic. In the 1976–77 excavations in the Ramkot area of Ayodhya (where the mosque is also located) Lal found that there was an urban settlement at the end of the sixth or during the first half of the fifth century B.C.[46] The question is, of course, whether this settlement is the Ayodhya of the *Ramayana*. The archeologist M. C. Joshi has thrown doubts on such an idea, arguing that Ayodhya is purely a mythical city. In reaction to Joshi's argument Lal claims that what he has found in present-day Ayodhya is the Ayodhya of the *Ramayana*.[47]

A rather convincing argument about these matters has been brought forward by Hans Bakker, who identifies the site with Saketa, a city mentioned in Buddhist and Jain sources, and argues that the name was changed to Ayodhya by the Gupta rulers, who moved their capital from Pataliputra to that place in the fifth century A.D. The Guptas sought by this reification of the Ayodhya of the *Ramayana* to link their rule with that of the god Rama.[48] In an interesting way this reconstruction is supported by local tradition in Ayodhya, which has it that the Ayodhya of the *Ramayana* was destroyed during the world period (*yuga*) in which Rama lived but rediscovered by King Vikramaditya (a title that here refers to the ruler Skandagupta). This tradition mixes historical reality with the Hindu theory of cyclical world periods. That archeologists would find evidence of Rama's Ayodhya seems unlikely from this point of view, given that the period during which Rama lived supposedly ended over a million years ago. However, one would expect them to find evidence of the Gupta period and of Vikramaditya. One would also expect them to find the temple built by Vikramaditya on Rama's birthplace under the mosque built by Babar. The problem here is that, as Lal reports, "the Gupta period is not significantly indicated at this site."[49] Another problem is that there is no evidence of temples dedicated to Rama in the first millennium A.D., except for a temple in Ramtek, near Nagpur. Moreover, the oldest Rama image found is a Chola bronze found in Tamil Nadu that dates to around A.D. 950. Bakker concludes on the basis of the first text concerned with the worship of Rama, which was composed in the twelfth century, that the temple cult of Rama only becomes prominent in the eleventh and twelfth centuries A.D.

Nevertheless, in a BBC interview in 1991, Lal argued that there had been a Hindu temple for Rama/Vishnu on the spot now occupied by the mosque and that pillars of that temple had been used in constructing the temple. Lal suggested that further digging should be carried out in order to come up with more evidence—a suggestion that was denounced in the press by the historian Irfan Habib and others as a ploy to demolish the mosque. Lal's views are supported by some archeologists, such as S. P. Gupta and B. P. Sinha, but rejected by others, such as R. S. Sharma.

Unlike the archeological evidence in the case of Somanatha, the findings by authorities like Lal have not gone unchallenged by other authorities. These findings provoked an interesting debate in Indian newspapers, in which well-established academics engaged in a good deal of mud-slinging. A particularly strong position was taken by historians connected to the Centre for Historical Studies at Jawaharlal Nehru University. These historians raised two questions: whether Ayodhya is the birthplace of Rama and whether present-day Ayodhya is the Ayodhya of the *Ramayana*. Although they do not explicitly refer to Bakker, their argument is largely based upon his hypothesis that the town Saketa was renamed Ayodhya by a fifth-century Gupta king in order to create a link between his rule and the ideal rule of lord Rama. These historians argue that "if present day Ayodhya was known as Saketa before the fifth century, then the Ayodhya of Valmiki's Ramayana was fictional. If so, the identification of *Ramajanmabhumi* (Rama's birthplace) in Ayodhya today becomes a matter of faith, not of historical evidence." Further, they argue that there is no evidence that the mosque has been built on the site of a temple, commenting that "it is in the nineteenth century that the story circulates and enters official records. These records were then cited by others as valid historical evidence on the issue."[50] The implication here is that the British found the "facts" that fitted their master narrative of the perpetual hostility between Hindus and Muslims. The solution to the problem proposed by these historians is to declare the disputed area a national monument.[51]

One of the problems with the above argument is that the British were not very interested in the Hindu history of Ayodhya. The most important British archeologist of India in the nineteenthth century was Alexander Cunningham. He did come to Ayodhya, not to dig up evidence of Hindu-Muslim enmity but to look for the Buddhist monuments of Saketa/Ayodhya—monuments that nobody locally was interested in, then or now.[52] Patrick Carnegy, the commissioner, argued that the pillars of the mosque—which are now ascribed to a Hindu temple by Lal and others—strongly resemble Buddhist pillars, although he did accept the local tradition that Babar built

his mosque on the "birthplace" temple. However, he also accepted
the local tradition that Hindus and Muslims used to worship together in this mosque-temple until the disturbances of 1855.[53] The
suggestion that the local tradition is entirely invented by the British
thus seems disingenuous. Moreover, the suggestion that the place
should become a national monument shows the extent to which
these historians want to replace religious nationalism with secular
nationalism.

However, the clash between the two is exactly the issue here.
This becomes even clearer in a book on the Ayodhya debate edited
by Sarvepalli Gopal, a scholar from Jawaharlal Nehru University.
In his introduction Gopal argues that after Independence "the log-
ical attitude of getting rid of religion altogether was too utopian for
Indian society, where many religions were deeply entrenched. So
the more practical answer was not opposition to religion but the
removal of religion from public affairs, the separation of the State
from all faiths, the insistence on religion as a private matter for the
individual with no bearing on civic rights and duties, and freedom
for the profession of diverse forms of religious worship provided
they did not come into conflict with each other." Although this is
straight Nehruvian secularism, Gopal also partakes in the discourse
of Hindu spirituality: "This common element in the faith which
binds together those who call themselves Hindus in the various
parts of India is the acceptance of religion as spiritual experience,
as the direct apprehension of the reality of the one supreme Universal Spirit. Devotion to truth and respect for all human beings, a
deepening of inner awareness and a commitment to compassion,
form the essence of the Hindu religion."[54] In this way Gopal shows,
inadvertently, how close the discourses of tolerance and secularism,
of Gandhi and Nehru, in fact are. Whatever the merits of the
arguments made by the contributors to this volume on the Ayodhya
issue, it should be clear that they are arguments made *within* the
debate about the nation, not arguments outside of it, discussing the
nature of the debate itself.

That Mahmud of Ghazni destroyed the Somanatha temple in
1026 is a celebrated fact in "official" Indian history not disputed by
anyone, Muslim, Hindu, or otherwise. That Babar destroyed Rama's temple in Ayodhya has not, however, acquired textbook status.
The common reaction of Indians outside of Ayodhya to the issue—

whatever their present position may be—is that they had never heard of the whole problem before the VHP took action in the 1980s. On the local level, the perception is naturally quite different. In research carried out in the 1970s both Bakker and I relied heavily on the local tradition that Babar's general had destroyed a temple built on Rama's birthplace. This tradition is supposedly corroborated by the fact that in the mosque are pillars of a temple (which Bakker ascribes to the eleventh century). The same kind of pillars are also used in the grave of a Muslim *pir* who is in the local tradition considered to have been instrumental in the demolition of the temple. But all this has become the subject of bitter dispute ever since the VHP attempted to incorporate local tradition into a history of the Hindu nation. Such an attempt implies that local tradition should be vindicated by scientific inquiry and is thus open to attack from those who oppose the move made by the VHP. While Bakker and I could naively accept local tradition, this cannot be done any longer. For example, one could argue that the fact that there are temple pillars in the mosque does not tell you much. They could have been taken from anywhere and not from a demolished Rama temple.[55]

Local tradition has now definitely been incorporated in the encompassing discourse of Hindu nationalism. But it is not only the VHP's activities that have brought about this incorporation. A major element in the process was the broadcasting of Rama's story, the epic *Ramayana*, as a television serial starting in January 1987. The success of this serial was enormous; streets in India were deserted during transmission time. The story of the *Ramayana*, in which Ayodhya figures as Rama's capital, is well known to every Hindu. Now, however, national television brought Ayodhya to millions of Hindus simultaneously in the privacy of their homes. This dramatic presentation cannot but have aided the VHP's cause of turning a black page in the history of the Hindu nation by "liberating Rama's birthplace."

Religious shrines are, for believers, beyond time and history. These shrines were also subject to violent contest between power brokers long before the advent of colonialism and nationalism. What nationalism does, though, is to reinterpret the nature of the contest in the past to serve its purposes in the present. Hindu nationalism provides the link between Somanatha and Ayodhya. However, there are also striking differences. In the case of Somanatha the reconstruction was largely a symbolic act guided by Patel and Munshi, leaders of the Congress party, which had led India to Independence, with indirect support from the state. There was no opposition from Muslims. The Ayodhya case involved a direct confrontation between the state and Hindu nationalists, led by a major opposition party, in 1949 and again in 1990. It has also involved direct confrontations between Hindus and Muslims in many parts of the country. The most striking difference appears to be the decline of the ability of the Congress party to project a convincing pluralist and moderate version of Hindu nationalism and thereby contain the extremist version of the VHP.

Conclusion

The case of Somanatha shows the extent to which the Indian state and the Congress party have been involved in the construction of the history of the Hindu nation, although in this case no confrontation with Muslims was involved. In the Ayodhya case it is Hindu nationalist opposition to the "secularism" of the state that leads to agitation, this time involving a confrontation with Muslim opposition. The latter case has therefore resulted in violence on the streets and heated debate among scholars. It is here that the politically contested nature of history becomes perfectly clear.

It is obviously not the case that historiography and archeology always simply follow religious discourse, filling in the "facts." On the contrary, there is a constant interaction between the empiricist insistence on the "facts," scientifically established, and orientalist and nationalist narratives. This may lead a researcher like B. B. Lal to question aspects of religious discourse. However, as we have seen, this takes place in the rarefied arena of archeological scholarship and does not result by itself in confrontations with established worldly or religious authorities. His scholarly testimony only becomes important when there is a public debate, as in the mosque issue. Here he does not confront religious-nationalist opinion, but his support is sought.

An example of what leads to a confrontation with religious leaders who are backed by the state can be found in a recent dispute in Gujarat between scholars and leaders of the Swaminarayan sect. In

1988 the Gujarat government sanctioned the prosecution of three scholars in connection with a research paper written by the historian Makrand Mehta. The paper, entitled "Sectarian Literature and Social Consciousness: A Study of the Swaminarayan Sect, 1800–1840," appeared in the October–December issue of *Arthat*, a Gujarati quarterly published by the Centre for Social Studies in Surat. The argument in this paper is consistent with what I described in chapter 2 as the close collaboration between the Swaminarayan movement and the British, which is, of course, in post-Independence India a source of embarrassment for this movement. Warrants were issued against the writer and the editors of the journal, Ghanshyam Shah and Achyut Yagnik. The mere fact that the journal is published in Gujarati, rather than English, and that it enjoys a wide circulation immediately implies that it reaches beyond scholarly circles and enters the public sphere. As its legal ground for the prosecution of the author and editors the government argued that the writing is "bound to be regarded by any reasonable man as grossly offensive and provocative and deliberately intended to outrage the feelings of the followers of Swaminarayana sampradaya."[56]

An interesting aspect of the case is that the Swaminarayan sect credited much of its success in the nineteenth century to the way it opposed the "libidinous" ways of another Hindu movement in Gujarat, the Pushtimarg, or Vallabhacharyas. The "objectionable" practices of the leaders of this movement became the subject of a libel case brought by a Pushtimarg leader against a book reporting these practices. This case harmed the Pushtimarg immensely and helped the Swaminarayanis at the same time. Whether the Swaminarayanis will now take the risk of bringing a libel suit may depend on their assessment of the constantly shifting political situation in Gujarat, in which their supporters are a powerful group, whereas in the British period the author of criticism of "Hindu ways" could count on the support of the judge and the administration.

A major problem facing scholars concerned with religious nationalism is that they tend to deconstruct the historical or archeological base of certain arguments but, at the same time, are confined to a narrative that attracts less and less support outside of scholarly circles. On the one hand, one wonders what the so-called interventions in journals like *Seminar* or in books by eminent Jawaharlal Nehru University scholars really mean when there is little or no public support beyond a few English-language newspapers for these arguments. On the other hand, there is no alternative for scholars but to enter public debate, and the editorial pages of the Indian newspapers give ample evidence of the liveliness of that debate. A discourse focusing on separating "facts" from "fiction" and bent on the construction of "national monuments" should, however, explicitly acknowledge that it is not value-free but based on political choices and political power, lest it remain, in the end, marginal.

Chapter Six

Words and Gestures

Introduction

As we saw in chapters 1 and 3, language is commonly seen as the basis of collective identification. The construction of a national language is considered to be an absolutely crucial step on the road to modernity. In *Nations and Nationalism* Ernest Gellner focuses on the creation of a national language as an institutional effect of schooling, a primary function of the state. In *Imagined Communities* Benedict Anderson shifts the attention somewhat to the role of "print-capitalism" and the rise of the novel in the emergence of a national language. While there can be no doubt about the importance of the language community and the establishment of a national language, one should be aware of the "openness" of the linguistic construction of identity.[1] People can command several languages and opt for one or another of them according to the demands of the situation. This is particularly clear in the Indian case, where we find some fifteen hundred languages and dialects spoken by some 800 million people, in which approximately thirty languages have a million speakers or more. Moreover, printed language can have only limited effects given the sort of literacy rates we find in India.

Our argument in chapter 3 was therefore that printed language had to be studied in relation to other verbal and nonverbal ways of communicating identity. While our focus in that chapter was on ritual, I want now to draw attention to the politics of language in textual and theatrical performance. I will deal first with the changing relation between the languages of sacred communication and those of profane communication, which will lead to a discussion of the

165

"nationalization" of language. Second, I will consider the relation between different modes of language performance: the epic, the novel, and the religious soap opera.

Sanskrit and Arabic/Persian, Hindi and Urdu

Sanskrit and Arabic are sacred languages. Sanskrit is the language of the Hindu gods and thus also that of their human representatives, the Brahmans. It is the language of civilization, and indeed the word *sanskriti* means exactly that. In the long process of "civilizing" India's population Sanskrit has therefore played a crucial role, as one Brahman anthropologist, M. N. Srinivas recognized when he coined the term *Sanskritization*.[2] This refers to the spread of Brahman communities over the Indian subcontinent and the growing influence of their ideas and practices on the people they interacted with. Sanskritization is, then, the gradual reshaping of local beliefs and practices in the direction of Brahmanical ideals. To some extent Sanskritization is synonymous with Hinduization, in that Brahman priestly communities as well as ascetic orders play a crucial role in converting tribals to Hinduism. Sanskritization, however, is a never-ending process. Even after a given group has accepted a certain position in the caste hierarchy, the possibility of Sanskritization remains open.

Brahmans used Sanskrit sacred formulas (*mantras*) in their rituals, and these *mantras* were themselves believed to have sacred power. Ultimately the language did not have to refer to anything outside itself. The *mantra* as sound without meaning connects the one who utters it with the ultimate meaning of the universe. The notion of the sacredness and perfection of Sanskrit is developed very early in the Brahmanical theory of sacrifice and in linguistic theories that originated in that sacrificial theory. In later ascetic and devotional religion, which does not pay much attention to the Brahmanical sacrifice, the notion of the *mantra* nonetheless continues to have great importance.

By way of example, let me quote the *mantra* theory as it occurs in the theology of Rama, as explained by Hans Bakker on the basis of the twelfth-century *Agastyasamhita*:

The highest reality has two aspects: it is supreme light (*parajyotis*) which is homologised with the sound RA, and it is the essentia of all phaenomena (*prapancatman*), homologised with the sound MA. These together form the highest reality, RAMA. This transcendent reality manifest itself in the form of a phonic body comprised of the fifty syllables of the Nagari alphabet (including "ksha"), and out of this "body" all phenomenal realities evolve. All deities, powers and realities are thus homologised with a particular combination of sounds. *Mantras* are therefore not merely formulae that refer to a particular god or force but are in fact this god or force itself. To utter a *mantra* in the proper way is to manipulate a particular divine cosmic force. Because all sounds directly evolve from Rama, Ramaite *mantras* constitute the most important and powerful of divine and cosmic realities and forces. Worship of Rama is thought to be the most effective since it makes use of such *mantras*.[3]

This may seem very esoteric and accessible only to a religious elite, but that impression is wrong. Commonly, when Hindus in North India carry their dead to the cremation ground, they repeat "Rama, Rama" over and over again, since this *mantra* is viewed as a *taraka mantra*, a formula that ensures salvation. According to an almost clichéd description of Mahatma Gandhi's death, he uttered "Rama, Rama" when he was killed. It is also significant that the power of the *mantra* is often seen in Hinduism as enabling low-caste people to attain salvation. The famous North Indian weaver-turned-poet Kabir supposedly discovered the path leading to salvation when the saint Ramanand stumbled over him and uttered "Rama, Rama." It is in the *nirguna sant* tradition, to which Kabir belonged, that the sacred language of the guru in fact replaces sacred images. In the Sikh tradition this leads ultimately to the replacement of the guru by the book, the *Guru Granth Sahib*. It is the language of this scripture, Punjabi, along with its script—appropriately called *gurmukhi*—that is one of the main rallying points of Sikh nationalism.

As V. D. Savarkar argued in *Hindutva*, Sanskrit is the language of the Hindu gods and prophets, people, race, and nation. Nevertheless, despite the fact that the sacredness of Sanskrit sound continues to be stressed, a major shift from the use of Sanskrit to that of regional languages in devotional Hinduism was already occurring in the first centuries of the second millennium A.D. In South India the Tamil *prabandham*, a collection of devotional hymns, became the vehicle of the spread of a new theology. In the North, Hindi,

Bengali, Marathi, Gujarati, and so on were the languages of medieval devotional poetry. I cannot trace the complicated history of these languages here, but let me note that these languages are used in both sacred and profane communication; Sanskrit, however, is not entirely discarded but continues to be an important element of formalized ritual. Moreover, the vocabulary of these "new" languages is to a great extent derived from Sanskrit, something that is true not only for the Indo-Aryan languages of North India but also for a Dravidian language like Tamil. The Sanskrit aspect is most emphatically present in religious communication. What is also important is the adaptation of Sanskrit lore in the vernaculars. A good example of this is the *Ramcaritmanas*, an adaptation of the Sanskrit *Ramayana* composed in a literary dialect of Hindi by the sixteenth-century poet Tulsi Das.

The important transformation wrought by the *Ramcaritmanas* is that Sanskrit, "the language of the gods," has been displaced by Hindi, "the language of the people." Or rather, Tulsi's text elevated the vernacular to to the status of a sacred language, and the first step had thereby been taken toward making Hindi the language of the Hindus in the North Indian arena. It has never become the language of the entire Hindu nation, though, despite strenuous efforts on the part of the Indian state after Independence. These efforts were resisted in many parts of India, but especially in the South. The fact that the languages of South India were Dravidian, whereas Hindi and Sanskrit were Indo-Aryan, was interpreted in more general racial and cultural terms. In Tamil Nadu this interpretation inspired a broader anti-Brahman, Dravidian movement, in which Brahmanical Hinduism, Sanskrit, and Hindi were seen as aspects of a long history of racist domination of the South by the North. The native Tamilians had to liberate their language and their culture from this oppression. All this is quite ironic when one realizes that the formulation of modern devotional Hinduism in the North was deeply influenced by South Indian poetic and philosophical movements.

As a result of the split between South and North on the Hindi issue, English has remained the language for elite communication in the country as a whole.[4] For our purposes, however, a more important corollary of the development of Hindi as the language of the Hindu nation is the emergence of Urdu as the language of the

Muslim nation. Urdu is very similar to Hindi except in two respects. First, unlike Hindi, Urdu is written in the Arabic script. Second, where standard Hindi employs Sanskrit-derived words, Urdu uses words derived from Persian and Arabic. Like Sanskrit, Persian and Arabic are the languages of civilization. Persian is the language of the court and of court poetry; Arabic is the language of the Qur'an and therefore the language of God. The words of the Qur'an have a power that goes beyond their direct, literal meaning, very similar to the Sanskrit *mantra*. This is quite evident in Islamic magic, which gives every word in the Arabic alphabet a number. A verse from the Qur'an is chosen for a particular magical purpose, its numerical value determined, and then the number is manipulated using a special numerical table to yield an amulet, a slip of paper with the numbers written on it. This amulet is then swallowed or worn on the body. It is the direct power of the words that brings about a certain desired result. "Knowing" the Qur'an, then, is a knowledge (*'ilm*) required for the theological and juridical pursuits of the *'alim* but also for the magical pursuits of the Sufi adept. In that sense Clifford Geertz's term *scripturalism* to describe the anti-Sufi tendencies in Islam is not entirely apposite, since it is orthodoxy, the right way of dealing with the scripture, that is at issue in Islamic debate, not the status of the scripture itself.

Persian was for a long time the administrative language of India. This implies that, until the end of the nineteenth century, Hindus who wanted to become members of the bureaucracy had to learn Persian. My Brahman informant and friend, the late Ram Raksha Tripathi, who guided me during my study of Ayodhya, was a man in his sixties when I first met him in 1977. He told me that, although his father had been the religious advisor of the Maharaja of Ayodhya, he had not taught him Sanskrit in his early years but Persian, to prepare him for an administrative career. Tripathi ended up as a teacher of English and Hindi, but as a poet he still loved Persian and continued to write poetry in Urdu. This anecdote serves to convey the complex language picture at the beginning of the twentieth century, in which a son of a Brahman priest might well learn Persian but not Sanskrit.

As the language of the Qur'an but not of government, Arabic remained more limited in India. Arabic is the language of prayer and of recitation and, to some extent, is taught in Qur'anic schools, but it is only clerics who have any real command of the language. Moreover, with the advent of the British Persian was gradually replaced by English, which remains the dominant administrative language in India. It is thus Urdu, with its distinctive script and vocabulary, that has become the characteristic idiom of Muslims. Urdu is the language in which lay people converse about religious matters. But, as in the case of Hindi, it is also a literary language, which brings us to the relation between the spoken and the written in Urdu and Hindi.

In a recent paper David Lelyveld examines some general trends in the creation of "communal" languages in the colonial period and the eclipse of a language called Hindustani.[5] This language was "discovered" by John Gilchrist, a Scottish physician and sometime indigo farmer. According to Gilchrist, Hindustani was a unified language that had three major dialects, which could be distinguished by the extent to which they used Sanskrit, Persian and Arabic, or ordinary Hindi words. Gilchrist was prepared to publish his lexicon of Hindustani in both the Arabic script and *nagari* (the Sanskrit script), as well as in Roman transliteration. The important point Lelyveld makes is that Gilchrist's project, undertaken at the end of the eighteenth century, to publish a Hindustani lexicon and grammar based directly on speech was very similar to language projects in England and France during the same period. Here, however, the clientele was not indigenous but were the officers of the East India Company. It was above all else a colonial project intended to further rapport with the natives. This project continued in a transformed manner when India became part of the British empire in the latter half of the nineteenth century. Colonial empiricism was responsible for the creation of linguistic surveys to identify the spoken languages of India in order to replace Persian with "vernacular" languages. Gilchrist's Hindustani now came to be equated with Urdu, which was standardized and given official status over a large part of North India, while a number of geographically defined dialects of Hindi were also distinguished. Urdu, Hindi, and Hindustani are all three literary languages, constructed to suit the purposes of literate elites. The spoken languages show an enormous variation within a strongly multilingual context. It is therefore especially by their script—the *nagari* of Sanskrit and the Arabic script— that Hindi and Urdu are identified. It is also in their written form that they tie up with the idea of civilization, which is simultaneously that of religion.

It was in the early nineteenth century, when Persian was gradually being replaced by Urdu as the "vernacular" to serve as the administrative language in a growing colonial bureaucracy, that both British educators and certain Hindu elites started to press for a standardized Hindi as an alternative to Urdu. Urdu was seen as too Persianized and still too far from the language of the people to bring the administration in touch with those it governed. This trend crystallized in the 1860s in opposing language movements, which supported either Hindi or Urdu. The Hindi movement identified Hindi with the Hindu majority and Urdu (with its "foreign" script) with the Muslim minority. The defenders of Urdu pointed to the indigenous character of the language, the long history of the use of Arabic script for administrative and poetic purposes, and its close relation to everyday speech. In the end the latter accepted the imposed "minority" status of Urdu and defended it as such.

A catalyzing role in this linguistic identification was played by the employment policy of the colonial government. In 1877 the government of Awadh and the Northwestern Provinces demanded an examination to prove competence in the "vernacular" as a qualification for government service. The competition was mainly between Hindu Kayasths and Muslims, who favored using Urdu, on the one hand, and high-caste Hindus (Brahmans, Rajputs, Khatris, and Baniyas) wanting to promote Hindi, on the other.[6] As Christopher King rightly observes, the economic well-being of these elite groups depended very much on the outcome of this language conflict. However, rather than seeing the language issue as simply a set of symbols manipulated by the elite to advance their own interests, the issue is, in my view, an excellent example of how in the colonial period older discourses about language and religious community came to be transformed into linguistic nationalism.

Of course, the development of Hindi as the language of Hindus and Urdu as the language of Muslims is as fraught with contradictions as any other aspect of religious nationalism. Lelyveld provides us with the fascinating story of the role played by All-India Radio. In 1940 A. S. Bukhari, director-general of All-India Radio, appointed two well-known writers of Hindi and Urdu, respectively, to prepare a lexicon for Hindustani news broadcasts. Between the two of them they had to find the most common, precise, and, if possible, neutral term from either Urdu or Hindi to create a new Hindustani, a language, so to say, of secular nationalism. The lexicon took five years to prepare and, at that point, it was already a lost cause, given the chaos of partition. What emerged with partition was Urdu as the official language of Pakistan and of the Muslim minority within India, and Hindi as an all-India language, a position shared with English, as well as the main language of Hindu nationalism.

Whatever the official language policy of the state in Pakistan or in India it remained far from successful. East Pakistan became Bangladesh as a result of Bengali nationalism, in which language was a prime symbol of identity. In India language diversity continued to play an important role in conflicts about state boundaries within the Indian union, in Maratha nationalism, in Tamil nationalism, and in Punjabi/Sikh nationalism. The languages of education are Hindi, English, and, when the official language of the state is not Hindi, another language. The situation therefore remains multilingual. Moreover, in an interesting twist of history, Urdu, which is acknowledged by Hindus and Muslims alike to be a great language for love poetry and songs, has been adopted in a more or less "refined" way in film songs. Therefore, ironically, while Hindi is both promoted and resisted in South India as an official language policy, Urdu/Hindustani infiltrates via films and songs. English has remained the language of the higher echelons of the administration and, more and more, is the language of modern literature and fashion. The English influence is also "brought home" by significant transnational Indian populations, whose movements affect fashions in metropoles like Bombay.

The *Ramayana*

The production of a national language is sometimes accompanied by the production of a national text. This indeed seems to be the case in Hindu nationalism. The earliest and most influential text we have of the story of Rama is the Sanskrit *Ramayana*, attributed to the poet Valmiki and probably composed in the first few centuries B.C. The earliest major vernacular retelling of the story was written in Tamil by the twelfth-century author Kampan. It was only in the sixteenth century that the poet Tulsi Das managed to create a highly influential North Indian vernacular version of the story. This became the authoritative text for the worship of Rama in the following centuries to the extent that the British deemed it "the Bible of North India" or, in F. S. Growse's words, "the best and most trustworthy guide to the popular living faith of its people."[7] Very striking in this kind of devotional text is that it is simultaneously available in a written and in an oral form. It thus bridges the gap between orality and literacy of which Jack Goody makes so much. So, while people do read the *Ramcaritmanas*, many know it only from recitation by relatives or by professional reciters. It has a metric form that makes it easy to memorize at least parts of it, so that in everyday conversation with "civilized people" one is regularly confronted with an appropriate homily from Tulsi Das's story. It has also been adopted in street theater and even cultural performances of grand scale, such as the Ram Lila of Banaras, which is sponsored by the raja of Banaras.[8]

There is no evidence at all that the spread of the printed *Ramcaritmanas* has marginalized the oral performance. On the contrary, one might perhaps argue that the oral performance of this text in all its diversity has been furthered by "print-capitalism." The Gita Press, located in Gorakhpur, Uttar Pradesh, and founded in the early 1920s by Hanuman Prasad Poddar, a member of an orthodox Marwari merchant family, has played a significant role in making printed texts of the *Ramcaritmanas* available in pocket as well as folio editions. Philip Lutgendorf quotes the 1983 edition of the pocket version, which notes in its title page that the book has gone through seventy-two printings for a total issue of 5,695,000 copies, with two printings of 100,000 copies each in 1983 alone.[9] Lutgendorf goes on to show how these printed editions are used in recitations and are themselves the object of veneration.

A fascinating "framing" of the recitation of the text takes place in so-called *mahayajnas* (great sacrifices), often sponsored by rich businessmen, in which 108 (a sacred number) Brahmans recite the text. Here the "ancient" Vedic ritual of sacrifice provides a Sanskritizing frame for the reading of a vernacular devotional text. To some extent, one may argue that this amounts to a reappropriation of a devotional tradition by the Brahman voices of orthodoxy, but we have to realize that in fact the *Ramcaritmanas* and its theology has become the orthodoxy and that Brahmans have to position themselves in relation to that orthodoxy by claiming it as their own. This is certainly an important part in the construction of *sanatana dharma* as the religion of the Hindu nation, and it is thus not surprising that, according to Lutgendorf, the first of these "sacrifices" seems to have been inspired by Swami Karpatri, a Shaivite ascetic and founder of an extremist Hindu nationalist party, the Ram Rajya Parishad.[10] Despite Karpatri's reactionary tendency to go back to a long outlived Brahman Vedic orthodoxy, he was able to assist in this cultural bricolage of sacrificial and devotional elements. It is this same bricolage that has proved so successful in the VHP's staging of Vedic "sacrifices" as political rituals.

When Mahatma Gandhi wanted to communicate his political ideal of *ramrajya*, the ideal social order of lord Rama in Ayodhya, he turned to the language of Tulsi Das. Gandhi continually quoted the *Ramcaritmanas*, with which most literate Hindus would be familiar, in order to bolster his political views. If Indians were able to live according to the high ideals of this text, they would be able to overcome poverty, untouchability, and foreign rule. There is little doubt that, at least in North India, Gandhi's constant reference to Rama and Rama's just rule, *ramrajya*, had an almost millenarian impact on the Hindu population. It is also clear that it was the sort of appeal that totally ignored and alienated the "Muslim other" in India. Even though Gandhi gave his usual "inclusivist" interpretation of the *Ramcaritmanas*, Hindu radicals were prone to use the devotional message for "antidemonic" purposes. The struggle between Rama the good and Ravana the evil can easily be used as a conceptual framework to understand and legitimize the struggle of Hindus against Muslims.

This is not to say, of course, that the Hindu nationalist reading is the only way Indians can interpret and use the *Ramayana* politically. Interestingly, at the same time that Gandhi gave his inclusivist interpretation of the text, it was also used precisely to resist that inclusion. In the South the *Ramayana* played a significant role in the articulation of the Dravidian movement. E. V. Ramasami Naicker, the most prominent leader of the Dravidian movement, developed from the 1920s onward a consistent attack on the *Ramayana* as a text of Brahmanical hegemony. In his pamphlets he attacked the worship of Rama, whom he depicted as a depraved character, while defending the demon king Ravana as a Dravidian hero. In his view the *Ramayana's* story of the march of the North Indian Rama on Lanka, the capital of the South Indian Ravana, tells of the Hindu subjugation of Dravidian culture. This interpretation allowed him to promulgate a cultural separatism and mount an attack on Brahman privilege in the South. As Paula Richman shows in a recent article, Ramasami's dramatic campaign, which culminated in a highly publicized burning of pictures of Rama in 1956, was inherited by the leaders of Dravidian parties, who moved from pamphlets to film as the preferred form of propaganda for their cause.[11]

Obviously, regional and political differences in narration and interpretation have continued to exist. However, according to some observers, the television broadcast of the *Ramayana* has been an important step in the homogenization of the narrative and interpretive tradition.[12] Between January 1987 and July 1988 a serialized adaptation of the *Ramayana* in seventy-eight episodes was broadcast on national television. It not only became the most popular program ever seen on Indian television but also turned out to be a social event of great significance. Put on twenty-six video cassettes it became available for worldwide sale, adorned with the following blurb: "The Greatest Indian Epic. Treasured for over 10,000 years. Enshrining Ideals That Are Ageless. Teaching Lessons That Are Timeless." Though based primarily on Valmiki's Sanskrit *Ramayana* and Tulsi Das's Hindi *Ramcaritmanas*, other regional retellings were used to create the all-India television version. Lutgendorf quotes a figure according to which some 80 to 100 million people watched the most popular episodes.[13] Part of the reason the series could attract such a huge audience—roughly twice the estimated daily viewership of 40 to 60 million—was that many television sets were mounted in public locations. Even those who did not understand Hindi still watched. Newspaper reports say that Indian life ground to a standstill at the time of the broadcast. Hindus all over the country watched with a religious attitude, having in fact a *darshan*, a glimpse of the sacred, on *durdarshan*, television. A particularly striking response was that of untouchable sweepers in North India, some of whom call themselves "Balmiks," claiming descent from the Sanskrit sage Valmiki, the alleged composer of the Sanskrit *Ramayana* and the guru of Rama. When they learned that there were no plans to depict the events of the final book of the epic—Sita's exile in Valmiki's hermitage and his education of Rama's son—they launched a strike. Sanitation workers all over North India stopped doing their job and forced the union government to prolong the series to include these episodes.[14]

The long, rambling television narrative continued the tradition of the extended oral narration of the epic. The serialized format was thus immediately recognizable to a huge audience already in some way acquainted with the story. Similarly, the very static television performance seemed to continue the tradition of tableaux vivants (*jhanki*) used in the theater performance of the Ram Lila. The actors were revered (as in the Ram Lila) as embodiments of the gods, and the director, who also acted as narrator, could not extract himself from the developing religious drama. He gave up tobacco and alcohol, and the entire film crew followed a vegetarian regimen. All this is squarely within the tradition of the Ram Lila. One has to realize here that in Hindu devotion theater is regarded as the higher reality of the gods, in which humans can participate by playing a part. Film and video are media that interact directly with this kind of devotional expectation. One does not simply watch the story of Rama unfold in many episodes, but as a viewer one is visually related to the cosmic drama of Rama's life. Television allows many millions to be connected at the same time and thereby creates the sensation of the unity of a religious gathering (*satsang*), while allowing everyone to stay home with their own family. This is exactly what Anderson has argued was the doing of the novel, namely, the imagining of a nation of individuals, and so it is not surprising that the success of this telecast has been related to the recent upsurge in religious nationalism.[15]

There is a long-standing relation between politics and cinema. This is especially true for South India, where movie stars like M. G. Ramachander and N. T. Rama Rao have become leading politicians who have used their films to convey political messages and their film personae to create populist leadership. This legacy has also been brought to North India, where movie stars such as Amitabh Bacchan have increasingly sought to begin a political career. In the case of the televised *Ramayana* one cannot argue that the political career of any particular movie star has been served. On a more subtle level, however, Romila Thapar wonders whether the state was not projecting a "mainstream national culture" through this broadcast.[16] She argues that the televised version "eliminates the range of folk and popular versions or alternative versions even within the same religious tradition. There is a very deliberate choice of one tradition and the elevation of this tradition (remoulded in accordance with contemporary tastes and values) to national status."[17] Lutgendorf has responded to this view, which is widespread among Indian intellectuals and in the Indian media, by arguing that such an interpretation gives television too much of a hegemonic force and that the *Ramayana* tradition remains open enough to allow for continuous reinterpretations and retellings.[18] In general I agree with that response, but I do think that Thapar and others are right in observing a tendency to use the *Ramayana* for the creation of a "Hindu nation." The point is, however, that the political use of the Rama story for the legitimation of political rule is already old. We have already seen such a use in the relation between Ayodhya and the Guptas in the fifth century A.D. In the age of nationalism the politics of Rama devotion has been transformed, so that the legitimation of a royal dynasty has been replaced by that of the "Hindu nation." The television *Ramayana* simply continues certain tendencies in the oral tradition that have always stressed the "national" character of the *Ramayana*, notably in the exegesis of the most famous present-day expounder, Ram Kinkar. The advantage of television is obviously that it reaches a much larger audience and can use special effects in the service of the nationalist enterprise.

One would perhaps expect Muslims to have distanced themselves from the national ritual of watching the *Ramayana* on television. There are no reliable data on this, but if my own observations count for anything here, I must report that many of my Muslim friends watched the drama as fervently as their Hindu neighbors. If I may add a random observation, it struck me that my Muslim acquaintances in general knew relatively little of the epic and thus saw the broadcast as a wonderful way to get introduced to it. Often they were quite thrilled by what they saw as a totally engrossing drama, but at the same time they distanced themselves through comments like "How can these Hindus believe all these things?" This makes at least one important thing clear, namely, that the telecast of a quintessentially Hindu drama had nothing to do with an attempt to convert Muslims to Hinduism or to a Hindu nation. One might perhaps even argue that it reinforced the boundaries between the two communities by informing Muslims about Hindu practice and belief, with its multitude of gods and demons. The objective of those who controlled the broadcast was to enhance the multiculturalist project of the state, first by showing that various regional Hindu traditions had contributed to this television version and, second, by attempting to incorporate non-Hindu contributions by citing an Urdu *Ramayana* in the credits and by making occasional references to Jesus, Buddha, and Mohammad in the text.

Despite this pluralist slant of the telecast I would suggest that it has facilitated the Ayodhya campaign of the VHP and BJP. It is difficult to imagine the "naturalness" of L. K. Advani's impersonation of Rama in his campaign without taking the recent telecast into account. Anuradha Kapur has argued that the televised *Ramayana* emphasized an image of Rama as a crusader, a warrior for the good, thereby transforming the tranquil Lord of the Universe.[19] This is indeed evident in the iconography of Rama in the propaganda of the VHP, in which Rama is shown as a heavily armed warrior. The devotional movement toward sweetness and femininity in the worship of Rama seems to have been jolted toward militancy as a result of this more martial portrayal of Rama and his actions in the *Ramayana*. Moreover, through the power of television, Ayodhya and Rama's life in and return to that city are brought very close to the viewer. The scenes in Ayodhya may seem to a Westerner rather unrealistic. Nonetheless, the tremendous success of the telecast attests to its emotional impact. While the effect of the telecast is in principle not different from what a whole range of media has been doing over a long period of time, namely, spreading the story of Rama throughout India, the televised version made the tale more compelling for a nation of Hindu viewers. There can be little doubt that Ayodhya, as a real, historical place in Uttar Pradesh, has been effectively connected by the VHP and BJP campaign to the Ayodhya of television. It comes, then, as no surprise that Hindus felt outraged by the idea that the birthplace of this god, whose televised life they had been so touched by, had been "demolished by Muslims." It is striking how history and televised story have become intermingled in the emotions related to the Ayodhya affair, and on a national scale, no less.

The Novel and Rushdie's Novel

The birth of the novel is often seen as connected to that of the nation. According to Benedict Anderson, the novel and the newspaper were the forms used for representing the imagined nation.[20] The emergence of the novel as a literary genre was taken as a national allegory. What Anderson sees as crucial in the great shift from "traditional" texts, such as the epic, to the novel is the importance given in the novel to homogeneous time, measured by clock and calendar. The modern novel links its "interior time" with the "exterior time" of the readers, so that both the characters and the readers are moving in the same manner through calendrical time and sociological space.[21] To show that the novel is indeed different from previous literary forms, Anderson draws attention to an early nineteenth-century Tagalog text that takes place in a fabulous land removed in time and place from the Philippines. This text was meant to be sung, not read. It did not have a chronological order; rather, the story was conveyed through a series of flashbacks.[22] It was a traditional epic, which had, in Anderson's view, a form totally different from that of a novel. Anderson compares this epic with the first Filipino novel, written by Jose Rizal, an "Indio" who is called the "Father of Filipino Nationalism."

Of course Anderson is right in assuming that, if the novel is truly novel, it has indeed to distinguish itself from previous literary forms, most obviously that of the epic. Whereas the epic shows the roots of the present in an ancient past, the novel addresses contemporary everyday reality. Whereas the epic depends on oral tradition, the novel only emerges with the advent of printing. According to Timothy Brennan, "the epic's 'ritual' view gives way to the novel's political one."[23] The epic uses a sacred language; the novel speaks in the national language, with its many references to class difference. However, it is remarkable in both Anderson's and Brennan's arguments to what extent this discussion by literary theorists reproduces the dichotomy of the "traditional" and the "modern."

This dichotomy has recently been overshadowed by another dichotomous opposition, namely, that between "first-world novels" and "third-world novels." According to the literary theorist Fredric Jameson, the third-world novel "will not offer the satisfactions of Proust or Joyce," but it still has the power for political and social critique, which has been lost by the first-world modernist novel.[24] Thus, Jameson argues, all third-world texts have to be read as national allegories: "The story of the private individual destiny is always an allegory of the embattled situation of the public third-world culture and society."[25] Moreover, these texts use satire to criticize a politically and economically corrupt present in order to point toward a social utopia. In Jameson's view, therefore, the connection between nationalism and the novel exists only in the early novels of the West and in the "third-world novel" of today. Jameson's argument is flawed, as Aijaz Ahmad has convincingly shown.[26] Obviously, the "third-world" category is untenable. The texts Jameson writes about form but a minor fraction of the total number of texts in Asia and Africa, and most of these texts have never been translated into English. Jameson thus refers to texts that are in an interesting way more part of the canon of "world literature" than of a marginal "third-world" literature.

Little of India's contribution to this "world literature," which principally appeals to metropolitan readers, comes from translations of texts written in Indian languages. India has a sizeable "Indo-English" literature associated with famous contemporary writers like R. K. Narayan and Bharati Mukherjee. As is to be expected with a category like "Indo-English," it becomes fuzzy at the edges. Can V. S. Naipaul and his brother Shiva Naipaul, third-generation descendants from Indian indentured laborers in Trinidad, be counted among the "Indo-English" writers? V. S. Naipaul would deny it, since he sees his literary production as part of an English-language world literature. One might speculate that he would see the fact that he writes in English as ultimately connected to a world history of which transcontinental labor migration and the new literary form of the novel are different, but related, aspects. Indeed, Naipaul makes at points an explicit comparison between the journey of his forefathers to Trinidad, Gandhi's imagination of the nation in South Africa, and his own form of investigative journalism and literary realism.

Rather than defining the novel in terms of its formal aspects as different from the epic Naipaul defines it in terms of its content as "a form of social inquiry, and as such outside the Indian tradition."[27] Naipaul emphasizes the fact that the British introduced the novel to India. When he goes on to discuss the work of one of India's most admired contemporary novelists, R. K. Narayan, he gets down to what he sees as a fundamental lack in Narayan's work, namely, a lack of a modern sense of history and thereby of human possibility.[28] Naipaul sees Narayan's work as religious, as "intensely Hindu." To the extent that Narayan in his later work allows history to intrude into the equilibrium of Hindu civilization, it is indeed an "intrusion," a violation, and the only response of the characters a "retreat."[29] This is all Naipaul's interpretation of Narayan's work, and it is a perfect example of a modernist reading. Needless to say it does not exhaust possible interpretations, but that is not the point here. It is important to see that Naipaul argues that one can have the modern form of the novel but still retain the religious attitude that limits its content of social inquiry. Certainly Narayan does write about contemporary life in a frame of time and space that relates himself, his characters, and his readers in a way different from that of the "traditional storyteller." He writes about an imaginary place, Malgudi, which can be seen as a "typical" Indian town, and not about a mythological place where the gods reside. But how different is this from the approach of the "traditional storyteller" who constantly interlaces his text with references to the present? To what extent is "social inquiry" or even the sense that the life of the characters is contemporaneous with that of the reader (or listener, or viewer) bound to one literary form? Moreover, one may ask, is "the novel" really only one literary form?

What I would suggest is that the literary form of modernity portrays itself as "novel" but that on close examination there is a great deal of continuity in form and content between the epic and the novel. A crucial transformation is that brought about by printing, but it is important to realize that not only the novel is printed but also the Bible and the Qur'an and the *Ramcaritmanas*, so that reading in social isolation while being aware that a million others are doing the same is not restricted to what Brennan calls the "mass ceremony" of the novel.[30] Indeed, one might perhaps argue that Protestantism stimulated a direct communion with the divine through the private reading of the Bible and that printing made this possible. Thus, not only does the novel allow for an imagining of the nation but other textual forms may do so as well. I would suggest that, in the novel and *Nationalliteratur* as such, one finds the secular nation imagined and that Protestantism has aided the transition from religious text to literature as the site of highest values. While in Western Christian societies this transition has been at least partly accomplished, in other societies religious texts have continued to dominate value orientations. It is thus in texts like the Qur'an and the *Ramayana* that one finds the religious community as the basis of the nation imagined. The clash between the novel and the sacred text and thus between opposed imaginings of community forms the core of the Rushdie affair, which we will discuss later in this section.

While, as we have seen, a "traditional text" like the *Ramayana* can be "nationalized" and become the form in which the nation is imagined, an important side of the modern novel may well be that it is not written with reference to the nation as a bounded group of "national readers." Narayan, however Hindu he may be, does not write for a national audience. Rather, he writes in English for a transnational audience and takes care that his references to Hindu tradition do not require too much prior knowledge. It is precisely this literary objectification of culture for a transnational audience, however, that produces national culture. It is in the dialectic of the national and the transnational that the late-twentieth-century novel situates itself.

A simple but important observation here is that there is an "Indo-English" literature. The continuing importance of English for elite communication makes it the main language of the Indian Administrative Service, the all-India bureaucratic framework of the Indian state. Moreover, in 1983 English-language newspapers accounted for some 19 percent of the total number of newspapers in the country.[31] A relatively broad national elite continues to read the news in English, watch English news on television, and send their children to English-medium schools. This implies that those who want to use English for their literary activities will find an English-reading public in India of considerable magnitude. Since English not only connects people within India but also connects Indians to non-Indian English speakers, Indian writers contribute to that growing category of transnational literature in the English language, to which the "English" born in Britain, Americans, Australians, Africans, and Asians, as well as various diasporic peoples, also contribute. An interesting reflection of this can be seen in the 1991 Booker Prize contest. Three of the five contestants for Britain's largest literary prize were "immigrants" to Britain. The prize went to a Nigerian-born author. Of course, not only English allows for this transnational phenomenon, but also Arabic, French, and Spanish. Moreover, it is interesting to see how the limitations of translation regulate the communication between these larger transnational linguistic communities, so that Gabriel García Marquez, writing in Spanish, comes to India in English translation rather than in Hindi or any of the regional languages of India.

The writing and reading of English is sometimes seen as a sign of the colonization of the mind, of Westernization and thus alienation. The very widespread use of English as a language of culture in India by the huge urban middle class, however, has more or less removed the emphasis from "foreignness" to class distinction. Much fun was made of Rajiv Gandhi's attempts to speak Hindi, and his failures were interpreted as a sign of his "alienation" from "the people." The Nehru family was certainly not viewed as un-Indian, but simply as a Westernized elite. It is thus not at all "unnational" to write and read English and, as in the case of the writer R. K. Narayan, not at all "un-Hindu" either. However, it does link one's national identity with a cosmopolitan community of readers and writers. One interesting outcome of Lord Macauley's colonial project to make Indians read British literature in order to civilize them is that a metropolitan literary audience has begun to read English-language novels written by Indian writers.

The complications and intricacies of the modern, transnational novel today are revealed in the work of Salman Rushdie, who is, by now, the most famous Indo-English novelist. Rushdie's literary project refutes V. S. Naipaul's claim that Indians have to get rid of their mythical fantasies to be able to use the novel as a tool for social and political inquiry into the real world. It is interesting to see that the notion of the "national allegory" fits Naipaul's modernist realism much less well than it does Rushdie's postmodernist "magical realism." Rushdie's work is deeply allegorical in the sense that its spirit is, to use Jameson's words, "profoundly discontinuous, a matter of breaks and heterogeneities, of the multiple polysemia of the dream rather than the homogeneous representation of the symbol."[32] Nevertheless, despite enormous literary and political differences, both Naipaul and Rushdie belong squarely to a secular Enlightenment tradition in their rejection of religious culture. Rushdie's literary device is the "traditional" frame story that encompasses myths, family chronicles, and all kinds of other digressions. At the same time, his emphasis on comic dialogues and his juxtaposition of seemingly incongruous scenes resembles the "modern" narrative of the Bombay movie. Rushdie's first claim to fame was an epic novel that won the Booker Prize in Britain, *Midnight's Children* (1981). This book deals with the modern history of independent India, mingling acid references to Mrs. Gandhi's Emergency with Hindu myths. His work is related to the so-called magical realism developed in Latin American literature by writers such as García Marquez but also to eighteenth-century English works such as Laurence Sterne's *Tristram Shandy*. In another celebrated novel, *Shame* (1983), Rushdie deals in a similar way with the modern history of Pakistan. In these two works religion and politics, democracy and totalitarianism are confronted head on in a form that might be called a "bricolage" of epic, novelistic, and cinematic styles. The language of these novels is English, sometimes mixed with Urdu terms (for example, "this Angrezi I am forced to write," in *Shame*). While these novels were mostly read in the West and drew critical acclaim from a small section of the reading public—what one might call the "literary audience"—his subsequent novel, *The Satanic Verses* (1988), found a response far beyond that audience.

India banned the book on 15 October 1988. Demonstrations in Bradford—including the burning of the book—followed in February 1989. And on 14 February the publication of the book turned into the Rushdie affair when the call to Muslims all over the world to execute Rushdie was issued by the Iranian leader, the Ayatollah Khomeini. Much has been written about the Rushdie affair in the meantime, including several books, so I will limit myself to a discussion of some of the most salient aspects in the context of my larger argument. It should be clear that the issues raised by the Rushdie affair—transnational migration, the political and religious imagination of community, literature and revelation, gender and sexuality—are very much the same as those raised in the rest of this book.

The central character in *The Satanic Verses* is a movie actor who has played all the mythological parts in Bombay's dream factory but now starts to dream of himself as the archangel Gibreel. He has a vision in which he sees God sitting on a bed, a man of about the same age as himself, of medium height, fairly heavily built, with salt-and-pepper beard cropped close to the line of the jaw. What struck him most was that the apparition was balding, seemed to suffer from dandruff and wore glasses. This was not the Almighty he had expected. "Who are you?" he asked with interest. . . .

"Ooparvala," the apparition answered, "The Fellow Upstairs."

"How do I know you're not the other One," Gibreel asked craftily, "Neechayvala, the Guy from Underneath?"[33]

This short, funny, but if you wish, blasphemous passage shows a God who strikingly resembles the author. Indeed, whatever Gibreel sees or does in dreaming or in waking originates in the imagination of his creator. The passage serves the novel's most ambitious goal: to explore the boundaries between sacred texts and fiction, between divine revelation and literary inspiration. We may discern three interrelated themes in *The Satanic Verses*, namely, migration, love, and religious inspiration. It is the last one that triggered the international Muslim reaction, although the other two are germane to the nature of the reaction. The absolute Truth, revealed to Muhammad through Gibreel, is juxtaposed and compared to Rushdie's inspiration. This is a legitimate exploration in the post-Enlightenment world of the writer and his "literary audience," and by no stretch of the imagination can it be seen as unacceptable to Muslims. However, when this theme is combined with a satire of the sexual politics of the Prophet and of Islam in general—a subject already broached in *Shame*—it becomes an insult to the Muslim community and its religious discourses.

Despite its treatment of Islamic history and of South Asian Muslims, as well as its occasional use of Urdu idioms and film songs, it is clear that the book was not written with a South Asian Muslim audience in mind. It was written for a post-Christian, secular, Western audience that could be amused by a literary treatment of exotic beliefs and histories. I call this audience post-Christian because I think that the lampooning of the Prophet has a particular history in Christian-Muslim rivalry, which has been inherited by the modern readership. That practicing Muslims would take note of what were for them insulting passages in the book came as a surprise to both the author and the literary audience. It came as even more of a surprise that they would not accept it as literature, a higher good, but would react to it politically as blasphemy.

A danger of my formulation thus far is of course that it gives the impression that there was a unified, homogeneous Muslim outrage. The opposite is the case, and one might even argue that the articulation of the Rushdie affair in terms of an internal debate among Muslims has given it its particular dynamics. We have to consider at least three interconnected levels at which the affair emerged. The first Muslim reaction to *The Satanic Verses* came from Muslim politicians in India, whose demand for a ban on the book was quickly accepted by Rajiv Gandhi's government. This course of events can only be appreciated if we recall that these Muslim politicians had recently won success in mobilizing Muslim opinion and had voted against a Supreme Court decision that interfered with Muslim personal law, the Shah Banu case (discussed in chapter 3). Gandhi's government obviously wanted to avoid a renewed mobilization in the face of already heightened communal tensions produced by the Ayodhya affair. While Rushdie reacted angrily to this ban in an open letter to Rajiv Gandhi printed in the *New York Times* (19 October 1988), throwing doubt on the secular and democratic nature of Indian society ("the right to freedom of expression is at the foundation of any democratic society"), the fact that India did not allow a novel to be imported did not, predictably, cause the metropolitan "literary audience" great concern.

Despite all the emphasis in literary criticism on exile literature as a special category, writers are not the only migrants. Indeed, one of the important features in the "decolonization" of South Asia is the increased settlement of South Asian migrants in the land of their former colonizer. The second phase of the Rushdie affair, the loud protest by South Asian Muslims in Britain—a part of "the West"—was rather more difficult to ignore than the banning of the book in India. The fact that the migrant community with which Rushdie, as a South Asian migrant himself, felt such a strong solidarity turned against him came as a terrible blow to the author. However, the whole affair shows the extent to which Rushdie, as a regular liberal spokesman for the civil rights of this community and against the racism afflicting it, had been out of touch with what goes on in it. This is at least partly a result of class difference. Most of the South Asian immigrants are members of the working class who were compelled by economic reasons to migrate and have been badly hit by the recession and by unemployment, whereas Rushdie is a highly educated, very successful member of a cosmopolitan South Asian elite. There is little doubt that religion and religious community play a totally different role in the lives of most immigrants and in that of the celebrated author. To be subjected to everyday racism in British society was one thing, but to have their Prophet insulted by someone who was at least partly one of their own must have been felt as treason.

The third phase of the Rushdie affair was initiated by Khomeini's call for the execution of the author. This related the plight of British Muslims with the struggle for power in the international Muslim community between Sunni Saudi Arabia and Shiʿa Iran, which has come to several outbursts during the hajj. In Britain, as in other European countries with large groups of migrant workers, there is a competition between Iran and Saudi Arabia in terms of funding for Islamic organizations. In the context of this struggle, Khomeini's intervention established that Iran dared to speak up against the Satanic West on behalf of all Muslims.

However, this claim was at once rejected by Sunni Muslims in Surat, amongst whom I was living at the height of the affair in 1989. Both Khomeini's intervention and the simultaneous anti-Rushdie riots in Bombay, engineered by Imam Bukhari of Delhi, were denounced as political games in the same way as Rushdie himself denounced them. Moreover, Indian Sunnis tended to see Khomeini as a typical Shiʿa radical who wanted himself to usurp the place of the Prophet and was as such a greater danger to Islam than Rushdie. The simple fact that there is this major schism between Shiʿites and Sunnis should alert one to the fact that, far from being a consensus, there is instead a constant, sometimes violent, debate about orthodoxy. One should also not underestimate the extent to which South Asian Muslims both allow and enjoy satire about the institutions of Islam. As Barbara Metcalf shows, a book can be popular in Pakistan even though the author shows contempt for the clerics of Islam and claims space for Muslims like himself who are torn between faith and skepticism.[34]

Nevertheless, even if Muslims both in South Asia and Britain might well have wanted to reject the radical leadership of Khomeini, their cause was now inextricably tied to international political re-

lations between Iran and the West. Thus, in the West, their reaction
to Rushdie's book came more and more to be interpreted as an
Islamic threat to the Western secular nation-state, and the book
itself came to stand for Western secular values, foremost that of
freedom of expression. At the same time, the book was constructed
by Khomeini as an insidious attack by the Christian West on the
Islamic East, thereby reinterpreting the insult felt by South Asian
Muslims in the British context.

Rushdie's book has thus come to play a fascinating role in the
clash between the secular cultural project of the British state and
the projects of Muslim organizations in the immigrant communities.
Perhaps nothing represents this clash better than the highly publicized burning of the book by Muslims in Bradford. As Talal Asad
argues, not only does the anger of South Asian Muslims over the
publication of the book require analysis but also the outrage felt by
liberal opinion at this symbolic act.[35]

First of all, there is the issue of freedom of the press, which is a
core value of the Enlightenment. It is interesting in this connection
that Rushdie's first public appearance in the United States after the
death threats was at a celebration of the First Amendment held
at Columbia University on 12 December 1991. In his lecture he
said: "Sometimes I think that one day, Muslims will be ashamed of
what Muslims did in these days, will find the "Rushdie Affair" as
improbable as the West now finds martyr-burning. One day they
may agree that—as the European Enlightenment demonstrated—
freedom of thought is precisely freedom from religious control,
freedom from accusations of blasphemy. . . . 'Free Speech is a non-
starter,' says one of my Islamic extremist opponents. No, sir, it is
not. Free speech is the whole thing, the whole ball game. Free
speech is life itself."[36] The book burning is a straightforward rejection
of the Enlightenment value of free speech. It places religious sentiment above that value. It is clear that strong discourses that form
the basis of the construction of different kinds of community clash
here.

Second, what is involved here is not the burning of a book, but,
as Talal Asad rightly notes, of literature itself, which is as sacred to
the enlightened, literary audience as the Qur'an is to Muslims. One
of the main themes of *The Satanic Verses* is a comparison of the
revelation of the Prophet with the creation of literature. And this

is precisely what is going on in this affair: the clash of different textual imaginations of community.

Third, book burning reminds a Western audience of the Nazi period and its view of *entartete Kunst*. The interesting difference is, however, that in this case it is not the state burning the books of a despised racial and religious minority but a similar minority burning a book that is defended by the state. It is not the repression of free speech by the state and its powerful institutions but a political demonstration by a marginal immigrant community—which has not resulted in a ban on the book in Britain.

The book burning in Bradford followed the banning of *The Satanic Verses* in India, another secular state but one with a very different configuration of discourses on the nation-state, as we have seen. The difference in reaction suggests that, despite the colonial project to introduce India to modernity, the novel, or literature in its modern, secular sense, is in India not as sacred as a religious text, like the Qur'an. A simple petition by Muslim spokesmen to the prime minister of India had the required effect. This easy success in India may suggest that South Asian immigrants in Britain expected the British state to act in ways similar to those of the Indian state—both the colonial state and its postcolonial successor—namely, to recognize "communal" difference and to develop policies based upon that recognition. Instead, they found that the project of the British state was not only to make them British citizens but to transform their moral identities. Englishness had to come first, before being Muslim. In a multicultural society one does not have to become a nonbeliever, but religious identity is a private matter in civil society, not a collective matter in political society. While these ideas were also prevalent in India, the politics were more those of accommodation than of integration.

In Britain Muslims were faced by a culture that, I would suggest, had in fact been formed to distinguish the British rulers from the colonized largely on the basis of the distinction between the religious and the secular. The demise of the British empire had already shown that the colonized had rejected the superiority of the British race and, while accepting elements of British cultural discourse, had not become "brown Englishmen." The politics of difference were, in a literal sense, brought home to British public opinion by the Rushdie affair, which showed that the immigrants were not merely low-class workers but citizens with a different culture, which they wanted to protect. For the Muslim immigrants, however, the affair must have shown them that the space in which to negotiate their identity is much smaller in Britain than in India.

Conclusion

Language is certainly one of the main aspects of national identity. Hindi and Urdu are the successors of the sacred languages, Sanskrit and Arabic, and, as such, they have come to stand for the Hindu and Muslim nations of India. Hindi and English are the successors of the administrative and cultural language, Persian. Moreover, Hindi has come to stand for the present nation-state of India and English for its all-India elite. English has continued to play such an important role in India, rather than being replaced by Hindi, because there is such a great number of strong "subnational" linguistically, historically, and culturally unified regions in India. Language as the expression of national culture has played an important role in Sikh/Punjabi and in Tamil nationalisms, and it will continue to do so.

The question of which theatrical gestures, which literary forms, and which cultural media express the imagery of the nation and of the religious community deserves a more complex answer than Anderson has given. It is the epic *Ramayana* in its many forms that is constantly invoked as a repository of images of the Hindu nation. The printing of the epic has not made other forms of it disappear. Rather, it has enhanced its popularity. The televising of the *Ramayana* has done a great deal toward creating a nation of viewers, each family in its own living room but all sharing an experience of the struggle between good and evil as a historical drama. There is little doubt that the televised *Ramayana* has helped to link the imagination of the Hindu nation with a struggle against the Muslim powers of evil in the Ayodhya case. Nevertheless, the use of the *Ramayana* is not without its contradictions, as is shown in the way E. V. Ramasami used the struggle of Rama against the demon Ravana as historical evidence of the Brahmanical colonization of the Dravidian South.

The Rushdie case demonstrates the extent to which the global production and consumption of a transnational English literature is paralleled by a transnational Muslim reaction, which is refracted in a number of national arenas. The reading of Rushdie's novel as a Christian-Western attack on Islam was used in India to represent Muslims in their struggle against Hindu communalism, in Britain to preserve Muslim "honor" in a racist society, and in Iran to gain the high ground in a modern-day jihad against the satanic West. Indians in India and Britain contribute not only to English literature but also to the rejection of some of the basic Enlightenment values related to literature. Indo-English literature is undoubtedly transnational, but the Rushdie affair shows how transnational literature can still play a part in the construction of national identities, both in Britain and in India.

Epilogue

The issues raised in this book are ultimately connected to the problem of the interpretation of culture and history. We argue that nationalism is a discourse that transforms preexistent forms of culture. By this we say, in effect, that nationalism produces national culture but that the production of culture does not start with nationalism. Rather than existing in a prehistorical vacuum, "proto-nationalist" forms of culture have been produced by specific historical processes. It is important to understand the history of these cultural configurations in order to understand the way nationalist discourse transforms them. No doubt, nationalist discourse attempts to establish its authority by denying historical change, but it is not monolithic or inpenetrable. On the one hand, it holds that the nation has always existed, that the culture we see today is an entity, an unchanging national truth. On the other hand, its very logic allows for the contingencies of history, since it argues that the nation is never entirely secure. Indeed, it is always threatened by forces from outside, such as the nationalisms of others, or by betrayal from inside. In that way it resembles religious discourse, which establishes primeval, transcendental truth as orthodoxy but acknowledges the constant threat of heresy.

History is not a simple representation of "the past." Its narrative production is, in many complex ways, connected to nationalist discourse. In his famous lecture on what constitutes a nation, Renan saw serious historical scholarship as a danger to nationalism, since "forgetting and even the historical error are an essential factor of the formation of a nation."[1] Eric Hobsbawm agrees with Renan's point, arguing that a serious historian of nations and nationalism cannot be a committed political nationalist.[2] There is, of course, some truth in this, and a "serious historian" can play a role by exposing nationalist history as myth, but the matter is more complicated than Hobsbawm allows. Benedict Anderson reflects in an interesting way on nationalist "forgetting" by quoting another passage from Renan's lecture in which Renan claims that nationalism implies that "every French citizen should already have forgotten Saint Bartholomew's day, the massacres of the Midi in the thirteenth century."[3] There is an interesting contradiction here. Renan recalls these historical facts in his lecture and assumes that the audience knows them, but at the same time he argues that they "should have been forgotten already."[4] It is Anderson's argument that this is indeed how the "lessons of history" work, namely, through the remembering or forgetting of historical experiences within the national narrative. Hobsbawm's "serious historian" thus provides the "facts" for this particular process of remembering and forgetting in the historical fictions of the nation.

I find Anderson's argument very persuasive. The only problem I have with it is that it does not deal with the politics of selection of what is remembered or forgotten. It leaves too little room for contestation, for resistance within the nationalist paradigm, as well as for the existence of external discourses. Sitaram's history of Ayodhya, from which I quoted in chapter 5, falls largely outside the paradigm of nationalist narration. It does not record facts in terms of secular, serial time. As religious discourse, it remembers/forgets in a way that differs from nationalist discourses, whether secular or religious. Religious nationalism articulates religious discourse of the Sitaram type by using modern historical and archeological discourse. It remembers only a very small selection of historical data and forgets the rest. It also creates its own facts by "reconstructing" temples, such as Somanatha and the projected temple in Ayodhya. The "serious historian" may well contest the facts of these nationalist histories, as the historians at Jawaharlal Nehru University have done in the Ayodhya case. As we have seen, however, their contestation really serves another, secular narrative of the Indian nation (as befits historians at a university named after Nehru). To an important extent the reconstruction of the past implies a clash of stories deeply enmeshed in the discursive construction of present identities. That is why history is so important, because it is a part of what we think we are; it is a part of our culture.

The anthropological study of culture is as much tied to nationalist discourse as the study of history is. Clifford Geertz argues that culture "denotes an historically transmitted pattern of meanings embodied in symbols, a system of inherited conceptions expressed in symbolic forms by means of which men communicate, perpetuate, and develop their knowledge about and attitudes toward life."[5] Talal Asad has pointed out that in that definition "the very expressions 'knowledge *about*' and 'attitudes *toward*' suggest a distanced spectator-role, as compared to 'knowledge from' and 'attitudes in' living."[6] Asad's point is that Geertz defines culture in such a way as to suggest that "knowledge" and "attitudes" are isolated from the very social practices and discourses that produce and authorize them. In other words, Geertz's definition of culture allows for the separation of culture as a "thing" from the historical struggle out of which, in fact, more than one cultural form emerges. One can easily see how such a definition of culture—which is a fairly typical one in anthropology—colludes with the nationalist desire to produce a "national culture" that transcends history and life itself.

I accept Richard Handler's argument that "boundedness, continuity, and homogeneity encompassing diversity" dominate nationalist discourse and social-scientific discourse to the same degree.[7] No doubt, the study of "aspects of culture," and especially of "traditional culture," does much to freeze and objectify culture as a specific heritage, as an objective sign of a common identity. Handler's discussion of the construction of "folklore" as a cultural domain through the study of that folklore is a fine example of how cultural objectification works. In the Indian context, K. M. Munshi's Hindu nationalist activities provide a good example. Munshi's founding of the publishing house Bharatiya Vidya Bhavan for the "integration of the Indian culture in the light of modern knowledge and to suit our present-day needs and the resuscitation of its fundamental values in their pristine vigour," as well as his plans for the "reconstruction" of the Somanatha temple with the help of archeologists, show how both the publication of "national literature" and the building of "national monuments" create a national reality in which people then come to live.

While Munshi's activities can be squarely understood as part of the project of Hindu nationalism, it is also important to consider the relation between professional anthropology and the nationalist project in India. As we saw in chapter 1, the anthropology of India has done much to gather the facts for the construction of a "traditional culture," characterized by a caste system and autarkic villages. Moreover, by portraying Indian culture as dominated by an essentialized "religion" it effectively characterized this culture as "the oriental other." The anthropology of India has to an important extent inherited the orientalist perspectives of the colonial period. Indian culture is, in the view of leading anthropologists like Dumont and Marriott, a Hindu civilization.[8] In fact, Dumont does not seem even to have second thoughts about speaking of the Hindu ideology of Indian society. Such anthropological writings do much to construct the image of an integrated, unified whole, an endeavor very similar to that of nationalist ideologues.

As I have argued elsewhere, the Muslim presence in India is either ignored or marginalized.[9] The two common ways of dealing with the considerable fact of Indian Islam are either to argue that Muslims have an entirely separate culture or to argue that they share basically the same culture with Hindus. There is very little anthropological study of Muslim societies in South Asia, because anthropologists want to make a contribution to the understanding of what is understood to be the "dominant" culture of the majority. They thereby unwittingly support Hindu nationalism. However, as I have tried to demonstrate in this book, India's Hindu and Muslim cultures have been produced through a historical process in which movements, led by Brahmans and ascetics, *'ulama'* and Sufis, have played a major role. Nationalist discourse impinges on these movements and on the discourses and practices produced by them. It attempts to essentialize and reify culture to suit the narrative of the nation, a project that is supported by a "traditionalizing" anthropological and historical scholarship.

The contested nature of culture and history should be clear by now. No doubt, national traditions are "invented," as Hobsbawm and Ranger argue, and nations are "imagined," as Anderson argues, but that is not all there is to it. It is not a question of one monolithic imagination or invention, but of several contested versions. Moreover, the cultural material used for invention and imagination is historically produced and thus has to be understood historically.

The process of invention and imagination does not start with the rise of nationalist discourse; it is the process of history and culture itself.

Whether one speaks of "invention" or of "imagination," a sharp opposition between tradition and modernity seems hard to avoid in theories of nationalism. This is not surprising given that these theories are, as we have observed, often closely tied to a master narrative of modernity. Since modernity is in this narrative always secular, such theories can hardly account for the religious nationalisms we find in India. As nationalisms go, Hindu and Muslim nationalisms are "derived" from Western models, but only to a certain extent.[10] As we have seen, they are combinations of the discourses of modernity with discourses of religious community. So, indeed, in the end it seems that it is the place of religion that makes all the difference—provided one realizes that there is no such thing as "Hinduism" or "Islam." Instead, there are Hindu and Muslim religious discourses that try to establish their authority in changing societal configurations. They are internally divided and fragmented as well as contested by "external" secular discourses. It is this cultural field of debate that I have tried to sketch.

It could be argued that my account conflates and confuses "religious" discourse with "religious" nationalism. The social philosopher and psychologist Ashis Nandy, for example, sees religious and nationalist discourses as entirely separate from, and even opposed to, each other. According to Nandy, "Hinduism is a faith and a way of life," while *Hindutva*, Hindu nationalism of the Savarkar type, is "an ideology for those whose Hinduism has worn off."[11] But this line of reasoning, which makes a clear-cut distinction between an unadulterated "culture" (to be found in rural areas) and a Westernized reformist ideology (to be found in the cities), is a romantic simplification. It assumes that "culture," the "Hindu way of life," is not influenced by nationalist discourse and survives without being affected by history. This is plainly contradicted by the very broad appeal of Muslim reformist movements or the Cow Protection Movement in both rural and urban areas. It is also contradicted, at the level of religious organization, by the fact that the VHP has been able to bring major religious leaders from different parts of the country onto one platform.

In the same article, Nandy suggests that Mahatma Gandhi, as a representative of "real" Hinduism, was the enemy of *Hindutva*. Nandy might be right if he argued that Gandhi's version of Hindu nationalism was opposed to Savarkar's version, but I see no reason to assume that Gandhi's version is nearer to "the faith by which a majority of Indians still live" than is Savarkar's. This faith must then be Hindu in the Gandhian sense, but, ironically, Nandy does not realize that it was Gandhi's inclusivist "Hindu" tolerance that made the nationalism of the Congress party so alienating to Muslims. What we must understand is that there is an internal cultural debate about Hinduism and the Hindu nation in which every participant, including Nandy, claims to be a spokesman for "the people." This is certainly not a static debate, isolated from the larger context of historical change. Hindu nationalism has been strong from the days of the Cow Protection Movement in the nineteenth century through to the present day, and it belongs to the mainstream of Indian nationalism. However, there is more than one version of it, and these versions have enjoyed more or less support at different points in time.

Elsewhere, Nandy develops his distinction between faith and ideology somewhat further. By faith he means "religion as a way of life, a tradition which is definitionally non-monolithic and operationally plural." By ideology he means "religion as a sub-national identifier of populations contesting for or protecting non-religious, usually political or socio-economic interests."[12] Nandy sees religious ideology and secularism as opposed but kindred ideologies of the modern world, whereas faith is an Indian worldview in which tolerance and a fluid definition of the self provide an alternative to the boundedness of these ideologies. Nandy's message is a very good example of the ideology of tolerance in Hinduism, which I discussed in chapter 2. He does not seem to realize that his views have the same genealogy as those of the VHP, the movement he attacks, namely, Vivekananda's construction of an "Indian spirituality." His construction of the "nonmodern faith" of Indians is precisely a legacy of the very orientalism that he blames for the gradual destruction of this faith.

Nandy's argument also perpetuates a well-established view among Indian intellectuals that Indian culture, at the grass-roots level, is syncretistic and that you need political intervention from outside, as it were, in order to draw communal boundaries. Syncretism is, of course, a term as complex as the term *religion* or *culture*. It refers to the "borrowing, affirmation, or integration of concepts, symbols, or practices of one religious tradition into another by a process of selection and reconciliation."[13] While syncretism is often seen as a gradual process of melting and mixture, of "growing together," it should be understood that the "process of selection and reconciliation" is simultaneously one of rejection and contestation. Obviously, we should realize that, rather than being a bounded "thing," religion is constantly being discursively identified. It always draws upon "foreign" elements to the extent that historians often cannot unravel what comes from where. What is frequently striking in the use of the term *syncretism* is that it hides the relation of syncretism to processes of religious expansion and conversion. Syncretism as a historical phenomenon is often not a "natural" process of growth, a random combination of heterogeneous elements, but rather an appropriation of religious symbols in the construction of religious regimes.

There is an interesting link between the use of the notion of "syncretism" in a society such as India, in which religion plays a central social and political role, and the notion of "multiculturalism" in secular societies such as the United States. What we can see in multiculturalism as a project is a distinction between the "private" and the "public," in which the private extends beyond the individual to his ethnic community but in which the public remains the "common whole" of the nation. Debate about multiculturalism touches the core of the cultural project of the modern nation-state as much as debate about syncretism touches the heart of religious expansion.

The issues of syncretism and multiculturalism are crucial for the project of the contemporary Indian nation-state. A powerful strand in Indian nationalism, which has become the official ideology of the Congress party, argues for multiculturalism, for the possibility of peaceful coexistence among different ethnic and religious communities under the umbrella of a secular state that does not interfere with the religious practices of those different communities. This kind of argument is related to a discourse on Indian society as essentially "pluralist" and "tolerant," a discourse we find, albeit in different ways, in the writings of Gandhi and Nehru. So, where does all this tolerance leave Muslim citizens in India? The discursive move made in scholarly writing about Indian Islam in the post-

Independence period is to link this discourse about the "pluralist" nature of Indian society with an interpretation of Sufism as "syncretistic." This move is exemplified in the writings of Imtiaz Ahmad, who emphasizes the coexistence of formal, textual Islam with local Islam, validated by indigenous (i.e., Indian or Hindu) custom, "as complementary and integral parts of a single common religious system."[14] This kind of argument—that Indians are syncretistic or multicultural at the "folk level" and that the communal difference between Hindus and Muslims only emerges when political parties (or fanatic *maulvis* or Brahmans) try to mobilize the common folk— is also part of constant media propaganda in India. On a sort of commonsense level it is also the view many Indian intellectuals have of "folk culture." Participation by Hindus and Muslims in Sufi saint worship, for example, is often portrayed as a sign of grassroots tolerance.

In a recent essay, Francis Robinson not only criticizes the particulars of Ahmad's argument, such as the contention that saint worship is essentially a Hindu institution that was absorbed within Indian Islam, but also the general project in which Ahmad and his colleagues are involved.[15] According to Robinson, they have developed their particular angle on Indian Islam in their desire to show that Indian Muslims have their roots deep in Indian society and that they are therefore good and loyal citizens of India. Robinson goes on to emphasize a long-term process of Islamization by which local customs were either infused with new meanings or were eradicated. Such an interpretation attempts to demonstrate the gradual marginalization of Sufism and the slow victory of "pure" Islam through reform, with some assistance by the institutions of the modern state. In a sharp reaction to this essay Veena Das wonders whether Robinson's article ultimately shows support for repressive Muslim regimes (such as that of Pakistan) that force their subjects to follow the right path.[16]

This goes some way toward illustrating the extent to which the discussion of syncretism in India reflects the larger discourses of nationalism and the nation-state. An important aspect of the discussion among scholars is what it leaves out. Major sites of ritual construction of identity such as mosque and temple are omitted from the picture. Instead, the site under discussion is simply the Sufi tomb. Most of the historical evidence for "syncretism" deals

with the appropriation of pre-Islamic religious sites for the construction of Sufi tombs. However, this appropriation is seldom viewed
in relation to the process of religious expansion and conversion,
since the whole issue of conversion to Islam is such a hot potato in
modern India. The anthropological literature on the Sufi tomb notes
the "participation" of Hindus in the worship of the buried saint but
does not discuss what this participation means. There is little or no
discussion of the kinds of interactions between Hindus and Muslims, or of the constraints on those interactions. In fact, we do not
know much about "syncretism" in India; it is a trope in the discourse
of "multiculturalism."

So much for contemporary syncretism and tolerance. There is
no reason to argue that India was a syncretistic and tolerant society
in the precolonial period but has become the opposite as a result of
the colonial construction of communalism. It is good to realize that
such terms as *tolerance* and *syncretism* belong to discursive strat-
egies that try to determine the "national culture." At the same time,
there is also no reason to argue that antagonistic Hindu and Muslim
nations existed before the nineteenth century. On the contrary,
nationalist discourses emerged in India in the same period that
thinkers in Europe tried to formulate them. Only then could Hindu
and Muslim movements, like so many of their counterparts in the
rest of the world, start to transform a plethora of religious communities, which indeed were often antagonistic, into Hindu and
Muslim nations. This process remains unfinished and is in its very
nature always partial.

Without denying the importance of state projects in the construction of communities, the argument in this book has tried to escape
from the hegemony of the discourse on state hegemony. Community
formation has a variety of sources, but in the case of religious
nationalism we have to focus more than we often do on religious
movements and institutions, as well as on the disciplinary practices
connected to them. Nationalism reinterprets religious discourse on
gender, on the dialectics of masculinity and femininity, to convey a
sense of belonging to the nation. It appropriates the disciplinary
practices, connected to the theme of the management of desire, in
the service of its own political project. Nationalism also grafts its
notion of territory onto religious notions of sacred space. It develops
a ritual repertoire, based on earlier rituals of pilgrimage, to sanctify

the continuity of the territory. While developing a rhetoric of the "sons of the soil," it also plays with religious transnationality in "Hindu spiritualism" and in the Muslim *umma*. In all its ambiguities and dialectical transformations religious nationalism in India has a history of its own, which cannot be reduced to the master narrative of European modernity.

Notes

Preface

1. See Eric Hobsbawm, *Nations and Nationalism since 1780*, chapter 2. Although Hobsbawm acknowledges that there can be close links between religion and national consciousness, he has difficulty dealing with the Muslim nationalism that led to the formation of Pakistan (see p. 70).

2. See Peter van der Veer, *Gods on Earth: The Management of Religious Experience and Identity in a North Indian Pilgrimage Centre*.

3. For an account of this campaign, see Peter van der Veer, "God Must Be Liberated: A Hindu Liberation Movement in Ayodhya."

4. Parts of the present book concerning the interpretation of the Ayodhya case and the description of one of the Hindu movements involved in it appear as "Hindu Nationalism and the Discourse of Modernity: The Vishva Hindu Parishad," in *Accounting for Fundamentalisms*, ed. Martin Marty and Scott Appleby.

5. Richard Gombrich and Gananath Obeyesekere, *Buddhism Transformed: Religious Change in Sri Lanka*.

6. Richard Handler, *Nationalism and the Politics of Culture in Quebec*, 7.

7. For a discussion of this concept, see Jonathan Spencer, "'Writing Within': Anthropology, Nationalism, and Culture in Sri Lanka."

Chapter One

1. The Congress (I) party won 225 seats and 37 percent of the vote, which allowed it to form a (minority) government.

2. V. D. Savarkar, *Hindutva*, 1. Savarkar was the leader of the Hindu

Mahasabha, the most important Hindu nationalist party before Independence.

3. A very detailed report on the Bombay riots appeared in the national magazine *Frontline*, 30 January 1993.

4. For eyewitness accounts of the Seelampur riots, see *Seelampur 1992: A Report on the Communal Violence in Seelampur New Delhi 1992*, a report published by the Sampradayikta Virodhi Andolan/People's Movement for Secularism, n.d.

5. For the former, see Michael Carrithers, "Passions of Nation and Community in the Bahubali Affair"; for the latter, Richard Gombrich and Gananath Obeyesekere, *Buddhism Transformed*.

6. On temple complexes, see Christopher J. Fuller, *Servants of the Goddess: The Priests of a South Indian Temple*; for Sufi shrines, Katherine Ewing, "The Politics of Sufism: Redefining the Saints of Pakistan."

7. For more on this contested site, see Roger Friedland and Richard Hecht, "The Politics of Sacred Space: Jerusalem's Temple Mount/*al-haram al-sharif*," in *Sacred Spaces and Profane Places*, ed. Jamie Scott and Paul Simpson-Housley, 21–61.

8. T. N. Madan, "Secularism in Its Place."

9. Ralph Grillo, ed., *"Nation" and "State" in Europe: Anthropological Perspectives*, 1.

10. Ernest Gellner, *Nations and Nationalism*.

11. Ibid., 57.

12. Ibid., 77, 142.

13. Sally Falk Moore, "The Production of Cultural Pluralism as a Process."

14. Nicholas Abercrombie and Bryan S. Turner, "The Dominant Ideology Thesis."

15. Gellner, *Nations and Nationalism*, 64–73.

16. Benedict Anderson, *Imagined Communities*, 12–22.

17. Ibid., 36.

18. Ibid., 25.

19. Ibid., 104–28.

20. Ibid., 36.

21. Louis Dumont, *Homo Hierarchicus*, 107.

22. Simon Commander, "The Jajmani System in North India: An Examination of Its Logic and Status across Two Centuries." See also Christopher J. Fuller, "Misconceiving the Grain Heap: A Critique of the Concept of the Indian Jajmani System," in *Money and the Morality of Exchange*, ed. Jonathan Parry and Maurice Bloch, 33–63.

23. Frank Perlin, "The Material and the Cultural: An Attempt to Transcend the Present Impasse," 387.

24. Ibid., 389.

25. Louis Dumont, "Nationalism and Communalism," Appendix D in *Homo Hierarchicus*, 314–34. I offer an elaborate critique in "The Foreign Hand: Orientalist Discourse in Sociology and Communalism," in *Orientalism and the Postcolonial Predicament: Perspectives on South Asia*, Carol A. Breckenridge and Peter van der Veer, eds., 23–44.

26. Partha Chatterjee, *Nationalist Thought and the Colonial World: A Derivative Discourse?* 42.

27. For an excellent exploration of the subject, see B. S. Cohn, "The Census, Social Structure and Objectification in South Asia," in his *An Anthropologist among the Historians and Other Essays*, 224–55.

28. See, for example, Nicholas Dirks, "The Invention of Caste: Civil Society in Colonial India."

29. Edward Said, *Orientalism*.

30. See, for example, the discussion of James Mill's *History of British India* (1858) in Ronald Inden, *Imagining India*, 90–93.

31. The classic text is W. W. Hunter, *The Indian Musalmans*. See also Gyanendra Pandey, "The Bigoted Julaha," in his *Construction of Communalism in Colonial North India*, 66–109.

32. Pandey, *Construction of Communalism*, 8, 9.

Chapter Two

1. For more on the subject of Muslim conversion, see Peter Hardy, "Modern European Explanations of Conversion to Islam in South Asia."

2. For further discussion, see Peter Hardy, "The Authority of Muslim Kings in Medieval South Asia."

3. See Robert E. Frykenberg, "The Concept of 'Majority' as a Devilish Force in the Politics of Modern India: A Historiographic Comment."

4. See Eleanor Zelliott, "Gandhi and Ambedkar: A Study in Leadership," and Owen Lynch, "Dr. B. R. Ambedkar: Myth and Charisma," both in J. Michael Mahar, ed., *The Untouchables in Contemporary India*, 69–96 and 97–113.

5. See Abdul Malik Mujahid, *Conversion to Islam: Untouchables' Strategy for Protest in India*.

6. A recent scholarly expression of that opinion can be found in the introduction to Richard Burghart and Audrey Cantlie, eds., *Indian Religion*. In my opinion, Islam and Christianity in India are also Indian religions.

7. For a discussion of this and other metaphors used in describing Hindu society, see Ronald Inden, *Imagining India*.

8. See Gyanendra Pandey, *The Construction of Communalism in Colonial North India*. See also the debate between Paul Brass and Francis

Robinson in *Political Identity in South Asia*, ed. David Taylor and Malcolm Yapp.

9. Talal Asad, "Anthropological Conceptions of Religion: Reflections on Geertz."

10. Ernest Gellner, *Nations and Nationalism*.

11. B. S. Cohn, "The Anthropology of a Colonial State and Its Forms of Knowledge."

12. See Andreas Höfer, *The Caste Hierarchy and the State in Nepal*.

13. Richard Burghart, "The Formation of the Concept of Nation-State in Nepal."

14. I am indebted here to Mart Bax, "Popular Devotions, Power, and Religious Regimes in Dutch Brabant."

15. Richard Eaton, *Sufis of Bijapur*, 33–43.

16. Lorenzen, "Warrior Ascetics in Indian History."

17. Eaton, *Sufis of Bijapur*, 39.

18. See Susan Bayly, "Islam and State Power."

19. This and the following paragraph are based on my own observations of a number of ʿurs celebrations in 1988 by the Rifaʿi Sufis in Surat.

20. See my "Playing or Praying: A Saint's Day in Surat."

21. Patricia Jeffery demonstrates the link between seclusion and status in her *Frogs in a Well*.

22. On the debate about prayer among Indonesian Muslims, see John Bowen, "Salat in Indonesia: The Social Meanings of an Islamic Ritual."

23. See Marc Gaborieau, "Les Oulemas/Soufis dans l'Inde Moghole: Anthropologie historique de religieux musulmans."

24. Ernest Gellner, *Muslim Society*.

25. See, for example, Bruce Lawrence, "Islam in India."

26. See Richard Eaton, "Court of Man, Court of God."

27. See Lawrence, "Islam in India," 34.

28. For an overview of what is known about this saint, see P. M. Currie, *The Shrine and Cult of Muʿin al-din Chishti*.

29. See Richard Eaton, "The Political and Religious Authority of the Shrine of Baba Farid," in *Moral Conduct and Authority: The Place of* adab *in South Asian Islam*, ed. Barbara Metcalf, 333–57. See also David Gilmartin, "Shrines, Succession, and Sources of Moral Authority," in the same volume, 221–41.

30. See Ernest Gellner, *Saints of the Atlas*.

31. This is the main argument in David Gilmartin, *Empire and Islam*.

32. In the Sufi initiation rituals I have witnessed in Gujarat the saint drinks from a glass and then hands it to the initiate, who puts his lips on the same spot and drinks. The initiate partakes of the power of the saint's spittle but would become polluted if he were a Hindu.

33. On this point, see Rafiuddin Ahmed, "Conflict and Contradictions in Bengali Islam," in *Shariʿat and Ambiguity in South Asian Islam*, ed. Katherine Ewing, 114–42.

34. Richard Eaton, "The Political and Religious Authority of the Shrine of Baba Farid," 352–55.

35. See Arjun Appadurai, "The Past as a Scarce Resource."

36. B. S. Cohn, "The Role of the Gosains in the Economy of Eighteenth- and Nineteenth-Century Upper India."

37. Christopher Bayly, *Rulers, Townsmen and Bazaars: North Indian Society in the Age of Expansion, 1770–1870*, 143.

38. See David Lorenzen, "Warrior Ascetics in Indian History."

39. See in particular Louis Dumont, "World Renunciation in Indian Religions," in his *Religion, Politics and History in India*, 33–60; and Madeleine Biardeau, *L'Hindouisme: Anthropologie d'une civilisation*.

40. David Pocock shows as much in his *Mind, Body and Wealth*.

41. On this point, see Richard Burghart, "The Disappearance and Reappearance of Janakpur."

42. Charlotte Vaudeville, "Braj, Lost and Found."

43. Richard B. Barnett, *North India between Empires: Awadh, the Mughals, and the British, 1720–1801*, 56.

44. For more on Anupgiri, see Jadunath Sarkar, *A History of the Dashanami Nagas*.

45. For Jai Singh's religious policies, see P. Mital, *Braj ke dharm-sampradayom ka itihas* (in Hindi); A. Roy, *History of Jaipur City*; and Monika Thiel-Horstmann, "Warrior Ascetics in Eighteenth-Century Rajasthan and the Religious Policy of Jai Singh II."

46. See Lorenzen, "Warrior Ascetics in Indian History."

47. See Willem van Schendel, "Madmen of Mymensingh: Peasant Resistance and the Colonial Process in Eastern India, 1824 to 1833."

48. See Raymond Williams, *The Swaminarayana Satsangh*, 1–24.

49. See Christopher J. Fuller, *Servants of the Goddess: The Priests of a South Indian Temple*.

50. See Charlotte Vaudeville, *Kabir*. My account of Sikh history is largely based on W. H. McLeod, *The Evolution of the Sikh Community*, and idem, *Who Is a Sikh? The Problem of Sikh Identity*.

51. On the militant tradition of the Jats, see Joyce Pettigrew, *Robber Noblemen: A Study of the Political System of the Sikh Jats*. Habib's theory is cited in McLeod's *Evolution of the Sikh Community*.

52. Quoted in Rajiv Kapur, *Sikh Separatism: The Politics of Faith*, 8.

53. Quoted in ibid., 8.

54. Richard G. Fox, *Lions of the Punjab: Culture in the Making*.

55. These connections are demonstrated in an admirable way for Sri

Lanka by Richard Gombrich and Gananath Obeyesekere, *Buddhism Transformed: Religious Change in Sri Lanka.*

56. For more on Sirhindi and the Naqshbandi Mujaddadi, see Yonathan Friedmann, *Shaikh Ahmad Sirhindi: An Outline of His Thought and a Study of His Image in the Eyes of Posterity.*

57. See Susan Bayly, "Islam and State Power," 149.

58. See Marc Gaborieau, "Les Oulemas/Soufis dans l'Inde Moghole."

59. Rafiuddin Ahmed, "Islamization in Nineteenth-Century Bengal," in *Contributions to South Asian Studies, 1,* ed. Gopal Krishna, 99.

60. See Barbara Metcalf, *Islamic Revival in British India: Deoband, 1860–1900,* 158.

61. See, for example, David Eickelman, *Moroccan Islam;* and Michael Gilsenan, *Saint and Sufi in Modern Egypt.*

62. Gilsenan, *Recognizing Islam* (London: Croom Helm, 1982), 249–50.

63. Katherine Ewing, "The Politics of Sufism: Redefining the Saints of Pakistan."

64. Gananath Obeyesekere, "Social Change and the Deities: Rise of the Kataragama Cult in Modern Sri Lanka," 388.

65. For more on this subject, see James Piscatori, *Islam in a World of Nation-States.*

66. See Richard Eaton, "Approaches to the Study of Conversion to Islam in India," in *Approaches to Islam in Religious Studies,* ed. Richard Martin, 121.

67. See my "Playing or Praying: A Saint's Day in Surat."

68. My analysis of this movement is largely based on Mumtaz Ahmad, "The Jamaat-i-Islami and the Tablighi Jamaat of South Asia," in *Fundamentalism Observed,* ed. Martin Marty and Scott Appleby.

69. See Talal Asad, "Anthropological Conceptions of Religion: Reflections on Geertz."

70. It is sometimes argued that the "tolerance" that characterizes Hinduism influenced the "tolerant" policies of "Indianized" Muslim rulers like the Mughal emperor Akbar. A sharp distinction is thus made between "tolerant" Muslim rulers and "fanatic" ones, such as the emperor Aurangzeb. All this assumes, however, that one can understand politics by looking exclusively at the religious worldview of rulers, as well as that one can understand these worldviews by anachronistically applying a modern understanding of "tolerance."

71. In an unpublished paper, entitled "Cultural Collusion in Ethnography: The Religious Tolerance of Hindus," Richard Burghart argues convincingly that we do not find a direct equivalent of the English term *tolerance* in Hindi or Nepali.

72. B. N. Halhed, *A Code of Gentoo Laws* (London, 1776), quoted in Wilhelm Halbfass, *Tradition and Reflection*, 74.

73. See Narendra K. Wagle, "Hindu-Muslim Interactions in Medieval Maharashtra," in *Hinduism Reconsidered*, ed. Gunter D. Sontheimer and Hermann Kulke, 51–67.

74. For a thorough discussion of Hacker's argument, which is found in a number of articles written between 1957 and 1977, see Wilhelm Halbfass, *India and Europe*, 403–18.

75. For a discussion of this concept, see, for example, Lawrence A. Babb, *The Divine Hierarchy*.

76. I believe this is my own term, although it is reminiscent of a general perspective on Hindu discourse shared by theorists like Louis Dumont and McKim Marriott—who in many ways have opposite views on Indian society (see Louis Dumont, *Homo Hierarchicus*; and McKim Marriott, "Hindu Transactions," in *Transaction and Meaning*, ed. Bruce Kapferer, 109–42). The term refers to the Hindu belief that there is a similarity in body and behavior between the believer and the god he chooses to worship (*istadevata*). A simple example would be that a vegetarian worships a vegetarian god.

77. This notion emerged clearly in the interviews I held with afflicted Hindus who visited Sufi shrines in Surat and the vicinity. It is also reported by Sudhir Kakar, *Shamans, Mystics and Doctors: A Psychological Inquiry into India and Its Healing Traditions*, 87.

78. Quoted in Halbfass, *India and Europe*, 409. Radhakrishnan's distinction between various "religions" and "religion" as the unifying essence of them makes the important move to equate "religion" with Hinduism as the spirit of India. See Robert N. Minor, "Sarvepalli Radhakrishnan and 'Hinduism,'" in *Religion in Modern India*, ed. Robert Baird, 421–55.

79. Tapan Raychaudhuri, *Europe Reconsidered*, 230.

80. On the RSS, see Walter Anderson and Sridar Damle, *The Brotherhood in Saffron: The Rashtriya Swayamsevak Sangh and Hindu Revivalism*.

81. Nita Kumar, *The Artisans of Banaras: Popular Culture and Identity, 1880–1986*.

82. See Peter van der Veer, "The Power of Detachment: Disciplines of Body and Mind in the Ramanandi Order"; and Joseph Alter, "The Sannyasi and the Indian Wrestler: The Anatomy of a Relationship."

83. Joseph Alter, *The Wrestler's Body: Identity and Ideology in North India*, 237–56.

84. A common argument heard in interviews I held with VHP members in Ayodhya in December 1990 was that Muslims should realize that they were in fact converted and should return to Hinduism. Reconversion is

seen as one task of the VHP. Some of this goes back to the purification (*shuddhi*) ceremonies of the Arya Samaj in the Punjab in the late nineteenth and early twentieth centuries. But this is not an extreme way of thinking in India. The government of India also sees it as its task to prevent conversion to Islam. It reacted negatively when untouchables converted to Islam in Meenakshipuram in 1981 and tried to prevent further conversions (see Jaswant Rae Gupta, *Role of Foreign Money in Conversion of Hindus*). A letter of the Home Ministry, published in the Muslim leader Shahabuddin's journal *Muslim India* (February 1984), asserts that "all precautionary measures have been taken to prevent *Adi Dravidas* (Tamil Untouchables) being converted to become Muslims" (quoted in Abdul Malik Mujahid, *Conversion to Islam: Untouchables' Strategy for Protest in India*, 97).

Chapter Three

1. See Benedict Anderson, *Imagined Communities*.

2. Jonathan Parry, "The Brahmanical Tradition and the Technology of the Intellect," in *Reason and Morality*, ed. Joanna Overing, 215.

3. Jack Goody, *The Domestication of the Savage Mind*.

4. Charles Taylor, "The Person," in *The Category of the Person: Anthropology, Philosophy, History*, ed. Michael Carrithers, Steven Collins, and Steven Lukes, 257–81.

5. Stanley Tambiah, "A Performative Approach to Ritual," in his *Culture, Thought and Social Action*, 128.

6. Bruce Kapferer, *A Celebration of Demons*, 96–97.

7. Maurice Bloch, *From Blessing to Violence*.

8. For more on this subject, see my *Gods on Earth*, 211–17.

9. For example, see the discussion of the way in which the rituals of the Tshidi in South Africa are a site of resistance to neocolonialism, in Jean Comaroff, *Body of Power, Spirit of Resistance*, 194–252.

10. Bruce Kapferer, *Legends of People, Myths of State: Violence, Intolerance, and Political Culture in Sri Lanka and Australia*.

11. Ibid., 82–83.

12. See Bryan S. Turner, *The Body*, 115.

13. Marvin Harris, *Cows, Pigs, Wars and Witches*.

14. See especially Deryck O. Lodrick, *Sacred Cows, Sacred Places: Origins and Survivals of Animal Homes in India*.

15. For a useful discussion of *sati*, see Catherine Weinberger-Thomas, "Cendres d'immortalité: La Crémation des veuves en Inde."

16. On this subject, see Françoise Mallison, "A Note on Holiness Allowed to Women: Pativrata and Sati."

17. I discuss this subject in greater detail in "The Power of Detachment: Disciplines of Body and Mind in the Ramanandi Order."

18. See Deryck O. Lodrick, *Sacred Cows, Sacred Places.*

19. Rajiv Kapur, *Sikh Separatism: The Politics of Faith,* 36.

20. On the Cow Protection Movement, see Peter Robb, "The Challenge of Gau Mata: British Policy and Religious Change in India, 1880–1916."

21. See Sandria Freitag, *Collective Action and Community: Public Arenas and the Emergence of Communalism in North India,* 150.

22. Gyanendra Pandey, *The Construction of Communalism in Colonial India.*

23. See Ibid., 152–54. See also Freitag, *Collective Action and Community,* 166–70.

24. See my *Gods on Earth: The Management of Religious Experience in a North Indian Pilgrimage Centre,* 211–17.

25. Gyanendra Pandey gives a number of examples of these "snowball" letters in *The Construction of Communalism,* 263–66.

26. See, for example, Thomas Metcalf, *Land, Landlords and the British Raj,* 352. For Ayodhya in particular, see my *Gods on Earth,* 39 and 272–75.

27. See Anand Yang, "Sacred Symbol and Sacred Space in Rural India: Community Mobilization in the 'Anti–Cow Killing' Riot of 1893."

28. Ibid., 594.

29. John McLane, *Indian Nationalism and the Early Congress,* 290.

30. Lloyd Rudolph and Susan Rudolph, *The Modernity of Tradition.*

31. Homer A. Jack, ed., *The Gandhi Reader,* 170.

32. See Shahid Amin, "Gandhi as Mahatma: Gorakhpur District, Eastern UP, 1921–1922," in *Selected Subaltern Studies,* ed. Ranajit Guha and Gayatri C. Spivak, 288–351.

33. Quoted in Ved Mehta, *Mahatma Gandhi and His Apostles,* 175–76.

34. See the discussion in Catherine Thomas, *L'Ashram de l'amour: Le Gandhisme et l'imaginaire,* 118–23.

35. Bhikhu Parekh, *Colonialism, Tradition and Reform: An Analysis of Gandhi's Political Discourse,* 189.

36. Quoted in ibid., 195.

37. See Barbara Metcalf, "Islamic Reform and Islamic Women: Maulana Thanawi's *Jewelry of Paradise,*" in *Moral Conduct and Authority: The Place of adab in South Asian Islam,* ed. Barbara Metcalf, 184–96.

38. For more on this distinction, see D. A. Jacobson, *Hidden Faces: Hindu and Muslim Purdah in a Central Indian Village.*

39. Patricia Jeffery, *Frogs in a Well,* 25.

40. Marcel Mauss, "Les Techniques du corps," in his *Sociologie et anthropologie*.

41. Metcalf, "Islamic Reform and Islamic Women," 190. The foregoing description of this text is largely based on Metcalf's article.

42. See Jeffery, *Frogs in a Well*, 20–21.

43. Quoted in Aziz Ahmad, *Islamic Modernism in India and Pakistan*, 213.

44. Quoted in Barbara Metcalf, "Islamic Arguments in Contemporary Pakistan," in *Islam and the Political Economy of Meaning*, ed. William Roff, 147.

45. For more on this subject, see Anita Weiss, "Implications of the Islamization Program for Women," in *Islamic Reassertion in Pakistan*, ed. Anita Weiss, 97–115.

46. For more on this case, see Zakia Pathak and Rajeswari Sunder Rajan, "Shahbano."

47. Salman Rushdie, *Shame*, 173.

48. See my "Satanic or Angelic: The Politics of Religious and Literary Inspiration." I will have more to say about Rushdie in chapter 6.

Chapter Four

1. See V. D. Savarkar, *Hindutva*, 1.

2. Louis Dumont, "Nationalism and Communalism," in his *Religion, Politics and History in India*, 108.

3. Sandria B. Freitag, *Collective Action and Community: Public Arenas and the Emergence of Communalism in North India*, 178.

4. See Ferdinand Tönnies, *Gemeinschaft und Gesellschaft*.

5. For a discussion of the notion of a village community, see Louis Dumont, "The 'Village Community' from Munro to Maine," in his *Religion, Politics and History in India*, 112–32. For the application of the notion of a village republic to Bali and for Wittfogel on Bali, see Clifford Geertz, *Negara*.

6. See Dirk Kolff, *Naukar, Rajput and Sepoy: The Ethnohistory of the Military Labour Market in Hindustan, 1450–1850*, on which the following discussion is based.

7. For a description of ascetic soldiers, see my *Gods on Earth: The Management of Religious Experience and Identity in a North Indian Pilgrimage Centre*, 130–59.

8. The classic study of the indenture system is Hugh Tinker, *A New System of Slavery: The Export of Indian Labour Overseas, 1830–1920*.

9. Geertz, *Negara*, 3–10.

10. The 'natural' emphasis on family reunification in the film may be

debatable, depending on the extent of a tradition of single male migration among Patels as compared to other migrant groups.

11. See Myron Weiner, "International Migration and Development: Indians in the Persian Gulf."

12. See John Kelly, *A Politics of Virtue: Hinduism, Sexuality, and Countercolonial Discourse in Fiji*, 26–66.

13. See Peter van der Veer and Steven Vertovec, "Brahmanism Abroad: On Caribbean Hinduism as an Ethnic Religion."

14. *Ghadr*, November 1913, quoted in Rajiv Kapur, *Sikh Separatism: The Politics of Faith*, 55.

15. *The Aryan*, March–April 1912, quoted in Kapur, *Sikh Separatism*, 54.

16. See Kapur, *Sikh Separatism*, 57.

17. Peter Robb, "The Impact of British Rule on Religious Community: Reflections on the Trial of Maulvi Ahmadullah of Patna in 1865," paper delivered at the Eleventh Conference on Modern South Asian Studies, Amsterdam, July 1990, 7.

18. Muhammad Khalid Masud, "The Obligation to Migrate: The Doctrine of *hijra* in Islamic Law," in *Muslim Travellers: Pilgrimage, Migration, and the Religious Imagination*, ed. Dale F. Eickelman and James Piscatori, 29–50.

19. In 1920 there in fact was an actual, though extremely marginal, *hijra* movement among certain Muslims, who emigrated from British India to Afghanistan on religious grounds.

20. See Aliya Azam Khan, "The Muhajir Qaumi Movement," M.A. thesis, University of Pennsylvania, 1990.

21. See Eric Hobsbawm, *The Age of Empire, 1875–1914*, chapter 6. Hobsbawm makes also a striking observation, arguing that "the nationalist movements which gained genuine mass support in our period . . . were almost invariably those which combined the appeal of nationality and language with some more powerful interest or mobilizing force, ancient or modern. Religion was one" (p. 162).

22. See, for Vivekananda, George Williams, "Svami Vivekananda," in *Religion in Modern India*, ed. Robert Baird, 313–43.

23. Gananath Obeyesekere, "Sinhalese-Buddhist Identity in Ceylon," in *Ethnic Identity: Cultural Continuities and Change*, ed. George de Vos and Lola Romanucci-Ross, 231–58.

24. Gananath Obeyesekere, "The Buddhist Pantheon in Ceylon and Its Extensions," in *Anthropological Studies in Theravada Buddhism*, ed. Manning Nash, 1–26.

25. Eric Wolf, "The Virgin of Guadaloupe: A Mexican National Symbol," 38.

26. M. N. Srinivas, "The Cohesive Role of Sanskritization," in *India and Ceylon: Unity and Diversity*, ed. Philip Mason, 74.

27. David Mandelbaum, *Society in India*, 401.

28. Sandria Freitag, *Collective Action and Community*, 6.

29. For more on these developments, see my *Gods on Earth*, 213–17.

30. A full description of this nationwide ritual is contained in the VHP publication, *Ekatmata yajna*, New Delhi, n.d. I am indebted to Lisa McKean for providing me with a copy of this publication.

31. Ibid., 13.

32. Ibid.

33. For the application of this argument to Malaysia, see Mary Byrne McDonnell, "Patterns of Muslim Pilgrimage from Malaysia, 1885–1985," in *Muslim Travellers*, ed. Eickelman and Piscatori, 111–31.

34. P. M. Currie, *The Shrine and Cult of Muʿin al-din Chishti of Ajmer*, 119.

35. For more on Ilyas and his movement, see Anwar ul-Haq, *The Faith Movement of Mawlana Muhammad Ilyas*; and M. M. Quraishi, "The Tabligh Movement: Some Observations."

36. See, for example, Felice Dassetto, "The Tabligh Organization in Belgium," in *The New Islamic Presence in Western Europe*, ed. Tomas Gerholm and Yngve Lithman, 159–73.

37. "Message and Activities," VHP pamphlet, New Delhi, 1982.

38. "The Birth of Vishwa Hindu Parishad," *Hindu Vishwa*, July 1982, 3.

39. Walter Anderson and Sridhar Damle, *The Brotherhood in Saffron: The Rashtriya Swayamsevak Sangh and Hindu Revivalism*, 133.

40. "Message and Activities."

41. See, for example, Carol A. Breckenridge and Peter van der Veer, eds., *Orientalism and the Postcolonial Predicament: Perspectives on South Asia*.

42. See Robert E. Frykenberg: "The Concept of 'Majority' as a Devilish Force in the Politics of Modern India: A Historiographic Comment."

43. See Bruce Lawrence, *Defenders of God*.

44. See Robert E. Frykenberg, "The Emergence of Modern 'Hinduism' as a Concept and as an Institution: A Reappraisal with Special Reference to South India," in *Hinduism Reconsidered*, ed. Gunther D. Sontheimer and Hermann Kulke, 29–49.

45. "The Birth of Vishwa Hindu Parishad," 5.

46. The VHP quotes with approval a saying by the RSS chief, Balasaheb Deoras, "If untouchability is not wrong, nothing is wrong in this world," in *The Hindu Awakening: Retrospect and Promise*, VHP publication, New Delhi, n.d., 14.

47. This short "history" was told to me by a disciple of Chinmayananda during an interview in the Sandeepany Ashram, Bombay, in December 1990.

48. See Mattison Mines and Vijayalakshmi Gourishankar, "Leadership and Individuality in South Asia: The Case of the South Indian Big-Man," 781.

Chapter Five

1. V. S. Naipaul, *An Area of Darkness*, 202.

2. V. S. Naipaul, "Our Universal Civilization," *New York Times*, 5 November 1990.

3. See Georges Charbonnier, *Entretiens avec Claude Lévi-Strauss*, 37–49.

4. See André G. Frank, "The Development of Underdevelopment."

5. For more on this subject, see Bipan Chandra, *The Rise and Growth of Economic Nationalism in India, 1880–1905*.

6. For some telling quotations from these experts, see Sheldon Pollock, "Mimamsa and the Problem of History in Traditional India."

7. This formulation allows us to see the extent to which the discourse of history gives meaning to life and replaces religious discourse. This is particularly clear in modernist histories of the nation.

8. This argument is convincingly presented in Pollock's "Mimamsa and the Problem of History."

9. Sitaram, *Avadh ki Jhanki*; my translation. See also my discussion in *Gods on Earth: The Management of Religious Experience and Identity in a North Indian Pilgrimage Centre*, 105–6.

10. See Talal Asad, *The Idea of an Anthropology of Islam*, 15.

11. See, for example, Richard Burghart, "The Founding of the Ramanandi Sect"; and P. M. Currie, *The Shrine and Cult of Muʿin al-din Chishti of Ajmer*.

12. A successful attempt to do so is W. H. McLeod, *The Evolution of the Sikh Community*.

13. See David Ludden, "Orientalist Empiricism: Transformations of Colonial Knowledge," in *Orientalism and the Postcolonial Predicament: Perspectives on South Asia*, ed. Carol A. Breckenridge and Peter van der Veer, 250–78.

14. The term *orientalist* is used here in the broad sense given it by Edward Said and refers not only to those called such in the eighteenth and nineteenth centuries. The division of Indian history into three periods—Hindu, Muslim, and British—was first developed by the utilitarian James Mill in his *History of British India*. On this point, see Romila

Thapar, "Communalism and the Writing of Ancient Indian History," in *Communalism and the Writing of Indian History*, ed. Romila Thapar, Harbans Mukhia, and Bipan Chandra, 4.

15. Muslim nationalist history has a complicated relation to national territory since the ultimate point of reference is Mecca, which lies outside that territory. However, there is a strong identification in Muslim nationalism with the history of Muslim political power in India. Secularist history is not entirely able to get rid of the religious overtones of the glorification of the national past but attempts to emphasize the "tolerance" and "syncretism" of Buddhist and Muslim rulers like Ashoka and Akbar.

16. B. P. Sinha, "Indian Tradition and Archaeology," 109.

17. B. B. Lal, "Was Ayodhya a Mythical City?" 45.

18. Romila Thapar, "Puranic Lineages and Archaeological Cultures," 86.

19. Ibid., 98.

20. For a useful illustration of this point, see Madeleine Biardeau, "The Story of Arjuna Kartavirya without Reconstruction."

21. An earlier version of this section appeared in *Social Research* 59, no. 1 (1992): 85–111.

22. This section (and its title) is largely based on K. M. Munshi, *Somanatha: The Shrine Eternal*. The publisher of this work, Bharatiya Vidya Bhavan (Institute of Indian Culture), was founded by Munshi for the "reintegration of the Indian culture in the light of modern knowledge and to suit our present-day needs and the resuscitation of its fundamental values in their pristine vigour" (a statement that appears in every one of their books). Its book series includes English translations of Hindu classics. Munshi's book was first published in 1951, but the 1965 edition includes additional material, such as correspondence with Nehru, relating to Somanatha.

23. Munshi, *Somanatha: The Shrine Eternal*, 62.

24. Ibid., 67. Sardar Patel is a hero for members of the VHP nowadays, while Nehru is generally denounced as a "secularist" and Mahatma Gandhi regarded as the reason that Hindus are "second-rate citizens" in their own country. However, it is easily forgotten that, as home minister, Patel condemned the ally of the VHP, the Rastriya Swayamsevak Sangh, as a threat to the nation. He banned the RSS after the murder of Mahatma Gandhi by a former member of that organization. Patel was a Hindu nationalist but not an extremist.

25. Ibid., 83–84.

26. Quoted in ibid., 70–71.

27. Ibid., 176.

28. Ibid., 179.

29. Quoted in ibid., 104. A *linga* is a phallic aniconic form of the god Shiva.

30. Quoted in ibid., 125.

31. Quoted in ibid., 112.

32. Quoted in ibid., 104.

33. Mahmud of Ghazni has, of course, also been important in the Muslim historical imagination. However, it is striking that professional Muslim historians in the twentieth century have tended to give an economic interpretation of Mahmud's exploits. See, for example, Mohammad Habib, *Sultan Mahmud of Ghazni*.

34. See Richard Smith, "Rule-by-records and Rule-by-reports: Complementary Aspects of the British Imperial Rule of Law."

35. Romila Thapar, Harbans Mukhia, and Bipan Chandra, eds., *Communalism and the Writing of Indian History*, 8.

36. The reconstruction was, however, a clear demonstration of Hindu nationalism, supported by state institutions, which must have reinforced some doubts about the "religious neutrality" of independent India. But, considering that they had just lived through the events surrounding partition, the strength of Hindu nationalism cannot have come as a big surprise to Muslims.

37. Patrick Carnegy, *A Historical Sketch of Tahsil Fyzabad, Zillah Fyzabad*, 21.

38. G. D. Bhatnagar does not even mention the Babari Mosque in his account but calls it the Jama Masjid (see *Awadh under Wajid Ali Shah*).

39. Michael Fisher, *A Clash of Cultures: Awadh, the British and the Mughals*, 227.

40. This may look like "syncretism," but, as I will argue in the epilogue, the shared worship of a slab of stone does not necessarily imply a shared understanding of what that worship means. I would suggest that the place in question is contested terrain and that, at some point, Ramanandi militant ascetics are able to get it under their control.

41. Telegram from Jawaharlal Nehru to G. B. Pant, 26 December 1949, cited in Sarvepalli Gopal, "Introduction," in *Anatomy of a Confrontation: The Babri Masjid–Ram Janmabhumi Issue*, ed. Sarvepalli Gopal, 15.

42. The letter is reprinted in full as an appendix to A. G. Noorani, "Legal Aspects to the Issue," in *Anatomy of a Confrontation*, ed. Gopal; the quote is from p. 91.

43. Quoted in the *Indian Express*, 30 March 1986, which contained an account of these events.

44. His claim seems reliable to me, since I had already encountered strong indications that he had been involved when I did fieldwork in Ayodhya in the early 1980s. At that time, however, he could not have

made such a declaration of a criminal act in public. Another interesting side to this is, of course, that the "genuineness" of the whole appearance of lord Rama in the temple seems not to be put into doubt by such a declaration.

45. Nayar was forced to resign over this case, but his attitude made him a local hero (see Harold Gould, "Religion and Politics in a U.P. constituency," in *South Asian Politics and Religion*, ed. Donald Smith, 51–74). His portrait is now enshrined in a pavilion built by the VHP on the grounds of the mosque and devoted to a pictorial history of the Hindu struggle for Rama's birthplace.

46. See B. K. Thapar, ed., *Indian Archaeology, 1976–1977* (New Delhi: Archaeological Survey of India, 1980), 52.

47. See M. C. Joshi, "Archaeology and Indian Tradition—Some Observations"; and B. B. Lal, "Was Ayodhya a Mythical City?"

48. Hans T. Bakker, *Ayodhya*, part 1, chapter 1. Bakker deals with "the history of Ayodhya from the 7th century B.C. to the middle of the 18th century, its development into a sacred centre with special reference to the *Ayodhyamahatmya* and to the worship of Rama according to the *Agastyasamhita*." The larger part of his book of more than 700 pages is devoted to a critical edition of the *Ayodhyamahatmya*, a Sanskrit pilgrimage manual of Ayodhya.

49. Thapar, *Indian Archaeology*, 53.

50. Sarvepalli Gopal et al., eds., *The Political Abuse of History*, reproduced in V. C. Mishra, ed., *Ram Janmabhoomi Babri Masjid: Historical Documents, Legal Opinions and Judgements*, 179, 181.

51. The argument of these scholars has been disputed by, among others, the historian A. R. Khan. See the *Indian Express*, 25 February 1990, as well as the reply by the JNU historians and Khan's reaction to it, both in the 1 April edition.

52. See the *Archaeological Survey of India*, reports by Alexander Cunningham and others, 23 vols. (Simla and Calcutta: 1871–1887), especially 1:322–30.

53. Carnegy, *Historical Sketch of Tahsil Fyzabad, Zillah Fyzabad*, 20–21.

54. Gopal, "Introduction," in *Anatomy of a Confrontation*, ed. Gopal, 13, 14.

55. R. S. Sharma argues in his *Communal History and Rama's Ayodhya* that "the pillars used in the construction of Babri Masjid may have belonged to some Shaiva or Jain temple" (p. 28). His point is that there were many instances in which material from earlier buildings was used in new ones but that, in this case, such reuse does not have to mean that a temple was demolished. Moreover, Sharma sees it as highly unlikely that there

ever had been a Rama temple in Ayodhya. Sharma's position has been disputed by the historian S. P. Gupta: "Mr. Sharma has not given a single piece of archaeological or historical evidence in support of what he says. The archaeological and other evidence from art history indicate that there was a Brahminical temple at the place where the mosque stands today. The iconographical features like *vanamala* and *karandmukut* show that it was probably a Vaishnava temple" (*Times of India*, 1 October 1991).

56. See the report published in the *Indian Express*, 13 April 1988.

Chapter Six

1. See Etienne Balibar, "The Nation Form: History and Ideology," 352.

2. For more on this concept, see M. N. Srinivas, "A Note on Sanskritization and Westernization."

3. Hans T. Bakker, *Ayodhya*, 72.

4. Paul Brass, *The Politics of India since Independence*, 145.

5. David Lelyveld, "Colonial Knowledge and the Fate of Hindustani," in *Orientalism and the Postcolonial Predicament: Perspectives on South Asia*, ed. Carol A. Breckenridge and Peter van der Veer, 189–214.

6. Christopher R. King, "Forging a New Linguistic Identity: The Hindi Movement in Banaras, 1868–1914," in *Culture and Power in Banaras: Community, Performance, and Environment, 1800–1980*, ed. Sandria B. Freitag, 197.

7. Quoted in Philip Lutgendorf, *The Life of a Text: Performing the Ramcaritmanas of Tulsidas*, 1.

8. For more on this subject, see Linda Hess and Richard Schechner, "The Ram Lila of Ramnagar."

9. Lutgendorf, *Life of a Text*, 62.

10. Ibid., 96.

11. Paula Richman, "E. V. Ramasami's Reading of the Ramayana," in *Many Ramayanas: The Diversity of a Narrative Tradition in South Asia*, ed. Paula Richman, 195.

12. See, for example, Romila Thapar, "A Historical Perspective on the Story of Rama," in *Anatomy of a Confrontation: The Babri Masjid–Ram Janmabhumi Issue*, ed. Sarvepalli Gopal, 141–63.

13. Philip Lutgendorf, "Ramayan: The Video," 136.

14. Ibid., 140–41.

15. Benedict Anderson, *Imagined Communities*, 22–36.

16. Romila Thapar, "The Ramayana Syndrome," 74.

17. Thapar, "A Historical Perspective on the Story of Rama," in *Anatomy of a Confrontation*, ed. Gopal, 158.

18. Lutgendorf, "Ramayan: The Video," 168.

19. Anuradha Kapur, "Militant Images of a Tranquil God," *Times of India*, 1 October 1991.

20. Anderson, *Imagined Communities*, 25–36.

21. Ibid., 27.

22. Ibid., 28.

23. Timothy Brennan, "The National Longing for Form," in *Nation and Narration*, ed. Homi Bhabha, 50.

24. Fredric Jameson, "Third-World Literature in the Era of Multinational Capitalism," 65.

25. Ibid., 69.

26. See Aijaz Ahmad, "Jameson's Rhetoric of Otherness and the 'National Allegory.'"

27. V. S. Naipaul, *India: A Wounded Civilization*, 18.

28. Ibid., 21.

29. Ibid., 43.

30. Brennan, "National Longing for Form," 52.

31. Brass, *Politics of India*, 145.

32. Jameson, "Third-World Literature," 73.

33. Salman Rushdie, *The Satanic Verses*, 318.

34. See Barbara Metcalf, "An Islamic Ironist," *Times Literary Supplement*, 1 June 1990.

35. See Talal Asad, "Multiculturalism and British Identity in the Wake of the Rushdie Affair."

36. See the *New York Times*, 12 December 1991.

Epilogue

1. Ernest Renan, "Qu'est ce que c'est une nation?" 891; my translation.

2. Eric Hobsbawm, *Nations and Nationalism since 1780*, 12.

3. French original quoted in Benedict Anderson, *Imagined Communities*, 199; my translation.

4. Ibid., 200.

5. Clifford Geertz, *The Interpretation of Cultures*, 89.

6. Talal Asad, "Anthropological Conceptions of Religion: Reflections on Geertz," 239.

7. Richard Handler, *Nationalism and the Politics of Culture in Quebec*, 7.

8. See Louis Dumont, *Homo Hierarchicus*; and McKim Marriott, "Hindu Transactions: Diversity without Dualism," in *Transaction and Meaning*, ed. Bruce Kapferer, 109–42.

9. See my "The Foreign Hand: Orientalist Discourse in Sociology and Communalism," in *Orientalism and the Postcolonial Predicament: Per-*

spectives on South Asia, ed. Carol A. Breckenridge and Peter van der Veer, 23–44.

10. That nationalism in India has to be at least partly derivative is shown by Partha Chatterjee, *Nationalist Thought and the Colonial World: A Derivative Discourse?*

11. Ashis Nandy, "Hinduism versus Hindutva: The Inevitability of a Confrontation," *Times of India,* 18 February 1991.

12. Ashis Nandy, "The Politics of Secularism and the Recovery of Religious Tolerance," in *Mirrors of Violence,* ed. Veena Das, 70.

13. This is Judith Berlin's definition in *The Syncretic Religion of Lin Chao-En,* 9.

14. Imtiaz Ahmad, ed., *Ritual and Religion among Muslims in India,* 15.

15. Francis Robinson, "Islam and Muslim Society in South Asia," 187.

16. Veena Das, "For a Folk-Theology and Theological Anthropology of Islam."

Bibliography

Abercrombie, Nicholas, and Bryan S. Turner. "The Dominant Ideology Thesis." *British Journal of Sociology* 29 (1978): 149–70.

Ahmad, Aijaz. "Jameson's Rhetoric of Otherness and the 'National Allegory.'" *Social Text* 17 (Fall 1987): 3–26.

Ahmad, Aziz. *Islamic Modernism in India and Pakistan*. London: Oxford University Press, 1967.

Ahmad, Imtiaz, ed. *Ritual and Religion among Muslims in India*. Delhi: Manohar, 1984.

Ahmad, Mumtaz. "The Jamaat-i-Islami and the Tablighi Jamaat of South Asia." In *Fundamentalism Observed*, edited by Martin Marty and Scott Appleby. Chicago: University of Chicago Press, 1991.

Ahmed, Rafiuddin. "Islamization in Nineteenth-Century Bengal." In *Contributions to South Asian Studies, 1*, edited by Gopal Krishna, 88–119. Delhi: Oxford University Press, 1979.

———. "Conflict and Contradictions in Bengali Islam." In *Shari͑at and Ambiguity in South Asian Islam*, edited by Katherine Ewing, 114–42. Berkeley: University of California Press, 1988.

Alter, Joseph. "The Sannyasi and the Indian Wrestler: The Anatomy of a Relationship." *American Ethnologist* 19, no. 2 (1992): 317–37.

———. *The Wrestler's Body: Identity and Ideology in North India*. Berkeley: University of California Press, 1992.

Amin, Shahid. "Gandhi as Mahatma: Gorakhpur District, Eastern UP, 1921–1922." In *Selected Subaltern Studies*, edited by Ranajit Guha and Gayatri C. Spivak, 288–351. New York: Oxford University Press, 1988.

Anderson, Benedict. *Imagined Communities*. London: Verso, 1991.

Anderson, Walter, and Sridhar Damle. *The Brotherhood in Saffron: The*

Rashtriya Swayamsevak Sangh and Hindu Revivalism. Boulder, Colo.: Westview Press, 1987.

Appadurai, Arjun. "The Past as a Scarce Resource." *Man* (n.s.) 16 (1981): 201–19.

Asad, Talal. "Anthropological Conceptions of Religion: Reflections on Geertz." *Man* (n.s.) 18 (1983): 237–59.

———. *The Idea of an Anthropology of Islam.* Annual Distinguished Lecture in Arab Studies. Washington, D.C.: Georgetown University Press, 1986.

———. "Multiculturalism and British Identity in the Wake of the Rushdie Affair." *Politics and Society* 18, no. 4 (1990): 455–80.

Babb, Lawrence A. *The Divine Hierarchy.* New York: Columbia University Press, 1975.

Bakker, Hans T. *Ayodhya.* Groningen: Egbert Forsten, 1986.

Balibar, Etienne. "The Nation Form: History and Ideology." *Review* 13, no. 3 (1990): 329–61.

Barnett, Richard B. *North India between Empires: Awadh, the Mughals, and the British, 1720–1801.* Berkeley: University of California Press, 1980.

Bax, Mart. "Popular Devotions, Power, and Religious Regimes in Dutch Brabant." *Anthropological Quarterly* 56, no. 4 (1983): 167–78.

Bayly, Christopher. *Rulers, Townsmen and Bazaars: North Indian Society in the Age of Expansion, 1770–1870.* Cambridge: Cambridge University Press, 1983.

Bayly, Susan. "Islam and State Power." *Itinerario* 12 (1988): 143–63.

Berlin, Judith. *The Syncretic Religion of Lin Chao-En.* New York: Columbia University Press, 1980.

Bhatnagar, G. D. *Awadh under Wajid Ali Shah.* Varanasi: Bharatiya Vidya Prakashan, 1968.

Biardeau, Madeleine. "The Story of Arjuna Kartavirya without Reconstruction." *Purana* 12, no. 2 (1970): 286–303.

———. *L'Hindouisme: Anthropologie d'une civilisation.* Paris: Flammarion, 1981.

Bloch, Maurice. *From Blessing to Violence.* Cambridge: Cambridge University Press, 1985.

Bowen, John. "Salat in Indonesia: The Social Meanings of an Islamic Ritual." *Man* (n.s.) 24 (1989): 600–19.

Brass, Paul. *The Politics of India since Independence.* Cambridge: Cambridge University Press, 1990.

Brennan, Timothy. "The National Longing for Form." In *Nation and Narration,* edited by Homi Bhabha, 44–70. London: Routledge, 1990.

Burghart, Richard. "The Disappearance and Reappearance of Janakpur." *Kailash* 6 (1978): 257–84.

———. "The Founding of the Ramanandi Sect." *Ethnohistory* 25, no. 2 (1978): 121–39.

———. "The Formation of the Concept of Nation-State in Nepal." *Journal of Asian Studies* 44, no. 1 (1984): 101–25.

Burghart, Richard, and Audrey Cantlie, eds. *Indian Religion*. London: Curzon Press, 1985.

Carnegy, Patrick. *A Historical Sketch of Tahsil Fyzabad, Zillah Fyzabad.* Lucknow: Oudh Government Press, 1870.

Carrithers, Michael. "Passions of Nation and Community in the Bahubali Affair." *Modern Asian Studies* 22, no. 4 (1988): 815–44.

Chandra, Bipan. *The Rise and Growth of Economic Nationalism in India, 1880–1905.* New Delhi: Oxford University Press, 1966.

Charbonnier, Georges. *Entretiens avec Claude Lévi-Strauss.* Paris: Plon, 1961.

Chatterjee, Partha. *Nationalist Thought and the Colonial World: A Derivative Discourse?* London: Zed Press, 1986.

Cohn, B. S. "The Role of Gosains in the Economy of Eighteenth- and Nineteenth-Century Upper India." *Indian Economic and Social History Review* 1 (1964): 175–82.

———. *An Anthropologist among the Historians and Other Essays.* Delhi: Oxford University Press, 1987.

———. "The Anthropology of a Colonial State and Its Forms of Knowledge." Paper delivered at the Wenner-Grenn symposium on "Tensions of Empire: Colonial Control and Visions of Rule," Mijas, Spain, November 1988.

Cole, J. R. I. *Roots of North Indian Shi'ism in Iran and Iraq: Religion and State in Awadh, 1722–1859.* Berkeley: University of California Press, 1988.

Comaroff, Jean. *Body of Power, Spirit of Resistance.* Chicago: University of Chicago Press, 1985.

Commander, Simon. "The Jajmani System in North India: An Examination of Its Logic and Status across Two Centuries." *Modern Asian Studies* 17 (1983): 283–311.

Currie, P. M. *The Shrine and Cult of Mu'in al-din Chishti.* Delhi: Oxford University Press, 1989.

Das, Veena. "For a Folk-Theology and Theological Anthropology of Islam." *Contributions to Indian Sociology* (n.s.) 18, no. 2 (1984): 239–305.

Dassetto, Felice. "The Tabligh Organization in Belgium." In *The New Islamic Presence in Western Europe*, edited by Tomas Gerholm and Yngve Lithman, 159–73. London: Mansell Publishing, 1988.

Dirks, Nicholas. "The Invention of Caste: Civil Society in Colonial India." *Social Analysis* 25 (1989): 42–51.

Dumont, Louis. *Religion, Politics and History in India.* The Hague: Mouton, 1970.

———. *Homo Hierarchicus.* Chicago: University of Chicago Press, 1980.

Eaton, Richard. *Sufis of Bijapur.* Princeton: Princeton University Press, 1978.

———. "Court of Man, Court of God." *Contributions to Asian Studies* 17 (1982): 44–61.

———. "The Political and Religious Authority of the Shrine of Baba Farid." In *Moral Conduct and Authority: The Place of adab in South Asian Islam,* edited by Barbara Metcalf, 333–57. Berkeley: University of California Press, 1984.

———. "Approaches to the Study of Conversion to Islam in India." In *Approaches to Islam in Religious Studies,* edited by Richard Martin, 106–25. Tucson: University of Arizona Press, 1985.

Eickelman, David. *Moroccan Islam.* Austin: University of Texas Press, 1976.

Ewing, Katherine. "The Politics of Sufism: Redefining the Saints of Pakistan." *Journal of Asian Studies* 42, no. 2 (1983): 251–68.

Fisher, Michael. *A Clash of Cultures: Awadh, the British and the Mughals.* Delhi: Manohar, 1987.

Fox, Richard. *Lions of the Punjab: Culture in the Making.* Berkeley: University of California Press, 1985.

Frank, André G. "The Devlopment of Underdevelopment." *Monthly Review* 18 (1966): 17–31.

Freitag, Sandria B. *Collective Action and Community: Public Arenas and the Emergence of Communalism in North India.* Berkeley: University of California Press, 1989.

Friedland, Roger, and Richard Hecht. "The Politics of Sacred Space: Jerusalem's Temple Mount/*al-haram al-sharif.*" In *Sacred Spaces and Profane Places,* edited by Jamie Scott and Paul Simpson-Housley, 21–61. Westport, Conn.: Greenwood Press, 1991.

Friedman, Yonathan. *Shaikh Ahmad Sirhindi: An Outline of His Thought and a Study of His Image in the Eyes of Posterity.* Montreal: McGill University Press, 1971.

Frykenberg, Robert E. "The Concept of 'Majority' as a Devilish Force in the Politics of Modern India." *Journal of Commonwealth History and Comparative Politics* 25, no. 3 (1987): 267–74.

———. "The Emergence of Modern 'Hinduism' as a Concept and as an Institution: A Reappraisal with Special Reference to South India." In

Hinduism Reconsidered, edited by Gunther D. Sontheimer and Hermann Kulke, 29–49. New Delhi: Manohar, 1989.

Fuller, Christopher J. *Servants of the Goddess: The Priests of a South Indian Temple*. Cambridge: Cambridge University Press, 1984.

———. "Misconceiving the Grain Heap: A Critique of the Concept of the Indian Jajmani System." In *Money and the Morality of Exchange*, edited by Jonathan Parry and Maurice Bloch, 33–63. Cambridge: Cambridge University Press, 1989.

Gaborieau, Marc. "Les Oulemas/Soufis dans l'Inde Moghole: Anthropologie historique de religieux musalmans." *Annales* 5 (1989): 1185–1204.

Geertz, Clifford. *The Interpretation of Cultures*. New York: Basic Books, 1973.

———. *Negara*. Princeton: Princeton University Press, 1980.

Gellner, Ernest. *Saints of the Atlas*. Chicago: University of Chicago Press, 1969.

———. *Muslim Society*. Cambridge: Cambridge University Press, 1982.

———. *Nations and Nationalism*. Oxford: Basil Blackwell, 1983.

Gilmartin, David. "Shrines, Succession, and Sources of Moral Authority." In *Moral Conduct and Authority: The Place of* adab *in South Asian Islam*, edited by Barbara Metcalf, 221–41. Berkeley: University of California Press, 1984.

———. *Empire and Islam: Punjab and the Making of Pakistan*. Berkeley: University of California Press, 1988.

Gilsenan, Michael. *Saint and Sufi in Modern Egypt*. Oxford: Clarendon Press, 1973.

Gombrich, Richard, and Gananath Obeyesekere. *Buddhism Transformed: Religious Change in Sri Lanka*. Princeton: Princeton University Press, 1988.

Goody, Jack. *The Domestication of the Savage Mind*. Cambridge: Cambridge University Press, 1977.

Gopal, Sarvepalli, ed. *Anatomy of a Confrontation: The Babri Masjid–Ram Janmabhumi Issue*. Delhi: Viking, 1991.

Gopal, Sarvepalli, et al. *The Political Abuse of History*. Delhi: Centre for Historical Studies, Jawaharlal Nehru University, 1989.

Gould, Harold. "Religion and Politics in a U.P. Constituency." In *South Asian Politics and Religion*, edited by Donald Smith, 51–74. Princeton: Princeton University Press, 1966.

Grillo, Ralph, ed. *"Nation" and "State" in Europe: Anthropological Perspectives*. London: Academic Press, 1980.

Gupta, Jaswant Rae. *Role of Foreign Money in Conversion of Hindus*. Delhi: Vishva Hindu Parishad, n.d.

Habib, Mohammed. *Sultan Mahmud of Ghazni*. Delhi: S. Chand & Company, 1967.

Halbfass, Wilhelm. *India and Europe*. Albany: State University of New York Press, 1988.

———. *Tradition and Reflection*. Albany: State University of New York Press, 1991.

Handler, Richard. *Nationalism and the Politics of Culture in Quebec*. Madison: University of Wisconsin Press, 1988.

Hardy, Peter. "Modern European Explanations of Conversion to Islam in South Asia." *Journal of the Asiatic Society of Great Britain and Ireland* 2 (1977): 177–206.

———. "The Authority of Muslim Kings in Medieval South Asia." *Purushartha* 9 (1986): 37–55.

Harris, Marvin. *Cows, Pigs, Wars and Witches*. London: Fontana, 1977.

Hess, Linda, and Richard Schechner. "The Ram Lila of Ramnagar." *The Drama Review* 21, no. 3 (1977): 51–82.

Hobsbawm, Eric. *The Age of Empire, 1875–1914*. New York: Pantheon Books, 1987.

———. *Nations and Nationalism since 1780*. Cambridge: Cambridge University Press, 1991.

Höfer, Andreas. *The Caste Hierarchy and the State in Nepal*. Innsbruck: Universitätsverlag, 1979.

Hunter, W. W. *The Indian Musalmans: Are They Bound to Rebel against the Queen?* London: Trübner, 1876.

Inden, Ronald. *Imagining India*. Oxford: Basil Blackwell, 1990.

Jack, Homer A., ed. *The Gandhi Reader*. Bloomington: Indiana University Press, 1956.

Jacobson, D. A. "Hidden Faces: Hindu and Muslim Purdah in a Central Indian Village." Ph.D. diss., Columbia University, 1970.

Jameson, Fredric. "Third-World Literature in the Era of Multinational Capitalism." *Social Text* 15 (Fall 1986): 65–88.

Jeffery, Patricia. *Frogs in a Well*. London: Zed Press, 1979.

Joshi, M. C. "Archaeology and Indian Tradition—Some Observations." *Puratattva* 8 (1978): 98–102.

Kakar, Sudhir. *Shamans, Mystics and Doctors: A Psychological Inquiry into India and Its Healing Traditions*. New York: Alfred A. Knopf, 1982.

Kapferer, Bruce. *A Celebration of Demons*. Bloomington: Indiana University Press, 1983.

———. *Legends of People, Myths of State: Violence, Intolerance, and Political Culture in Sri Lanka and Australia*. Washington, D.C.: Smithsonian Institute Press, 1988.

Kapur, Anuradha. "Militant Images of a Tranquil God." *Times of India*, 1 October 1991.

Kapur, Rajiv. *Sikh Separatism: The Politics of Faith*. London: Allen & Unwin, 1984.

Kelly, John. *A Politics of Virtue: Hinduism, Sexuality, and Countercolonial Discourse in Fiji*. Chicago: University of Chicago Press, 1991.

Khan, Aliya Azam. "The Muhajir Qaumi Movement." M.A. thesis, University of Pennsylvania, 1991.

King, Christopher. "Forging a New Linguistic Identity: The Hindi Movement in Banaras, 1868–1914." In *Culture and Power in Banaras: Community, Performance, and Environment, 1800–1980*, edited by Sandria B. Freitag, 179–202. Berkeley: University of California Press, 1989.

Kolff, Dirk. *Naukar, Rajput and Sepoy: The Ethnohistory of the Military Labour Market in Hindustan, 1450–1850*. Cambridge: Cambridge University Press, 1990.

Kumar, Nita. *The Artisans of Banaras: Popular Culture and Identity, 1880–1986*. Princeton: Princeton University Press, 1988.

Lal, B. B. "Was Ayodhya a Mythical City?" *Puratattva* 10 (1979–80): 45–49.

Lawrence, Bruce. "Islam in India." *Contributions to Asian Studies* 17 (1982): 27–43.

———. *Defenders of God*. San Francisco: Harper & Row, 1989.

Lelyveld, David. "Colonial Knowledge and the Fate of Hindustani." In *Orientalism and the Postcolonial Predicament: Perspectives on South Asia*, edited by Carol A. Breckenridge and Peter van der Veer, 189–214. Philadelphia: University of Pennsylvania Press, 1993.

Lodrick, Deryck O. *Sacred Cows, Sacred Places: Origins and Survivals of Animal Homes in India*. Berkeley: University of California Press, 1981.

Lorenzen, David. "Warrior Ascetics in Indian History." *Journal of the American Oriental Society* 98, no. 1 (1978): 61–75.

Ludden, David. "Orientalist Empiricism: Transformations of Colonial Knowledge." In *Orientalism and the Postcolonial Predicament: Perspectives on South Asia*, edited by Carol A. Breckenridge and Peter van der Veer, 250–78. Philadelphia: University of Pennsylvania Press, 1993.

Lutgendorf, Philip. "Ramayan: The Video." *The Drama Review* 4, no. 2 (1990): 127–76.

———. *The Life of a Text: Performing the Ramcaritmanas of Tulsidas*. Berkeley: University of California Press, 1991.

McDonnell, Mary Byrne. "Patterns of Muslim Pilgrimage from Malaysia, 1885–1985." In *Muslim Travellers: Pilgrimage, Migration, and the Re-*

ligious Imagination, edited by Dale F. Eickelman and James Piscatori, 111–31. Berkeley: University of California Press, 1990.

McLane, John. *Indian Nationalism and the Early Congress*. Princeton: Princeton University Press, 1977.

McLeod, W. H. *The Evolution of the Sikh Community*. Oxford: Clarendon Press, 1976.

———. *Who is a Sikh? The Problem of Sikh Identity*. Oxford: Clarendon Press, 1989.

Madan, T. N. "Secularism in Its Place." *Journal of Asian Studies* 46, no. 4 (1987): 747–59.

Mahar, J. Michael, ed. *The Untouchables in Contemporary India*. Tucson: University of Arizona Press, 1972.

Mallison, Françoise. "A Note on Holiness Allowed to Women: Pativrata and Sati." *Ludwik Sternbach Felicitation Volume*. Lucknow: Akhil Bharatiya Sanskrit Parishad, 1979.

Mandelbaum, David. *Society in India*. Bombay: Popular Prakashan, 1972.

Marriott, McKim. "Hindu Transactions." In *Transaction and Meaning*, edited by Bruce Kapferer, 109–42. Philadelphia: Institute for the Study of Human Issues, 1977.

Masud, Muhammad Khalid. "The Obligation to Migrate: The Doctrine of *hijra* in Islamic Law." In *Muslim Travellers: Pilgrimage, Migration, and the Religious Imagination*, edited by Dale F. Eickelman and James Piscatori, 29–50. Berkeley: University of California Press, 1990.

Mauss, Marcel. *Sociologie et anthropologie*. Paris: Presses Universitaires de France, 1936.

Mehta, Ved. *Mahatma Gandhi and His Apostles*. Harmondsworth: Penguin, 1977.

Metcalf, Barbara. *Islamic Revival in British India: Deoband, 1860–1900*. Princeton: Princeton University Press, 1982.

———. "Islamic Reform and Islamic Women: Maulana Thanawi's *Jewelry of Paradise*." In *Moral Conduct and Authority: The Place of* adab *in South Asian Islam*, edited by Barbara Metcalf, 184–96. Berkeley: University of California Press, 1984.

———. "Islamic Arguments in Contemporary Pakistan." In *Islam and the Political Economy of Meaning*, edited by William Roff, 132–59. Berkeley: University of California Press, 1988.

———. "An Islamic Ironist." *Times Literary Supplement*, 1 June 1990.

Metcalf, Thomas. *Land, Landlords and the British Raj*. Delhi: Oxford University Press, 1979.

Mines, Mattison, and Vijayalakshmi Gourishankar. "Leadership and Individuality in South Asia: The Case of the South Indian Big-Man." *Journal of Asian Studies* 49, no. 4 (1991): 761–86.

Minor, Robert. "Sarvepalli Radhakrishnan and 'Hinduism.'" In *Religion in Modern India*, edited by Robert Baird, 421–55. Delhi: Manohar, 1989.

Mishra, V. C., ed. *Ram Janmabhoomi Babri Masjid: Historical Documents, Legal Opinions and Judgements*. Delhi: Bar Council of India, 1991.

Mital, P. *Braj ke dharm-sampradayom ka itihas*. In Hindi. Delhi: National Publishing House, 1968.

Moore, Sally Falk. "The Production of Cultural Pluralism as a Process." *Public Culture* 1, no. 2 (1989): 26–49.

Mujahid, Abdul Malik. *Conversion to Islam: Untouchables' Strategy for Protest in India*. Chambersburg, Penn.: Anima Books, 1989.

Munshi, K. M. *Somanatha: The Shrine Eternal*. Bombay: Bharatiya Vidya Bhavan, 1965.

Naipaul, V. S. *An Area of Darkness*. London: Penguin, 1968.

———. *India: A Wounded Civilization*. Harmondsworth: Penguin, 1979.

———. "Our Universal Civilization." *New York Times*, 5 November 1990.

Nandy, Ashis. "The Politics of Secularism and the Recovery of Religious Tolerance." In *Mirrors of Violence*, edited by Veena Das, 69–93. Delhi: Oxford University Press, 1990.

———. "Hinduism versus Hindutva: The Inevitability of a Confrontation." *Times of India*, 18 February 1991.

Obeyesekere, Gananath. "The Buddhist Pantheon in Ceylon and Its Extensions." In *Anthropological Studies in Theravada Buddhism*, edited by Manning Nash, 1–26. New Haven: Yale University Press, 1966.

———. "Social Change and the Deities: Rise of the Kataragama Cult in Modern Sri Lanka." *Man* (n.s.) 12 (1977): 377–96.

———. "Sinhalese-Buddhist Identity in Ceylon." In *Ethnic Identity: Cultural Continuities and Change*, edited by George de Vos and Lola Romanucci-Ross, 231–58. Chicago: University of Chicago Press, 1982.

Pandey, Gyanendra. *The Construction of Communalism in Colonial North India*. Delhi: Oxford University Press, 1990.

Parekh, Bhikhu. *Colonialism, Tradition and Reform: An Analysis of Gandhi's Political Discourse*. New Delhi: Sage, 1989.

Parry, Jonathan. "The Brahmanical Tradition and the Technology of the Intellect." In *Reason and Morality*, edited by Joanna Overing, 200–225. London: Tavistock, 1985.

Pathak, Zakia, and Rajeswari Sunder Rajan. "Shahbano." *Signs* 12, no. 3 (1989): 558–82.

Perlin, Frank. "The Material and the Cultural: An Attempt to Transcend the Present Impasse." *Modern Asian Studies* 22, no. 2 (1988): 383–416.

Pettigrew, Joyce. *Robber Noblemen: A Study of the Political System of the Sikh Jats*. London: Routledge, 1975.

Piscatori, James. *Islam in a World of Nation-States*. Cambridge: Cambridge University Press, 1986.

Pocock, David. *Mind, Body and Wealth*. Oxford: Basil Blackwell, 1973.

Pollock, Sheldon. "Mimamsa and the Problem of History in Traditional India." *Journal of the American Oriental Society* 109, no. 4 (1989): 603–10.

Quraishi, M. M. "The Tabligh Movement: Some Observations." *Islamic Studies* 28, no. 3 (1989): 237–48.

Raychaudhuri, Tapan. *Europe Reconsidered*. Delhi: Oxford University Press, 1988.

Renan, Ernest. "Qu'est ce que c'est une nation?" In *Oeuvres complètes*, 1:887–906. Paris: Calmann-Lévy, 1947–1961. Orig. publ. 1882.

Richman, Paula. "E. V. Ramasami's Reading of the Ramayana." In *Many Ramayanas: The Diversity of a Narrative Tradition in South Asia*, edited by Paula Richman, 175–201. Berkeley: University of California Press, 1991.

Robb, Peter. "The Challenge of Gau Mata: British Policy and Religious Change in India, 1880–1916." *Modern Asian Studies* 20, no. 2 (1986): 285–319.

———. "The Impact of British Rule on Religious Community: Reflections on the Trial of Maulvi Ahmadullah of Patna in 1865." Paper delivered at the Eleventh Conference on Modern Asian Studies, Amsterdam, July 1990.

Robinson, Francis. "Islam and Muslim Society in South Asia." *Contributions to Indian Sociology* (n.s.) 17 (1983): 185–203.

Roy, A. *History of Jaipur City*. Delhi: Concept, 1978.

Rudolph, Lloyd, and Susan Rudolph. *The Modernity of Tradition*. Chicago: University of Chicago Press, 1967.

Rushdie, Salman. *Midnight's Children*. London: Jonathan Cape, 1981.

———. *Shame*. London: Jonathan Cape, 1983.

———. *The Satanic Verses*. London: Viking, 1988.

Said, Edward. *Orientalism*. New York: Fontana, 1979.

Sarkar, Jadunath. *A History of the Dashanami Nagas*. Allahabad: Shri Panchayati Akhara Nirvani, n.d.

Savarkar, V. D. *Hindutva*. Poona: S. R. Date, 1942. Orig. publ. 1922.

Sharma, R. S. *Communal History and Rama's Ayodhya*. New Delhi: People's Publishing House, 1990.

Sinha, B. P. "Indian Tradition and Archaeology." *Puratattva* 14 (1984).

Sitaram. *Avadh ki Jhanki*. In Hindi. Prayag: n.p., 1930.

Smith, Richard. "Rule-by-records and Rule-by-reports: Complementary Aspects of the British Imperial Rule of Law." *Contributions to Indian Sociology* (n.s.) 19, no. 1 (1985): 135–76.

Spencer, Jonathan. "'Writing Within': Anthropology, Nationalism, and Culture in Sri Lanka." *Current Anthropology* 31, no. 3 (1990): 283–300.

Srinivas, M. N. "A Note on Sanskritization and Westernization." *Far Eastern Quarterly* 15 (1956): 481–96.

———. "The Cohesive Role of Sanskritization." In *India and Ceylon: Unity and Diversity*, edited by Philip Mason, 67–82. London: Oxford University Press, 1967.

Tambiah, Stanley. "A Performative Approach to Ritual." In *Culture, Thought and Social Action*, 123–66. Cambridge, Mass.: Harvard University Press, 1985.

Taylor, Charles. "The Person." In *The Category of the Person: Anthropology, Philosophy, History*, edited by Michael Carrithers, Steven Collins, and Steven Lukes, 257–81. Cambridge: Cambridge University Press, 1985.

Taylor, David, and Malcolm Yapp, eds. *Political Identity in South Asia.* London: Curzon Press, 1979.

Thapar, Romila. "Puranic Lineages and Archaeological Cultures." *Puratattva* 8 (1978).

———. "The Ramayana Syndrome." *Seminar* 353 (January 1989): 71–75.

———. "A Historical Perspective on the Story of Rama." In *Anatomy of a Confrontation: The Babri Masjid–Ram Janmabhumi Issue*, edited by Sarvepalli Gopal, 141–63. New Delhi: Viking, 1991.

Thapar, Romila, Harbans Mukhia, and Bipan Chandra, eds. *Communalism and the Writing of Indian History.* Delhi: People's Publishing House, 1969.

Thiel-Horstmann, Monika. "Warrior Ascetics in Eighteenth-Century Rajasthan and the Religious Policy of Jai Singh II." Paper presented at the Third Conference on Early Devotional Literature in New Indo-Aryan Languages, Leiden, 1985.

Thomas, Catherine. *L'Ashram de l'amour: Le Gandhisme et l'imaginaire.* Paris: Maison des Sciences de l'Homme, 1979.

Tinker, Hugh. *A New System of Slavery: The Export of Indian Labour Overseas, 1830–1920.* Oxford: Oxford University Press, 1974.

Tönnies, Ferdinand. *Gemeinschaft und Gesellschaft.* Leipzig: Fues, 1887.

Turner, Bryan S. *The Body.* London: Routledge, 1984.

ul-Haq, Anwar. *The Faith Movement of Mawlana Muhammad Ilyas.* London: Allen & Unwin, 1972.

van der Veer, Peter. "God Must Be Liberated: A Hindu Liberation Movement in Ayodhya." *Modern Asian Studies* 21, no. 2 (1987): 283–303.

———. *Gods on Earth: The Management of Religious Experience and Identity in a North Indian Pilgrimage Centre.* London School of Economics Monographs on Social Anthropology, 59. London and Atlantic Highlands, N.J.: Athlone Press, 1988.

———. "The Power of Detachment: Disciplines of Body and Mind in the Ramanandi Order." *American Ethnologist* 16 (1989): 458–70.

———. "Satanic or Angelic: The Politics of Religious and Literary Inspiration." *Public Culture* 2, no. 1 (1989): 100–105.

———. "Ayodhya and Somnath: Eternal Shrines, Contested Histories." *Social Research* 59, no. 1 (1992): 85–111.

———. "Playing or Praying: A Saint's Day in Surat." *Journal of Asian Studies* 51, no. 3 (1992): 545–65.

———. "The Foreign Hand: Orientalist Discourse in Sociology and Communalism." In *Orientalism and the Postcolonial Predicament: Perspectives on South Asia*, edited by Carol A. Breckenridge and Peter van der Veer, 23–44. Philadelphia: University of Pennsylvania Press, 1993.

———. "Hindu Nationalism and the Discourse of Modernity: The Vishva Hindu Parishad." In *Accounting for Fundamentalisms*, edited by Martin Marty and Scott Appleby. Chicago: University of Chicago Press, 1993.

van der Veer, Peter, and Steven Vertovec. "Brahmanism Abroad: On Caribbean Hinduism as an Ethnic Religion." *Ethnology* (1991): 149–66.

van Schendel, Willem. "Madmen of Mymensingh: Peasant Resistance and the Colonial Process in Eastern India, 1824 to 1833." *Indian Economic and Social History Review* 22, no. 2 (1985): 139–73.

Vaudeville, Charlotte. *Kabir*. Oxford: Oxford University Press, 1974.

———. "Braj, Lost and Found." *Indo-Iranian Journal* 18 (1976): 195–213.

Wagle, Narendra K. "Hindu-Muslim Interactions in Medieval Maharashtra." In *Hinduism Reconsidered*, edited by Gunther D. Sontheimer and Hermann Kulke, 51–67. Delhi: Manohar, 1989.

Weinberger-Thomas, Catherine. "Cendres d'immortalité: La Crémation des veuves en Inde." *Archives de Sciences Sociales des Religions* 67, no. 1 (1989): 9–51.

Weiner, Myron. "International Migration and Development: Indians in the Persian Gulf." *Population and Development Review* 8, no. 1 (1982): 1–36.

Weiss, Anita. "Implications of the Islamization Program for Women." In *Islamic Reassertion in Pakistan*, edited by Anita Weiss, 97–115. Syracuse: Syracuse University Press, 1986.

Williams, George. "Svami Vivekananda." In *Religion in Modern India*, edited by Robert Baird, 313–43. Delhi: Manohar, 1989.

Williams, Raymond. *The Swaminarayana Satsangh*. Cambridge: Cambridge University Press, 1980.

Wolf, Eric. "The Virgin of Guadaloupe: A Mexican National Symbol." *Journal of American Folklore* 71, no. 1 (1958): 34–39.

Yang, Anand. "Sacred Symbol and Sacred Space in Rural India: Community Mobilization in the 'Anti-Cow Killing' Riot of 1893." *Comparative Studies in Society and History* 22, no. 4 (1980): 576–96.

Index

Compositor:	Terry Robinson & Co.
Text:	11/13 Caledonia
Display:	Caledonia
Printer:	Edwards Brothers, Inc.
Binder:	Edwards Brothers, Inc.